Understanding Econometrics

Jon Stewart

Jon Stewart was born in 1944 and educated at Manchester University. In 1966 he gained a first class honours degree in Econometrics, and was awarded the Cobden prize. From 1966—68 he worked as a research assistant in Econometrics at Manchester, and in 1968 took his MA with distinction. He subsequently lectured in Economics for a year at the New University of Ulster, before returning to Manchester as a lecturer in Econometrics. Jon Stewart is married with four children.

Economics editor
Michael Parkin
Professor of Economics
University of Western Ontario

Understanding Econometrics

Jon Stewart

Lecturer in Econometrics
University of Manchester

Hutchinson of London

Hutchinson & Co (Publishers) Ltd
3 Fitzroy Square, London W1

London Melbourne Sydney Auckland
Wellington Johannesburg and agencies
throughout the world

First published 1976
© Jon Stewart 1976

Text set in 10/12 pt IBM Press Roman at The Pitman Press, Bath
Printed in Great Britain by the Anchor Press Ltd and bound by Wm
Brendon and Son Ltd both of Tiptree, Essex

ISBN 0 09 126230 5 (cased)
ISBN 0 09 126231 3 (paper)

330·018

20. JUL. 1976

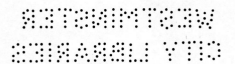

To S.S.L.

Contents

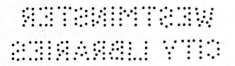

Preface

I have written this book in the belief that it is possible to present the methods of econometrics to a relatively wide audience. The topics covered are those that one would expect to find in a comprehensive introductory course, but very little mathematics is assumed and a prior knowledge of statistical method is not essential.

The key features of the presentation are as follows. First, it is necessary to explain what an economic model is and why such models are used. It is then necessary to explain why random disturbances are introduced and to show how this is achieved. In the course of this discussion, a statistical survival kit is provided, containing those components which are essential to an understanding of the nature of econometric methods. The various ideas can then be applied in the context of the two variable regression model and the extension to multiple regression is achieved by interpreting a multiple regression coefficient as a coefficient from a simple regression on adjusted data. This interpretation allows a full discussion of the use of the single equation linear model and topics such as the use of restrictions, specification error and multicollinearity are included. The later chapters cover disturbance problems, the use of lags, dynamic models and simultaneous equation methods.

It is explicitly recognized that the application of econometric techniques does require the use of a computer and, where possible, the calculations necessary under various extensions of the basic linear model are expressed in a form which is suitable for the application of a program designed for ordinary least squares estimation. Details which are more appropriate to hand calculation are not given and matrix algebra is not required. The emphasis is on understanding *why* particular techniques are used and this is always very carefully explained.

To all those who have helped with the production of this book, I extend my thanks. I received valuable comments from a number of people, but I would like to make special mention of the contributions made by Bill Farebrother, Ray O'Brien, Stuart Moore, George Hadjimatheou, Michael Parkin and Martin Timbrell. Nina Roach made a really excellent job of the typing and Anne Bennett gave invaluable help in the preparation of diagrams. My wife and children had to endure both my absence and my presence during long days of writing: to Christine and the boys, my thanks once more.

Jon Stewart
August 1975

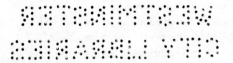

1 Introduction

1.1 The Nature of Econometrics

Econometrics is a discipline embracing aspects of methodology from
economics, mathematics and statistics. The econometrician is simply
an economist who, in trying to understand the working of economic
systems, makes use of techniques which are based primarily on the
methodology of statistics and which are often communicated in the
language of mathematics. This formal background to the subject is
sometimes a deterrent to those who would like to understand the nature
of econometrics and this book represents an attempt to explain how
and why econometric methods are used, avoiding formal mathematics
where possible and providing a detailed explanation of the statistical
concepts involved. Whilst the ideas introduced are precise and do
have to be carefully used, formal derivation and proof is not always
necessary and an explanation of why a particular result is likely to hold
can often provide an adequate alternative.

1.2 Economic Models

Before any progress can be made, it is necessary to understand exactly
what is meant by an *economic model*. Economic systems are undoubtedly
complex and the idea of using a model arises because of this complexity.
A model is an abstraction from reality, drawn in such a way as to reveal
the major features of the system. Clearly, there can be 'good' and 'bad'
models. If the abstraction is taken too far, the model may have little to
say about the corresponding real system. If, on the other hand, the
abstraction is taken insufficiently far, the model may be too complex to
be of value in gaining an insight into the working of the real system.

Models exist in many forms. The analysis of any system must be
based on a model, but the model need not necessarily be explicit.
Economic journalism provides many examples of analysis which is
obviously based on a set of assumptions, sometimes explicit, often not

so, which represent an underlying model. It is clearly advantageous
to those wishing to evaluate the analysis if the model can be given
some explicit form.

The models with which the econometrician is typically concerned
are expressed in mathematical form, but this is not true of explicit models
in general, nor of economic models in particular. A diagram, showing
the flows of goods, services and finance in the economy is a model, but
a model must be appropriate to the questions which the economist wishes
to ask and, if he is concerned about the *relationships* between the flows,
the flow diagram is unlikely to be sufficient on its own. In this case,
the level of abstraction is taken too far.

The discussion in the remainder of this chapter is based largely on the
example of a postulated relationship between consumers' expenditure
and personal disposable income at the macro-economic level. The asser-
tion that such a relationship should exist is a model, but one which is
insufficiently precise to answer questions concerned with the magnitude
of the response of changes in consumption to changes in income. To
make progress, the relationship must be given some explicit form. One
way in which this can be done is to start from a *theory* as to the way
individual consumers respond to changes in their income and, after
taking account of the *aggregation* of the behaviour of individuals, a
theoretical statement as to the relationship between consumption and
income in the macro-economy may be obtained. The development of
the theory might provide the exact form of the relationship, but this
is not always the case and a principle which is then often employed is
to make the relationship as simple as possible, until such time as there
is evidence, from observation of a real system, that the simple form is
untenable. This raises an interesting point. A model is an abstraction
from reality and a 'correct' model need not provide a complete description of how the real system works. If decision makers in the real system
behave *as though* they were following the rules of the model, this would
be quite sufficient. But a model would *not* be correct if some specific
assumption embodied in the model is violated in practice and the model
would be *seen* to be incorrect if any assumption is *seen* to be violated.
The testing of assumptions is a crucial objective of using econometric
techniques and there is a great deal more to be said about this in due
course.

1.3 A Simple Model

Suppose that, for a hypothetical economy, there exists a relationship between consumers' expenditure (*C*) and personal disposable income (*D*), which can be expressed as

$$C = 50 + 0{\cdot}8D \tag{1.3.1}$$

In this equation, *C* and *D* are *variables,* which can take different values at different points of observation of the economic system. The numbers 50 and 0·8 are constants. To fix ideas, suppose that consumption and income flows were observed for each of two time periods. Then, whereas consumption and income would generally take distinct values in each period, the existence of a fixed relationship would imply that the numbers 50 and 0·8 remain the same. Although the values of the variables change, the relationship between the variables does not.

The graph corresponding to equation (1.3.1) is shown in Fig. 1.1 and

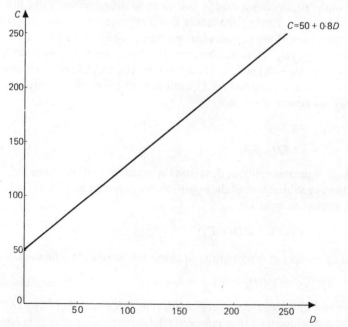

Figure 1.1

it can be seen that the equation represents a straight line. If consumption behaviour in the (hypothetical) economy is described by this equation, each pair of consumption and income values represent a single point which would lie on the straight line. It can also be seen, from the graph, that 50 is the value of consumption which, according to the equation, would hold if income were zero and that if income rises by 5 units, consumption rises by 4 units. Equivalently, if income rises by 1 unit, consumption rises by $4/5 = 0.8$ units. The number 0.8 therefore represents the effect on the *dependent* variable (consumption) of a *unit* change in the *explanatory* variable (income).

Equation (1.3.1) is a particular example of a straight line or *linear* relationship. More generally, a linear relationship between C and D can be written as

$$C = \alpha + \beta D \tag{1.3.2}$$

where α and β are the *parameters* of the relationship. In our hypothetical economy, $\alpha = 50$ and $\beta = 0.8$. In a second case, there might again be a linear relationship, but the values of the parameters could be different. The parameter α is called the *intercept* and β is the *slope*: the interpretation of the parameters is exactly that given to the numbers 50 and 0.8 in our example. To see algebraically that β represents the slope, suppose that the values of the variables for two time periods are written as C_1, D_1 and C_2, D_2. Then the *change* in D between the two time periods is given by $(D_2 - D_1)$ and the change in C by $(C_2 - C_1)$. If consumption behaviour is described by (1.3.2), both pairs of values of the variables satisfy the equation and so

$$C_1 = \alpha + \beta D_1 \tag{1.3.3}$$

$$C_2 = \alpha + \beta D_2 \tag{1.3.4}$$

If these equations are true, then so is the equation resulting from the addition or subtraction of the equations and, subtracting (1.3.3) from (1.3.4) gives an equation

$$(C_2 - C_1) = 0 + \beta(D_2 - D_1)$$

relating *changes* in consumption to *changes* in income. It follows that

$$\beta = (C_2 - C_1)/(D_2 - D_1) \tag{1.3.5}$$

If we now consider a unit change in income, this means that $(D_2 - D_1) = 1$ and the parameter β then represents the corresponding change in consumption. It should be noted that the change in consumption for a unit change in income is *always* β, irrespective of the particular point from which the unit change in income takes place.

In economic terminology, the relationship described above is a linear version of the *consumption function* and β is the *marginal propensity to consume*. The marginal propensity to consume is simply the slope of the consumption function, but it is important to realize that it is only in the case of a linear function that the slope is a constant, which does *not* depend on the values taken by C or D. The graph corresponding to a *nonlinear* relationship would be a curve rather than a straight line and, in the case of a curve, the slope *does* change as the values of the variables change.

In what follows, we shall concentrate largely on linear relationships and it is important, in several distinct contexts, to be able to recognize when a given relationship is linear. One could perhaps draw the graph corresponding to the relationship, but a much simpler test is to see whether the relationship can be written in the form of equation (1.3.2). The example

$$5C = 250 + 4D$$

does represent a linear relationship, because division by 5 on both sides gives

$$C = 50 + 0 \cdot 8D$$

which is in the standard linear form. In contrast, the equation

$$C = 20 + 10\sqrt{D}$$

is *nonlinear* in the variables C and D, because there is no way of writing the equation in exactly the same form as (1.3.2). At the risk of complicating the argument we should add that this last example *is* linear in the variables C and $\sqrt{D}$; if one were to draw a graph marking values of $\sqrt{D}$ on the horizontal axis, instead of values of D, the equation drawn would be a straight line. But a graph of C against D would produce a curve. This is illustrated in Fig. 1.2.

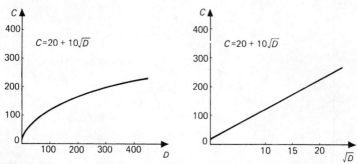

Figure 1.2

If it were true that there existed an exact linear relationship between consumption and income, then, by observing the flows for two periods of time, plotting the two pairs of values on a graph and joining the two points, the relationship would be known. That is, the values of α and β would be known and, by using the graph or the equation with the appropriate values of α and β written in, it would be possible to calculate the level of consumption for any given level of income. But if, for any real economy, one were to take figures for consumption and disposable income over a number of years and plot more than two points on the graph, it would not generally be possible to find a single straight line to pass through all the points. Perhaps one should therefore take an equation which represents a curve rather than a straight line? Actually, it is always possible to draw some curve through a given number of points, but inevitably, on taking an additional observation, one would find that it did not fall exactly on the chosen curve. Whilst the linear form is not always appropriate, choosing ever more complex curves is not the answer.

Fig. 1.3 shows a plot of consumers' expenditure at 1963 prices against personal disposable income at 1963 prices, based on data for the U K economy for the period 1963–72. Since it is apparent that it is not possible to draw a single straight line through all these points, it

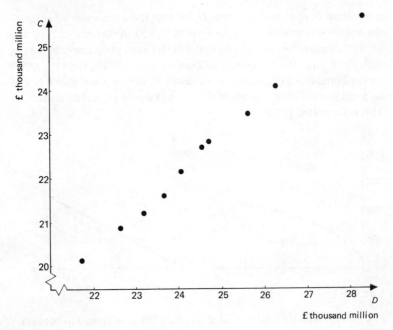

Figure 1.3

is clearly unreasonable to have a model which suggests that such a possibility exists. It is presumably true that there are links between consumption and income in the real system, but the model representing these links has to be changed. It is therefore assumed that a satisfactory model can be provided by an *inexact* linear relationship. This is written as

$$C = \alpha + \beta D + u \qquad\qquad (1.3.6)$$

where u represents a *disturbance* to the relationship between C and D.

Given the present specification for the main part of the model, the disturbance represents every error, whether avoidable or not, that is inherent in using the equation $C = \alpha + \beta D$ as the underlying economic hypothesis. If there are other important influences on consumption, these could simply be left as part of the disturbance, but it would presumably be more satisfactory to extend the list of explanatory variables, so that important influences are explicitly included in the main part of the model. The method for doing this is described in Chapter 3. There may, however, be other factors, which are not individually important and which cannot easily be measured. Since no other representation is possible, the disturbance is a convenient and legitimate device for including these factors. The implication is that (1.3.6) would be acceptable if income were the only major influence on consumption, but it would not be acceptable if there were other important influences which had been omitted from the main part of the model.

With this in mind, we shall impose a set of conditions on the disturbance term. These conditions are chosen in such a way that they are not likely to be satisfied unless the main part of the model does contain all the major influences on consumption. The main part of the model has also to be acceptable in other respects. It has been argued that choosing an alternative to the linear form will not remove the need to have a disturbance term. But the conditions on the disturbance are unlikely to be satisfied unless a linear relationship is reasonably good approximation to the links which exist between consumption and income in the real system.

The conditions to be imposed on the disturbance term are obtained by applying the concept of modelling to the process by which disturbance values are determined. The model used is similar to that which can be applied to a game of chance. A game of chance is described as such because it is impossible to determine, in advance, what the outcome of the game will be. This description actually implies a model: since it is very difficult to understand *why* a particular outcome occurs, the outcome is said to be determined 'by chance'. This does convey a vague impression of outcomes being chosen in some quite arbitrary way but, for our purposes, it is necessary to construct a much more explicit form of model. The modelling of a game of chance is not, in itself, of direct interest, but it will serve as a useful vehicle for introducing ideas which can then be applied to modelling the disturbance term in the consumption function.

1.4 A Model for a Game of Chance

Consider a game consisting of a single throw of a six-sided die, marked with the numbers 1 to 6. The possible outcomes of this game would be the distinct values 1, 2, 3, 4, 5 and 6. The essential characteristic of an outcome is that only one outcome can actually occur in a single play of the game. Outcomes are therefore said to be *mutually exclusive*. It is also possible to think of *sets* of outcomes which are said to consti-tute particular *events*, such as that described by obtaining a number greater than 3. This event would take place if one of the outcomes, 4, 5 or 6 were to occur. It is quite possible to define two events which *can* take place simultaneously. If one event is defined as the occurrence of a number greater than 3 and a second event as the occurrence of a number less than 5, *both* events would occur if the number shown on the die is 4. So outcomes are always mutually exclusive, but events may or may not be mutually exclusive.

When a die is thrown, there *is* presumably a reason, however complex, for obtaining a particular outcome. But, because the real mechanism is likely to be very complicated, it is much easier to think of the game in terms of a model. According to the model, each outcome is associa-ted with a measure to represent the chance or 'odds' for that particular outcome. More generally, such a measure is also associated with any event made up of the individual outcomes. This measure is the *probability* of an event and the measure has the following characteristics

1. The probability of an event is greater than (or equal to) zero.
2. The probability of an event which must take place is one.
3. For mutually exclusive events, the probability that one *or* other will occur is given by the *sum* of the individual probabilities.

From these *axioms* of probability, all other properties of the measure can be deduced. But all that we really need to know, to give an inter-pretation to the concept of probability, is that it is a number, between 0 and 1 in value and that the higher the probability, the more likely it is that the event will occur.

A complete description of the model for a single throw of the die would consist of a list of possible outcomes, together with the associated probabilities. A particularly simple version could be based on the assumption that all outcomes are equally likely, in which case the properties of the probability measure would dictate a probability of 1/6 for each outcome. One outcome *must* occur and so the probability of obtaining 1 *or* 2 *or* 3 *or* 4 *or* 5 *or* 6 must be 1. But outcomes are mutually exclusive, so the probability of obtaining 1 *or* 2 *or* 3 *or* 4 *or* 5 *or* 6 is equal to the sum of the individual outcomes. It follows that the sum of the individual probabilities must be 1 and if it is also assumed that each outcome has *equal* probability, this common probability must be 1/6.

The list of possible outcomes, together with the associated probabilities, is known as a *probability distribution.* It is possible to express the outcomes as the different values that can be taken by a variable, V. This variable can take as many distinct values as there are distinct outcomes and so, for throwing a die, the values are $V = 1$, $V = 2$, $V = 3$, $V = 4$, $V = 5$, $V = 6$. For each value, there is a corresponding probability, assumed to be 1/6. A variable, the value of which is determined according to the rules of a probability distribution, is said to be a *random variable.* So our model for throwing a die is based on the assumption that a variable representing the possible outcomes *can* be thought of as a random variable.

The example given above is fairly straightforward. The number of possible outcomes is small, it is very reasonable to assume that the individual probabilities are equal and, on this basis, it is easy to determine a complete probability distribution. We shall use similar principles in constructing a model for disturbances to the consumption function, but there are certain properties of random variables which are best introduced in the context of a relatively simple example. So, for the moment, we shall continue to discuss the die throwing game.

As a first step, consider the *expectation* or *expected value* of a random variable. To obtain the expectation, each possible value of the random variable is multiplied by the corresponding probability and the resulting products are then added together. For a random variable, V, the expectation is written as $E(V)$. So, for throwing a die

$$E(V) = 1/6(1) + 1/6(2) + 1/6(3) + 1/6(4) + 1/6(5) + 1/6(6)$$

$$= 3 \cdot 5$$

The value 3·5 can never actually occur as an outcome to the game. A single play will result in one of the outcomes $V = 1$ to $V = 6$. What the expectation represents is an average over all the values that *could* occur.

In general, it is *not* obtained by simply adding the values of all outcomes and dividing by the number of outcomes, because different outcomes may be more or less likely than others. Instead, we have a calculation in which each outcome is weighted by the corresponding probability. *In this particular case,* each outcome has the same probability and a simple average of outcomes *would* give the correct value for the expectation.

The expectation of a random variable is sometimes described as the *mean* of the corresponding probability distribution, or as the *population mean.* These descriptions refer to exactly the same concept and they are interchangeable. It is important to realize that $E(V)$ is not itself a random variable: it is a constant value which conveys a certain amount of information about the random variable, V.

Now consider the concept of *variance.* For a random variable, V, this is written as var(V) and defined as

$$\text{var}(V) = E([V - E(V)]^2) \tag{1.4.1}$$

The interpretation of this expression is not obvious and we shall calculate the variance for the die throwing game before attempting to explain what the variance represents. We know that $E(V) = 3 \cdot 5$, so $[V - E(V)]$ can take the values

$$1 - 3 \cdot 5 = -2 \cdot 5; \quad 2 - 3 \cdot 5 = -1 \cdot 5; \quad 3 - 3 \cdot 5 = -0 \cdot 5$$
$$4 - 3 \cdot 5 = 0 \cdot 5; \quad 5 - 3 \cdot 5 = 1 \cdot 5; \quad 6 - 3 \cdot 5 = 2 \cdot 5$$

Now consider the possible values of $[V - E(V)]^2$

$$\text{if } V = 1 \text{ or } V = 6, \text{ then } [V - E(V)]^2 = 6 \cdot 25$$
$$\text{if } V = 2 \text{ or } V = 5, \text{ then } [V - E(V)]^2 = 2 \cdot 25$$
$$\text{if } V = 3 \text{ or } V = 4, \text{ then } [V - E(V)]^2 = 0 \cdot 25$$

Since the outcomes $V = 1$ and $V = 6$ are mutually exclusive, the probability of obtaining $V = 1$ *or* $V = 6$ is the sum of the individual probabilities and is therefore $1/3$. So the probability that $[V - E(V)]^2 = 6 \cdot 25$ is also $1/3$. Similarly, it can be established that the two other values of $[V - E(V)]^2$ have a probability of $1/3$.

What we have shown is that $[V - E(V)]^2$ can take certain values, with certain probabilities or, in other words, that $[V - E(V)]^2$ is a random variable. Since we know the appropriate probability distribution, we can work out the expected value for this random variable

$$E([V - E(V)]^2) = 1/3(6 \cdot 25) + 1/3(2 \cdot 25) + 1/3(0 \cdot 25)$$
$$= 2 \cdot 92$$

According to the definition in (1.4.1), this quantity is the variance of
V.

Now consider the interpretation of var(V). Whereas $E(V)$ represents
an average over the values of V that could occur, var(V) summarizes, in
a single measure, the extent to which the individual values diverge from
the expectation. The variance is therefore a measure of *spread*. For
each outcome, the quantity $[V - E(V)]$ represents the *deviation* from
the expectation and one might consider taking the expectation of the
deviations, in order to produce an average value. But some deviations
are positive and some are negative and the expectation of the deviations
is actually zero (see exercise 1.2). In contrast, all the *squared* deviations
are positive and the expectation of the squared deviations is also positive.
By squaring the deviations, we ensure that positive and negative deviations both contribute in the same way to the measure of spread.

We have seen that, for the die throwing game, var$(V) = 2\cdot92$ and
we now know that this is a measure of spread, but it is still not entirely
clear what the value $2\cdot92$ actually tells us. In exercise 1.1, the reader
is asked to consider two variants of the game. In the first, the faces
of the die are marked with the numbers 7, 8, 9, 10, 11 and 12. In this
case the expectation is increased, but the variance does not change
since the *spread* of values is no greater than in the original game. In the
second variant, the scores are 2, 4, 6, 8, 10 and 12. In this case both
the expectation *and* the variance are increased. This illustrates an
important point. We may compare the variances obtained for two
different random variables or we may compare the variance of one
random variable with something else, but we do not usually consider
the variance in isolation. So it is not the number $2\cdot92$ that is important in itself: it is the comparison between this number and some
other quantity that will usually tell us something of interest.

Now suppose that the game consists of *two* throws of the die.
The outcomes for a two-throw game can be represented in terms
of *two* random variables, V_1 and V_2. The value taken by V_1 represents
the outcome from the first throw and the value taken by V_2 represents
the outcome from the second throw. This means that there are now
two probability distributions but, since there is no reason to believe that
the mechanism in the real system would be different as between the two
throws, we would assume that V_1 and V_2 have the same set of outcomes
and the same set of probabilities. The two distributions would then be
said to be *identical*. Amongst other things this means that both random
variables have the same expectation and that both have the same
variance. And, in the real system again, there is no reason to believe

that the value obtained on the first throw would have any influence on the value obtained on the second throw. This is reflected in the model by the assumption that the distributions are *independent*. We shall not give a precise technical definition of the concept of independence, but we shall note an important implication. In analysing the behaviour of two independent random variables, we can specify a distribution for each variable and this provides a complete description. There is no need to consider the interaction between the two variables, for independence implies that no such interaction exists.

The extension to a game consisting of n throws is immediate. The model would involve a set of n random variables, $V_1, V_2, \ldots, V_n$, each having the same distribution and each distribution being independent of all other distributions. There is an important reason for this extension. All that we have said so far relates to a theoretical model for throwing a die, but one could obviously take observations from the corresponding real system, by actually throwing a die and recording the results. Having collected this data, one would have a set of observations from the real system and a model which attempts to 'explain' these observations. In principle, one could then make comparisons between the model and the real system, on the basis of this set of observations. The model for a single throw would not be of much use because the corresponding observation on the real system would be the result of a single throw and it is doubtful whether this would tell us much about the real system. It is much more likely that one would take a *set* of observations and, if comparisons are to be made, it is the model representing the generation of a *set* of observations that is needed.

We now have a model which is similar, in many respects, to that which will be used for the disturbance term in the consumption function. There is, however, a small problem of interpretation. As we shall see, from the discussion in the next section, the data taken from the real economic system consists of a set of observations on consumption and income, usually relating to different periods of time. The natural representation for n observations on consumption is $C_1, C_2, \ldots, C_n$. But we shall also find that, according to the model, each observation on consumption is just one of the values that could have been assumed by a corresponding random variable. The crucial distinction here is between the use of the terms *variable* and *random variable* and a possible confusion arises from the use of the term variable, in the discipline to which the probability model is applied. Thus consumption is a single economic variable, but one can have a model which implies that each observation on consumption corresponds to a different random variable. To avoid a completely unworkable system of notation, the symbols $C_1, C_2, \ldots, C_n$ are also taken to represent a set of random variables, just as $V_1, V_2, \ldots, V_n$ are a set of random variables in the model for throwing a die. Having made this point, no confusion need arise, and it should be obvious from the context what is intended. If the symbols $C_1, C_2, \ldots, C_n$ appear in a formula giving instructions for a calculation to be performed on observed data, then, in carrying out the calculation, the symbols would be replaced by the values actually observed. But, in discussing the theoretical implications of the model, we may also take $C_1, C_2, \ldots, C_n$ to represent a set of random variables.

1.5 Random Disturbances

The ideas developed in the previous section are now applied to the disturbance term in the consumption function. The model suggested in equation (1.3.6) is

$$C = \alpha + \beta D + u \tag{1.5.1}$$

but, in practice, the model will be applied to a specific set of observations on consumption and income. Often these values relate to a single economy in different periods of time and this does assume that the consumption function remains the same over a certain time horizon. Alternatively, one might be prepared to specify that a number of different economies have the same consumption function and one could then take observations relating to different geographical areas. In either case, a set of n observations on consumption can be written as $C_1, C_2, \ldots, C_n$ or, more concisely as $C_t; t = 1, 2, \ldots, n$. The corresponding observations on income can be written as $D_t; t = 1, 2, \ldots, n$. The model, applied to these observations, would then be

$$C_t = \alpha + \beta D_t + u_t; t = 1, 2, \ldots, n. \tag{1.5.2}$$

which indicates that the model holds, for some constant α and β, for the n time periods identified as $t = 1, t = 2$, and so on. We shall generally refer to time periods, but it should be understood that the argument could equally well apply to any other type of observation. A set of observations relating to a single unit in different periods of time is called a *time series*. A set of observations relating to different units at a single point of time is a *cross-section*. In different contexts these units might be households, firms, industries, regions or countries. But, at least in macro-economics, time series are the most frequently used observations, and the discussion is continued on this basis.

It is now assumed that the disturbance in each time period behaves as though it were generated according to the rules of a probability distribution. In the simplest case, it is also assumed that the distributions are all *identical* and that they are all *independent*. There is thus a clear analogy between the model for a set of n disturbances and the model for n throws of a die. The same probabilities govern each throw of the die and the result of any one throw has no influence on the results obtained from the other throws. Similarly, the same probabilities apply to the generation of the disturbance value for each time period and the value obtained in one period has no influence on the values obtained in other periods.

As yet, nothing has been said as to the nature of the probability distribution associated with each disturbance term. In fact we need only consider a single disturbance, say u_1, because it has already been assumed that all other disturbances have identical distributions. Fig. 1.4 illustrates the distribution that we shall use. The horizontal axis

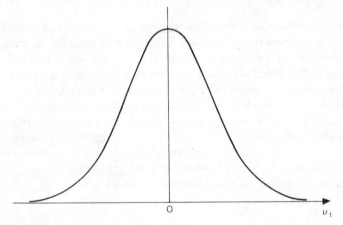

O u_1

Figure 1.4

represents the line of possible values for u_1 and, to satisfy the requirements of this distribution, u_1 must be considered to be a *continuous* random variable, which can take a value corresponding to any one of the infinite number of points on this line. Above the horizontal axis is a curve, which captures the idea that values of u_1 in an interval under the centre of the curve are more likely than values in a similar interval away from the centre. In the case of a continuous random variable, we do not refer to the probability of finding a particular point because, amongst the infinite number of possibilities, that probability must be very close to zero. Instead, we talk of the probability of finding values within a certain interval on the horizontal axis and this probability is given by the *area* bounded by the curve, the horizontal axis and the ends of the interval. So the height of the curve is connected with probability, but it does not actually *show* the probability directly. It should be noted that, in Fig. 1.4, the central value on the horizontal axis is zero and, by inspection, it is possible to see that positive and negative values of the disturbance occur with equal probability.

The distribution shown in Fig. 1.4 is a *normal* distribution. There are in fact many different normal distributions, all having the same characteristic bell shape, but differing in respect of their expectation and variance. As in the case of a discrete random variable, the expectation is an average over the values that could occur and the variance is a measure of spread. A rather special characteristic of a normal distribution is that one has only to know the expectation and variance in order to know which particular normal distribution is being used. The expectation and variance are said to be *parameters* of the distribution. A second characteristic is that the expectation falls under the centre of the curve and so the distribution shown in Fig. 1.4 has an expectation equal to zero. Remember that an exactly equivalent statement is that the *mean* of the distribution is zero. The assumption that the expectation is zero reflects the fact that the disturbance is supposed to represent many small influences on consumption, which cannot be built into the main part of the model. There is no reason to believe that such influences would increase or decrease consumption in a systematic way and, if this belief is correct, the assumption of zero expectation is quite reasonable.

To see exactly how the expectation of a continuous random variable is defined, it is useful to start with the discrete case and to consider what would happen if the number of outcomes could be increased. For a discrete random variable, the expectation is defined as a weighted sum of values of the random variable, the weights being the corresponding probabilities. If the number of outcomes is large, most of the probabilites must be very small and, in the case of a continuous random variable, the number of outcomes is infinite, but the probability attached to each must be very small indeed. In most cases, the result of the summation would still be a finite expectation. In the continuous case, the summation operation is replaced by an operation known as integration, but the interpretation is exactly the same and it is important to realize that one does not actually have to perform a summation or integration to make use of the concept of expectation. The purpose of this paragraph is simply to explain that the expectation can be defined for a continuous random variable and that the meaning is analogous to that in the discrete case. The same is true of the variance of a continuous random variable.

After a considerable amount of preparation, it is now possible to state a complete specification for the consumption function model. It is assumed that

$$C_t = \alpha + \beta D_t + u_t; t = 1, 2, \ldots, n \qquad (1.5.3)$$

and that the disturbances can be thought of as a set of random variables having identical and independent normal distributions. If the distributions are identical, they have the same expectation and the same variance and the common expectation is assumed to be zero. An important implication of the model is that each observation on consumption must be thought of as representing a single value taken by a corresponding random variable, because, according to the model, each value $C_1, C_2, \ldots, C_n$ is determined in part by the corresponding disturbance. To illustrate this point, take a single consumption term, say C_1, and consider what would have happened if the income value, D_1, had remained the same, but the disturbance value, u_1, had been different. The answer is that C_1 would have taken a different value. We know that, in practice, only *one* value of C_1 is observed, but this does not matter: the model is an abstraction and it is perfectly feasible to describe what would happen, in terms of the model, in a situation which cannot occur in practice.

So, in discussing the theoretical properties of the model, each observation on consumption is treated as being a single value taken by a corresponding random variable. But the model does not necessarily imply that the same is true of the observations on income. In fact the model does not explain how the income values are determined and it is convenient to assume, wherever possible, that the explanatory variable observations are fixed, non-random quantities. One could think of disposable income as being fixed by policy decision, although this is rather unrealistic. The alternative is to interpret the present analysis as being partial and conditional on the income values determined elsewhere. In either case, $D_1, D_2, \ldots, D_n$ can be considered to be non-random, and since the expression $(\alpha + \beta D_t)$ does not involve any random variables, this is described as the *deterministic* part of the model.

It is very important to note that we do not *know* the values of α and β for which the model is valid. Indeed we do not *know* whether the model is valid at all. We therefore have two crucial objectives. The first is to find a method of *estimation,* which will produce *estimates* of α and β. One possibility is to plot the observed values for consumption and income on a graph and to choose a straight line which looks as though it passes reasonably closely through the observed points. The intercept and slope of this line would then be estimates of α and β respectively. But there is more to estimation than simply producing a pair of numbers. The rather elaborate theoretical structure that we have developed does provide a model for the relationship between consumption and income, but it also makes it possible to say something about the behaviour of the estimates, at least for certain standard methods of estimation.

It is fairly obvious that any method of estimation would make use of the observed values of consumption and income. Now, according to the model, the observations on consumption correspond to random variables. A different set of disturbance values would imply a different set of consumption values and hence a different value for an estimate calculated from the consumption values. It follows that the estimate actually obtained is just one of the values that *could* have arisen. The rule defining a method of estimation, usually expressed as an algebraic formula, is called an *estimator*. Replacing elements in the formula by the values actually observed gives a particular value of the estimator and this is an estimate. Our argument suggests that an estimator defines a random variable and that an estimate is a particular value taken by the random variable.

In the consumption function model, both α and β are unknown and we would therefore need *two* estimators. The estimators are random variables and therefore have probability distributions and it is usually possible to deduce these distributions from assumptions concerning the disturbances. Given this development, it is possible to make probability statements about the closeness of the estimates to the unknown 'true' parameters. However, the validity of such statements depends on the truth of the underlying assumptions and this brings us to the second important objective. In subsequent chapters we shall develop methods of *testing* some of the assumptions embodied in the model, to see whether these assumptions are consistent with observations taken from the real system. We shall also consider various extensions of the model, to allow for more realistic representation of highly interdependent economic systems.

1.6 Some Further Preliminaries

The nature of the consumption–income model has now been explained in some detail and we have also given some indication as to how the model is to be used. The purpose of this section is to introduce one or two further ideas which are necessary to the discussion which follows.

In the literature of statistics, a model of the kind that we have used would be described as a two variable *regression* model and the twin problems of estimation and testing would be described as problems of *statistical inference.* According to the model, each observation on consumption is just one of the values that could have arisen and, in this sense, observation of the real system provides incomplete information about the model. Statistical inference is the process of trying to discover something about the model on the basis of this incomplete information. The set of observations actually obtained is described as a *sample*: we have one sample but, according to the model, there are many different samples that might have been obtained.

In describing a sample of observations, it is often useful to have a measure representing an average value and a second measure representing the spread of values. These measures are provided by the *sample mean* and the *sample variance.* There is a very useful shorthand device for stating the formulae for these quantities. Suppose that we have a set of n observations on consumption, written as $C_t; t = 1, 2, \ldots, n$. The operation of forming a sum of the values can be written as

$$\sum_{t=1}^{t=n} C_t$$

which means 'add all the values of the variable, in this case consumption, starting with C_1 and finishing with C_n'. Often, it is obvious from the context what the range of summation should be and, if so, the shortened form ΣC_t is used instead. It is also necessary to be able to carry out algebraic manipulation of expressions which involve the summation notation and the following rules are useful in this respect.

1. If c is a constant

$$\sum_{t=1}^{t=n} c = nc$$

2. If c is a constant and X is a variable
$$\Sigma(cX_t) = c \Sigma X_t$$

3. If X and Y are two variables

$$\Sigma(X_t + Y_t) = \Sigma X_t + \Sigma Y_t$$

Note, however, that it is not true that $\Sigma(X_t Y_t)$ is the same as $(\Sigma X_t)(\Sigma Y_t)$. Each of these statements can easily be verified by inventing a few numerical examples (see exercise 1.3).

Given the summation notation, the formula for the sample mean consumption is

$$\bar{C} = \Sigma C_t / n \qquad (1.6.1)$$

This formula represents a simple average of the observations and $\bar{C}$ is a conventional notation for the sample mean of the variable written underneath the bar. The sample variance is written as s_c^2, and defined as

$$s_c^2 = \Sigma(C_t - \bar{C})^2 / n \qquad (1.6.2)$$

There is obviously an analogy between these sample quantities and the expectation and variance of a probability distribution. The expectation and the sample mean both represent average values and the sample variance and variance of a probability distribution are both measures of spread. In the case of the sample variance, the deviations used are from the *sample* mean and the averaging process consists of taking the *sample* mean of the squared deviations. The actual calculation is illustrated by the solution to exercise 1.4. For both the sample variance and the variance of a probability distribution, there is an alternative measure obtained by taking the square root of the corresponding variance. These quantities are known as *standard deviations* and so the *sample* standard deviation would be

$$s_c = \sqrt{\Sigma(C_t - \bar{C})^2 / n} \qquad (1.6.3)$$

The advantage of this quantity is that the units of measurement are the same as those for the original sample. If the units for consumption are £ million, the units for the sample variance would be (£ million)^2. But, because of the square root operation in (1.6.3), the units of the (sample) standard deviation would again be £ million.

Although there are similarities between the measures relating to a probability distribution and those relating to a sample, there are also some crucial differences. The expectation and variance are theoretical concepts and they can only be evaluated by assuming that the underlying probabilities are known or, alternatively, by making some other assumption about an underlying model. The sample mean and sample variance can be calculated directly from a given set of observations. And there is also a more subtle difference. The expectation and variance of a probability distribution are fixed constants, but the formulae for the sample mean and sample variance *could* each define a random variable. According to our model, this would be true of the measures for a sample of consumption values, because observations on consumption are themselves values taken by a set of random variables. But it would not be true of the corresponding measures for income, because the observations on income are taken to be fixed, non-random quantities. In this case, the sample measures would be purely descriptive.

The discussion in this chapter has covered a number of important ideas and it is useful to present a brief summary. It has been argued that an exact relationship between economic variables will not generally correspond to what is observed in the real system and so disturbances are added to the model. Since the model is designed to explain the behaviour of the dependent variable, a necessary preliminary is to have some 'explanation' of how the disturbance values are generated. This is achieved by constructing a probability model for the disturbances and, to follow up the implications of the probability model, it is necessary to have some basic ideas of statistical method. To the reader who has not previously encountered statistical arguments, the range of ideas covered in this chapter might be somewhat daunting, but we have now covered the essentials of a statistical survival kit, which should be quite sufficient to enable the reader to understand the arguments which follow.

Exercises (solutions on page 228)

1.1 Consider two variants of the die throwing game, in which the values marked on the die are
   (a) 7, 8, 9, 10, 11, 12
   (b) 2, 4, 6, 8, 10, 12
   In each case, find the expectation and variance of a random variable representing the outcome of a single throw. Can you suggest, for each case, a rule which links the expectation of the modified random variable to the expectation in the original game?

1.2 If V is a random variable representing the possible outcomes from a single throw of a six-sided die, show that $E[V - E(V)] = 0$.

1.3 The variable X takes the values 1, 2, 3, the variable Y takes the values, 2, 4, 6, and c is a constant, equal to 10. Use these examples to demonstrate the validity of the rules of summation, given in Section 1.6.

1.4 The following data consist of observations on consumers' expenditure (C) and personal disposable income (D), for the U K economy, in £ million at 1963 prices, covering the years 1963–72. For each variable, calculate the sample mean and sample standard deviation

Year	t	C_t	D_t
1963	1	20 130	21 786
1964	2	20 830	22 663
1965	3	21 197	23 202
1966	4	21 628	23 697
1967	5	22 118	24 090
1968	6	22 687	24 574
1969	7	22 800	24 722
1970	8	23 413	25 601
1971	9	24 032	26 267
1972	10	25 618	28 316

Source: *Economic Trends,* October 1972 and July 1973

2 The Two Variable Linear Model

2.1 The Least Squares Principle

In Chapter 1, the consumption function was used to illustrate the nature of the two variable regression model, but very little was said about how parameter estimates could be obtained. We now start on a more systematic discussion of the use of the model and the first step is to introduce a general notation. The convention adopted is that Y represents the dependent variable and X the explanatory variable and so, in this general notation, the linear model becomes

$$Y_t = \alpha + \beta X_t + u_t; \; t = 1, 2, \ldots, n \tag{2.1.1}$$

If a line is estimated, perhaps by plotting points on a scatter diagram and choosing a line to go through the points, any given value of X_t can be used to generate an estimated or *predicted* value of the dependent variable. The algebraic representation of this would be

$$\hat{Y}_t = \hat{\alpha} + \hat{\beta} X_t; \quad t = 1, 2, \ldots, n \tag{2.1.2}$$

where $\hat{\alpha}$ and $\hat{\beta}$ represent *estimates,* as distinct from the true values α and β and where $\hat{Y}_t$ is the predicted value of the dependent variable, as distinct from Y_t, the observed value. Any point $\hat{Y}_t$ lies on the estimated line, whereas a point Y_t does not, in general, lie on the estimated line. So for each point there is an error

$$e_t = Y_t - \hat{Y}_t; t = 1, 2, \ldots, n \tag{2.1.3}$$

which represents the displacement of the observed point from the *estimated* line. These errors are described as *residuals.* Combining (2.1.2) and (2.1.3) gives an expression for the residuals in terms of the estimates $\hat{\alpha}$ and $\hat{\beta}$

$$e_t = Y_t - \hat{\alpha} - \hat{\beta} X_t; t = 1, 2, \ldots, n \tag{2.1.4}$$

The residuals must be carefully distinguished from the *disturbances,* used in writing down the model, which are

$$u_t = Y_t - \alpha - \beta X_t; t = 1, 2, \ldots, n \tag{2.1.5}$$

Since the true values of α and β are unknown and since it is highly improbable that a particular pair of estimates would coincide exactly with the true values, it follows that the disturbance values cannot be observed and that it is highly unlikely that they would be the same as the residuals defined in (2.1.4).

It would be very inconvenient to have to actually draw a scatter diagram to estimate the line and so we consider a method which allows estimates of the intercept and slope to be obtained from algebraic formulae. It is obviously desirable that the estimated line should pass as closely as possible through the observed points and this means that the residuals (e_t; $t = 1, 2, \ldots, n$) should be made as small as possible. To achieve this, the residuals corresponding to each point have to be taken together in some way and this collective measure has then to be minimized. One could consider taking the sum of the residuals, but, for any estimated line passing through the scatter of points, some observed points would be above the line and some would be below: hence some e_t values would be positive and some negative and there are actually many lines for which the sum of residuals is zero. We therefore consider the sum of *squared* residuals, which is a sum of non-negative quantities. The least squares principle is that the line (and hence the parameter estimates) should be chosen so as to make the sum of squared residuals as small as possible. Formally, this can be stated as

Choose $\hat{\alpha}$ and $\hat{\beta}$ to minimize $\Sigma e_t^2 = \Sigma(Y_t - \hat{\alpha} - \hat{\beta}X_t)^2$ (2.1.6)

There exists a well defined procedure in calculus for solving a problem such as (2.1.6). It is important to realize that the solution can be expressed by writing down formulae for $\hat{\alpha}$ and $\hat{\beta}$ and that the economist does *not* have to use calculus to get parameter estimates for a particular model. What the calculus does (see exercise 2.3) is to show that the values of $\hat{\alpha}$ and $\hat{\beta}$, which satisfy the minimization condition, are those values which satisfy a pair of equations, known as the *normal* equations

$$\Sigma Y_t = \hat{\alpha}n + \hat{\beta}\Sigma X_t \qquad\qquad (2.1.7)$$
$$\Sigma X_t Y_t = \hat{\alpha}\Sigma X_t + \hat{\beta}\Sigma X_t^2$$

In these equations, $\hat{\alpha}$ and $\hat{\beta}$ are unknowns and $\Sigma Y_t, n, \Sigma X_t, \Sigma X_t Y_t$ and ΣX_t^2 are all known, in the sense that, for any given set of data, a value can be calculated for each quantity. There are many values of $\hat{\alpha}$ and $\hat{\beta}$ which would satisfy *one* of the equations, but the least squares principle implies that the correct choice of estimates would be the particular values of $\hat{\alpha}$ and $\hat{\beta}$ which satisfy *both* equations.

This is one of the contexts in which it is important to be able to recognize linearity, for if two unknown quantities have to satisfy two linear equations, the only possible solution is a pair of values which define a point lying on both straight lines. Since two distinct straight lines can only cross at a single point, there can only be one value, for each unknown, which satisfies both equations. The only cases in which this conclusion does not hold are (a) when the two lines are parallel or (b) when the two equations represent exactly the same line. In the first case, no solution is possible and the equations are inconsistent. In the second case, there is really only one equation and any point on the corresponding line would be a solution: but such a solution is not unique and, to fit a single estimated line to observed points, we do need a unique solution. An example of this second case is provided by the equations

$$100 = 10\hat{\alpha} + 50\hat{\beta}$$
$$500 = 50\hat{\alpha} + 250\hat{\beta}$$

Division by 5 on both sides of the second equation would reproduce the first equation exactly: it seems, at first, that there are two equations, but, in fact, there is only one distinct line.

The equations in (2.1.7) are linear in $\hat{\alpha}$ and $\hat{\beta}$ and so it would usually be possible to obtain a unique solution. In fact, we do not need to worry about whether a solution will exist, because inconsistency cannot occur in this context and the two equations would only be the same in the highly unlikely case in which X_t has the same value in all time periods. Such a variable is unlikely to be the basis of a successful two variable model.

It would perhaps be useful to have an example at this point. The data are completely artificial, chosen only to make the arithmetic easy.

Observation	Y_t	X_t	$X_t Y_t$	X_t^2
1	14	10	140	100
2	18	20	360	400
3	23	30	690	900
4	25	40	1000	1600
5	30	50	1500	2500
$n = 5$	$\Sigma Y_t = 110$	$\Sigma X_t = 150$	$\Sigma X_t Y_t = 3690$	$\Sigma X_t^2 = 5500$

If these values are used in (2.1.7), the equations become

$$110 = 5\hat{\alpha} + 150\hat{\beta}$$
$$3690 = 150\hat{\alpha} + 5500\hat{\beta}$$

By multiplying the first equation by $(150/5) = 30$ and subtracting the result from the second equation, it is possible to eliminate $\hat{\alpha}$, leaving

$$3690 - 30(110) = [5500 - 30(150)]\,\hat{\beta}$$

or

$$\hat{\beta} = 390/1000 = 0.39$$

Then, using the first equation, it is possible to solve for $\hat{\alpha}$, given the value of $\hat{\beta}$, as

$$5\hat{\alpha} = 110 - 150(0.39)$$
$$\hat{\alpha} = (110/5) - [150(0.39)/5]$$
$$= 22 - 11.7$$
$$= 10.3$$

So the estimated line in this example would suggest that Y increases by 0·39 for each unit increase in X and that, when $X = 0$, Y would be 10·3.

This calculation involves numerical manipulation to eliminate $\hat{\alpha}$, to solve the reduced system for $\hat{\beta}$ and finally, to solve for $\hat{\alpha}$ in terms of the value of $\hat{\beta}$ which has been obtained. It is possible to express this sequence of operations algebraically, to provide explicit formulae for $\hat{\alpha}$ and $\hat{\beta}$. The result would be

$$\hat{\beta} = [\Sigma X_t Y_t - (\Sigma X_t / n)\Sigma Y_t] / [\Sigma X_t^2 - (\Sigma X_t / n)\Sigma X_t]$$

and

$$\hat{\alpha} = \Sigma Y_t / n - \hat{\beta}(\Sigma X_t / n)$$

or

$$\hat{\alpha} = \overline{Y} - \hat{\beta}\overline{X} \tag{2.1.8}$$

where $\overline{Y}$ and $\overline{X}$ are the sample means of Y and X. It is generally more convenient to express the result for $\hat{\beta}$ in a slightly different form, in terms of quantities expressed as deviations from the mean. If we define

$$y_t = Y_t - \overline{Y} \text{ and } x_t = X_t - \overline{X}; t = 1, 2, \ldots, n \tag{2.1.9}$$

then it can be shown (see exercise 2.4) that the expression for $\hat{\beta}$ becomes

$$\hat{\beta} = \Sigma x_t y_t / \Sigma x_t^2 \tag{2.1.10}$$

If (2.1.10) is used for the numerical example, the table of calculations is rather different

Observation	Y_t	X_t	y_t $=Y_t - \overline{Y}$	x_t $= X_t - \overline{X}$	$x_t y_t$	x_t^2
1	14	10	−8	−20	160	400
2	18	20	−4	−10	40	100
3	23	30	1	0	0	0
4	25	40	3	10	30	100
5	30	50	8	20	160	400
$n = 5$	ΣY_t $= 110$	ΣX_t $= 150$	Σy_t $= 0$	Σx_t $= 0$	$\Sigma x_t y_t$ $= 390$	Σx_t^2 $= 1000$

$$\overline{Y} = 110/5 = 22; \quad \overline{X} = 150/5 = 30; \quad \hat{\beta} = 390/1000 = 0.39;$$
$$\hat{\alpha} = 22 - 0.39(30) = 10.3$$

Although there are more steps involved when deviations are used, there are certain advantages to this formulation, which we shall discuss in due course.

Equations (2.1.8) and (2.1.10) represent shorthand expressions for a set of instructions, which can be applied to any set of data to produce estimates of the intercept and slope. The formulae define the *least squares estimators* and the values obtained from a particular set of data are the estimates for that data. You will notice that, at first, in defining the minimization problem which produces the formulae, $\hat{\alpha}$ and $\hat{\beta}$ were used to represent *any* estimators for α and β. From now on, this notation refers only to the *least squares* estimators, although we shall occasionally use the same symbols to refer to particular estimates.

2.2 The Correlation Coefficient

The least squares method produces an estimated line, which is the best fitting of all possible straight lines, at least in the sense of minimizing the sum of squared errors. But the best line in any particular case may not fit very closely to the observed points and so may not provide a particularly good explanation of the behaviour of the dependent variable. Fig. 2.1 shows two different situations, one in which all the points lie very close to the estimated line and one in which the points tend to lie well away from the line. In the first case, there is obviously a strong relationship between Y and X and an explanation relating the behaviour of Y to the behaviour of X does correspond to what is observed. In the second case, the explanation is poor and the linkage between Y and X is weak, if it exists at all. To give a precise numerical measure to

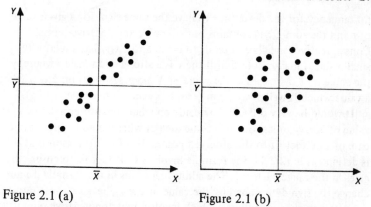

Figure 2.1 (a)   Figure 2.1 (b)

the strength of the relationship (sometimes called the 'goodness of fit'), the *correlation* coefficient is used. This is denoted by r and defined by

$$r = \frac{\Sigma x_t y_t}{\sqrt{\Sigma x_t^2} \; \sqrt{\Sigma y_t^2}} \qquad (2.2.1)$$

where, as before, $x_t = X_t - \bar{X}$ and $y_t = Y_t - \bar{Y}$.

To see why this formula does provide a measure of the strength of the relationship, consider again the two situations shown in Fig. 2.1. In both cases, the estimated line would actually pass through the point $(\bar{X}, \bar{Y})$, the point of sample means of the variables X and Y. This is a property of the least squares method and equation (2.1.8) shows this directly

$$\hat{\alpha} = \bar{Y} - \hat{\beta} \bar{X}$$

so

$$\bar{Y} = \hat{\alpha} + \hat{\beta} \bar{X} \qquad (2.2.2)$$

Equation (2.2.2) states that $\bar{Y}$ and $\bar{X}$ are particular values which do satisfy the equation corresponding to the estimated line. In the first case, shown in Fig. 2.1(a), nearly all the points for which X_t is greater than the mean, $\bar{X}$, are also points for which Y_t is greater than the mean, $\bar{Y}$, and nearly all the points for which X_t is less than $\bar{X}$ are also points for which Y_t is less than $\bar{Y}$. So positive deviations, $x_t = X_t - \bar{X}$, tend to go with positive deviations, $y_t = Y_t - \bar{Y}$ and negative values of x_t tend to go with negative values of y_t. Consequently, almost all the terms in the sum $\Sigma x_t y_t$ are the product of two positive numbers or the product of two negative numbers and, in either case, the product is positive. In a case like that shown in Fig. 2.1 (a), the value of $\Sigma x_t y_t$ will therefore tend to be large and positive. In the second case, there is no tendency for the deviations to have the same sign, for a given value of t and the sum $\Sigma x_t y_t$ contains both positive and negative terms. Consequently, cancellation tends to occur and $\Sigma x_t y_t$ has a relatively small value. Finally, note that if there is a strong relationship whereby the value of Y *decreases* as the value of X increases, the sum $\Sigma x_t y_t$ takes a value which is well away from zero, but which is *negative*.

It would be very difficult to decide on what constitutes a 'large' value of $\Sigma x_t y_t$, unless one had some idea of what would happen in the case of a perfect fit to the observed points. It is for this reason that r is defined as in (2.2.1): the formula involves scale factors to ensure that r lies in the range -1 to $+1$. The additional terms in the formula do not change the sign determined by the value of $\Sigma x_t y_t$, because these terms are based on sums of squares, which involve only non-negative quantities and it is understood that positive values are taken for the square roots. A perfect fit based on a positive relationship would give $r = 1$, a perfect fit based on a negative relationship would give $r = -1$ and a situation in which there was absolutely no connection between Y and X would give $r = 0$. But these are theoretical extremes and, in practice, one would obtain a value close to, but not equal to 1 for a strong positive relationship, close to -1 for a strong negative relationship and close to zero for a weak or non-existent relationship. It is often convenient to use r^2 rather than r, for then positive and negative slopes are treated in exactly the same way. The fact that r is bounded is not proved here, but the elements of a proof will be found in Section 3.3.

If the slope estimate has already been obtained by means of equation (2.1.10), it is relatively simple to extend the calculation to obtain the correlation coefficient. All that is needed is an extra column for the values y_t^2; $t = 1, 2, \ldots, n$ and, in the example used in the previous section, $\Sigma y_t^2 = 154$, so that

$$r = \frac{390}{\sqrt{1000} \sqrt{154}} = 0 \cdot 9938$$

This indicates that the artificial data shows a very strong positive association between Y and X, but this is a purely numerical illustration and, in practice, one would have to be very careful in trying to draw conclusions from as few as five observations.

2.3 Properties of the Least Squares Estimators

By application of the least squares principle, one can obtain estimators for the parameters of any economic relationship which corresponds to the two variable model

$$Y_t = \alpha + \beta X_t + u_t; \quad t = 1, 2, \ldots, n \qquad (2.3.1)$$

Remember that the estimators are rules, which can be applied to a given set of data to produce numbers which are the estimates based on that particular set of data. In Chapter 1, it was suggested that an estimator defines a random variable and that an estimate is a particular value taken by the random variable. If this is so, it would be misleading to treat estimates simply as point values and we should like to be able to say something about the quality of estimation and, in particular, about the probability of our estimates being close to the true values. To achieve this, it is necessary to establish the type of probability distribution associated with the least squares estimators and to find parameters such as the expectation and variance. The investigation of the statistical properties of the estimators will also provide some further criteria to justify the choice of least squares as a method of estimation. Although, for many economic applications, the two variable model is unduly restrictive, it is a useful vehicle for the discussion of estimator properties and the extensions introduced in the next chapter, to allow for further explanatory variables, are extensions of detail rather than of fundamental principle.

According to the model, the value taken by Y_t is determined by the value of X_t and by the value of the disturbance u_t. A different drawing from the probability distribution determining the value taken by the disturbance would imply a different value for the dependent variable and this in turn would imply a change in the scatter of observed points. Remember that the explanatory variable is assumed to take certain fixed values and that these would not change: the observed points would be different because of a change in the *dependent* variable values. If the observed points do change, one would expect a slightly different estimated line, which means that the parameter estimates would be different.

This argument should indicate why it is that the estimators are considered to be random variables. The random behaviour can be traced directly back to the random nature of the disturbance terms and this provides a clue as to how one can derive estimator properties. Since any random variable has a probability distribution, the least squares estimators have probability distributions. If all that is known about the disturbances is that they are random, there is nothing that can be said about the probability distributions of the disturbance process and the relationship between the estimators and the disturbances is of no help in trying to find the distributions of the estimators. If, however, we make certain plausible assumptions about the disturbance process, of the kind outlined in the previous chapter, the dependence of the estimators on the disturbances can be used. The precise nature of this dependence can be shown more concisely by means of an algebraic statement and the slope estimator

$$\hat{\beta} = \Sigma x_t y_t / \Sigma x_t^2 \qquad (2.3.2)$$

is used to illustrate this. The expression for the estimator contains the dependent variable values, in the form of deviations from the mean

$$y_t = Y_t - \bar{Y}; \ t = 1, 2, \ldots, n \qquad (2.3.3)$$

and the model states that

$$Y_t = \alpha + \beta X_t + u_t$$

By combining these three pieces of information, it is possible to show that

$$\hat{\beta} = \beta + \Sigma x_t u_t / \Sigma x_t^2 \qquad (2.3.4)$$

The full derivation of this expression is given in the solution to exercise 2.5, but our main concern is not with the algebraic detail, it is rather with the interpretation of the result.

Equation (2.3.4) shows clearly that the estimator does depend on the random disturbances, but it also conveys more specific information about the behaviour of $\hat{\beta}$. The estimator is made up of a non-random part, equal to the true parameter value, β, and a random part, based on the disturbances. It is clearly important, in trying to assess how well $\hat{\beta}$ performs as an estimator, to establish the connection between the estimator and the true parameter and equation (2.3.4) provides this link. If the random component was always equal to zero, the estimator would always provide an estimate equal to the true value, but we know that this does not happen in practice and it is necessary to look more closely at the behaviour of the random term.

According to equation (2.3.4) each individual disturbance, u_t, is *weighted* by the corresponding value of x_t and the weighted disturbances are then combined into the sum $\Sigma x_t u_t$. Finally, this sum is divided by Σx_t^2. The same result would be obtained if each term is *first* divided by Σx_t^2 and *then* added into the sum. Although these additions are not actually carried out in practice, the rules of summation still apply and this is nothing more than an application of those rules, but it tells us that (2.3.4) could be expressed as

$$\hat{\beta} = \beta + \Sigma(x_t/\Sigma x_t^2)u_t$$

or as

$$\tilde{\beta} = \beta + \Sigma w_t u_t \qquad (2.3.5)$$

where

$$w_t = x_t/\Sigma x_t^2; \ t = 1, 2, \ldots, n$$

The *weights*, w_t; $t = 1, 2, \ldots, n$, depend only on the deviations $x_t = X_t - \bar{X}$; $t = 1, 2, \ldots, n$ and hence on the values of X_t; $t = 1, 2, \ldots, n$. The weights are thus non-random. The particular form of equation (2.3.5) is important: a combination of the disturbances that can be written as $\Sigma w_t u_t$, for *any* set of non-random weights, is described as a *linear* combination and there are certain properties of a linear combination of random variables which can be used to derive the properties of $\hat{\beta}$.

As a first step, consider the *expectation* of $\hat{\beta}$. To make progress, it is necessary to assume something about the disturbance distributions and so it is assumed that each disturbance is represented by a random variable with zero expectation. This can be stated formally as

$$E(u_t) = 0; t = 1, 2, \ldots, n \qquad (2.3.6)$$

The problem is then to use this information to deduce the expectation of $\hat{\beta}$. It is easy to state the problem algebraically. Equation (2.3.5) shows that $\hat{\beta}$ is exactly equivalent to the expression on the right of (2.3.5) and so the *expectation* of $\hat{\beta}$ is given by the *expectation* of this expression

$$E(\hat{\beta}) = E(\beta + \Sigma w_t u_t) \qquad (2.3.7)$$

The solution to the problem then proceeds in stages

1. from the expectation of a single disturbance, say u_1, it is possible to deduce the expectation of $w_1 u_1$ and, by the same argument, the expectation of each term $w_t u_t$; $t = 1, 2, \ldots, n$
2. from the expectation of each term, $w_t u_t$; $t = 1, 2, \ldots, n$, it is possible to deduce the expectation of $\Sigma w_t u_t$.
3. from the expectation of $\Sigma w_t u_t$, it is possible to deduce the expectation of $\beta + \Sigma w_t u_t$, which, by (2.3.7), is the expectation of $\hat{\beta}$

The result obtained is rather important and each of these stages will be carefully explained. But, to make the objective clear, we shall first state the result and explain its significance. What we shall show is that the expectation of $\hat{\beta}$ is equal to the true parameter value

$$E(\hat{\beta}) = \beta \qquad (2.3.8)$$

For some sets of disturbance values, the slope estimate would be greater than the true value and, in other cases, it would be less. The *expectation* of $\hat{\beta}$ is an average over all the values that could arise and (2.3.8) states that there is no *systematic* tendency to either underestimate or overestimate the true parameter value. When the expected value of an estimator is equal to the true parameter, the estimator is said to be *unbiased*. The least squares slope estimator is therefore an unbiased estimator.

Now consider each of the stages outlined above. For a single disturbance, say u_1, the expectation is known and the only difference between the set of all possible values of u_1 and the set of all possible values of $w_1 u_1$ is that each value of u_1 is multiplied by the same non-random value, w_1. The effect of this is to multiply the expectation by the constant value w_1 (see exercise 1.1)

$$E(w_1 u_1) = w_1 E(u_1)$$

Exactly the same argument holds for each of the terms $w_t u_t$; $t = 1, 2, \ldots, n$

$$E(w_t u_t) = w_t E(u_t); t = 1, 2, \ldots, n \qquad (2.3.9)$$

But, since

$$E(u_t) = 0; t = 1, 2, \ldots, n$$

it follows that

$$E(w_t u_t) = 0; t = 1, 2, \ldots, n \qquad (2.3.10)$$

So the expectation of each term $w_t u_t$ is now known to be zero.

The next step is to derive the expectation of $\Sigma w_t u_t$. There are *two* types of summation implicit in finding this expectation. Although $\Sigma w_t u_t$ is a continuous random variable, the expectation would still effectively be obtained by summation over all possible values of $\Sigma w_t u_t$, using the corresponding probabilities as weights. Then the definition of $\Sigma w_t u_t$ involves a *second* summation, thus time over the n terms $w_t u_t$; $t = 1, 2, \ldots, n$. Neither of these operations is actually carried out in practice, but the rules of summation do indicate that the *ordering* of the two operations is irrelevant. One could first form the sum and then take the expectation or, alternatively, one could first take the expectation of individual terms and then form the sum.

Stated formally, this would give

$$E(\Sigma w_t u_t) = \Sigma [E(w_t u_t)] \qquad (2.3.11)$$

But in conjunction with (2.3.10), this implies that

$$E(\Sigma w_t u_t) = \Sigma [0] = 0 \qquad (2.3.12)$$

where we have used the fact that the sum of n zeros is just zero. So we now know that the expectation of $\Sigma w_t u_t$ is zero. Since $\Sigma w_t u_t$ is the random component in (2.3.5), it may now seem to be obvious that the expectation of $\hat{\beta}$ is equal to the non-random component β. But this too can be stated formally, as the final stage in the argument.

If the true parameter value, β, is added to the random variable $\Sigma w_t u_t$, each possible value of $\Sigma w_t u_t$ is increased by the *same* amount. The effect would be to increase the expectation by this constant value (see exercise 1.1)

$$E(\beta + \Sigma w_t u_t) = \beta + E(\Sigma w_t u_t) \qquad (2.3.13)$$

This, together with the earlier results, does imply that the expectation of $\hat{\beta}$ is equal to the true parameter value. Because this result is important, the derivation has been discussed in some detail and a formal proof is nothing more than a concise summary of the arguments that we have used. So, on this occasion, we depart from our usual practice by stating the complete proof

$$
\begin{aligned}
E(\hat{\beta}) &= E(\beta + \Sigma w_t u_t) && \text{from (2.3.7)} \\
&= \beta + E(\Sigma w_t u_t) && \text{from (2.3.13)} \\
&= \beta + \Sigma [E(w_t u_t)] && \text{from (2.3.11)} \\
&= \beta + \Sigma [w_t E(u_t)] && \text{from (2.3.9)} \\
&= \beta + \Sigma [w_t (0)] && \text{from (2.3.6)} \\
&= \beta + \Sigma [0] = \beta + 0 \\
&= \beta
\end{aligned}
$$

Having found the expectation of $\hat{\beta}$, the next step is to consider the *variance*, which acts as a measure of the extent to which individual estimates would be spread around the expected value. Just as the expectation of $\hat{\beta}$ is derived from an assumption about the expectation of the disturbance distributions, so here, it is necessary to make an assumption about the variance of the disturbance distributions and, initially, it is assumed that each distribution has the same variance, denoted as σ^2. It is also convenient to assume that the distributions are

independent, which means that the value taken by a single disturbance
has no influence on the values taken by other disturbances. Given this
assumption, it is not necessary to consider the interaction between the
behaviour of different disturbance terms, for independence implies that
no such interaction exists. So there is an advantage in making the
assumption that the disturbances are independent, unless there is
definite evidence to the contrary. On this basis, it can be shown that
the variance of $\hat{\beta}$ is given by

$$\text{var}\,(\hat{\beta}) = \sigma^2/\Sigma x_t^2 \qquad (2.3.14)$$

This result can be derived from the fact that $\hat{\beta}$ can be expressed as a
linear combination of the disturbances, but we shall not pursue this
line of argument. Instead, we shall pass directly to an interpretation
of the result.

Equation (2.3.14) suggests that the variance of $\hat{\beta}$ depends directly on
the variance of the disturbances (σ^2) and this is precisely what one would
expect. The estimate of the slope is determined by a particular choice
of disturbance values and changing the disturbances would alter the value
of $\hat{\beta}$. If the disturbances do show considerable variation, the effect on
$\hat{\beta}$ of choosing a different set of disturbances is likely to be greater than
would be the case if the disturbances show relatively little variation.
The other term in (2.3.14) is Σx_t^2. Now it is possible to compute a
sample variance for the observations on X, as a purely descriptive device
and this would give

$$s_X^2 = \Sigma(X_t - \bar{X})^2/n = \Sigma x_t^2/n \qquad (2.3.15)$$

Division by n is simply a means of scaling and the essential information
about the variation in the values of X is contained in the expression
Σx_t^2. So equation (2.3.14) suggests that the variance of $\hat{\beta}$ depends
inversely on Σx_t^2 and a relatively *wide* spread of values of the explanatory
variable produces a relatively *low* variance of $\hat{\beta}$.

It is clearly desirable that an unbiased estimator should have as small
a variance as possible, because this indicates that the estimator is distributed relatively closely about the expected value and, in the case of
an unbiased estimator, the expected value is equal to the true parameter
value. Given the assumptions concerning the common variance and
independence of the disturbance distributions, it can be shown that
the variance of the least squares estimator is at least as small as that of any
other *linear* unbiased estimator. The significance of linearity in this
context is that the least squares estimator can be expressed in terms
of a linear combination of the disturbances (see equation 2.3.5), but

by changing the definition of the weights, it would be possible to generate other linear unbiased estimators. The interesting feature of the result quoted here is that it enables us to say something about least squares as a method of estimation, without actually having to specify a list of alternatives. If any estimator has a variance which is always less than that of some other estimator, the first estimator is said to be the more *efficient*. An estimator which is at least as efficient as *any* other estimator of a given type is said to be the *best* estimator of that type. So our result can be stated by saying that the least squares slope estimator is a *best* linear unbiased estimator.

There is still some information to be obtained about the distribution of $\hat{\beta}$. If it is assumed that each disturbance behaves as though it has a normal distribution, it can be shown that the slope estimator also has a normal distribution. Once again, this result is based on a property of linear combinations. If a random variable is defined as a linear combination of other random variables, each having a normal distribution, the linear combination also has a normal distribution. So, if each disturbance, $u_t; t = 1, 2, \ldots, n$, has a normal distribution, it follows that $\Sigma w_t u_t$ has a normal distribution. It has already been established that $\Sigma w_t u_t$ has a zero expectation and equation (2.3.5) shows that the slope estimator is the sum of $\Sigma w_t u_t$ and the non-random true value, β. The only effect of adding β to $\Sigma w_t u_t$ is to shift the entire distribution through β units, so that $\hat{\beta}$ has a normal distribution with an expectation equal to β and a variance given by equation (2.3.14). When referring specifically to a probability distribution, it is usual to call the expectation the mean of the distribution, or simply the mean. In Chapter 1, it was stated that the expectation of a random variable and the mean of the corresponding distribution are identical concepts and, from now on, both descriptions are used.

In principle, we have now satisfied the objectives set at the beginning of this section. If the mean and variance of a normal distribution are known, it is possible to use published tables to make probability statements about the random variable in question. In the next section, we shall show how this idea is applied to the slope estimator, $\hat{\beta}$. The other objective was to provide some further criteria to justify the choice of least squares as a method of estimation and, to satisfy this objective, it has been argued that $\hat{\beta}$ is a best linear unbiased estimator. Given that we have assumed normality of the disturbance distributions, it is actually possible to strengthen this result. Under normality of the disturbances, $\hat{\beta}$ can be shown to be best amongst *all* unbiased estimators, without the constraint of linearity. It is true that best *linear* unbiasedness does not require the normality assumption, but if that assumption is made for other reasons, the stronger result of best unbiasedness also applies.

It is very important to understand that there are many ways of estimating any unknown parameter, but that there are certain criteria that an estimator should satisfy, if it is to be acceptable. On the basis of the criteria that we have discussed, the least squares estimator does have desirable properties, but this conclusion depends crucially on the *specification* of the model, which includes the form of the relationship and the additional assumptions that have to be made. There may eventually be enough evidence, from observation of the real economic system, to contradict one or more of these assumptions. In the meantime, the analysis can only proceed by using the model as though it were true.

The assumptions made play such an important role that it is worth restating the specification of the model in full. The dependent variable is assumed to behave as though the observed values are generated by, the relationship

$$Y_t = \alpha + \beta X_t + u_t; t = 1, 2, \ldots, n$$

where each X_t is considered to be non-random and where the disturbance values are assumed to be adequately represented as drawings from a set of n independent normal distributions, with zero mean and a common variance, σ^2. The complete model can thus be stated as a list of six assumptions:

(A) $Y_t = \alpha + \beta X_t + u_t; t = 1, 2, \ldots, n$

(B) X_t is non-random; $t = 1, 2, \ldots, n$

(C) $E(u_t) = 0; t = 1, 2, \ldots, n$

(D) var $(u_t) = \sigma^2; t = 1, 2, \ldots, n$

(E) The disturbance distributions are independent

(F) The disturbance distributions are normal

These assumptions were used, in the following way, to obtain the properties of the least squares slope estimator. From A, B and C, it was possible to derive the expectation of $\hat{\beta}$ and to show that $\hat{\beta}$ is an unbiased estimator. Then, by adding D and E, it was possible to argue that $\hat{\beta}$ is best linear unbiased, with variance given by equation (2.3.14). Finally, by adding F, it was possible to argue that $\hat{\beta}$ has a normal distribution and that $\hat{\beta}$ is best unbiased. But, in some respects, this argument is misleading. Assumption C is not actually necessary for the variance formula to be correct and assumptions C, D and E are not necessary for the normality of $\hat{\beta}$. To show exactly which assumptions are needed, the properties are summarized below, with the relevant assumptions listed alongside the statement of the property:

1. $E(\hat{\beta}) = \beta$, indicates unbiasedness (A, B, C)
2. var $(\hat{\beta}) = \sigma^2/\Sigma x_t^2$ (A, B, D, E)
3. best linear unbiasedness (A, B, C, D, E)
4. best unbiasedness (A, B, C, D, E, F)
5. normality (A, B, F)

A similar set of properties can be listed for the intercept estimator, $\hat{\alpha}$. Properties 3 to 5 hold as for $\hat{\beta}$ and the estimator is unbiased, but now

$$E(\hat{\alpha}) = \alpha \tag{2.3.16}$$
and
$$\text{var } (\hat{\alpha}) = \sigma^2 \left(1/n + \overline{X}^2/\Sigma x_t^2\right) \tag{2.3.17}$$

The various properties specified above hold for any set of observations which satisfy the assumptions, irrespective of how many observations there are. In Section 2.7, we obtain a further set of properties, which hold only approximately and then only when the number of observations is large. In later chapters, when the analysis has to be conducted under rather weaker assumptions, it will be necessary to use some of these alternative properties which an estimator may have.

2.4 Confidence Intervals

If a random variable has a normal distribution, with a specified mean and variance, it is possible to find the probability that the variable will take a value within any chosen range. This idea has already been mentioned briefly, but we shall now consider in detail how the probability statement is used. If the chosen range consists of an equal distance on either side of the mean, the probability of a value falling in that range depends only on the spread of the distribution, which can be measured either by the variance or by the standard deviation. This in turn implies that if the range is defined in terms of a certain number of standard deviations, we would have a probability statement which applies equally to *all* normally distributed variables. To illustrate the point, note that the probability of finding a value within one standard deviation, on either side of the mean, is 0·6826, that the probability for two standard deviations is 0·9544 and that the probability for three standard deviations is 0·9974. This information can be obtained from tables of the normal distribution, which can be found in almost any introductory statistics text, together with information on the use of the tables. It should be stressed that these probabilities are those for the normal distribution and that they do not apply to other probability distributions.

For our purpose, it is sufficient to know that there is a probability of approximately 0·95 attached to the event that a single value of a normally distributed variable will fall within 2 standard deviations of the mean. The range associated with a probability of *exactly* 0·95 is based on 1·96 standard deviations. It would make very little difference if the number 1·96 were to be rounded to 2, but it would perhaps be helpful to retain the rather distinctive value of 1·96 for the time being.

In the case of the normal distribution associated with the slope estimator, $\hat{\beta}$, the mean is β, the variance is $\sigma^2/\Sigma x_t^2$ and the standard deviation is the square root of this quantity. The standard deviation of a probability distribution associated with an estimator is usually called the *standard error* and, if the notation se( ) is used to represent this, the standard error of the slope estimator would be

$$se(\hat{\beta}) = \sigma/\sqrt{\Sigma x_t^2} \qquad (2.4.1)$$

The value of Σx_t^2 can, of course, be computed from the data, but equation (2.4.1) cannot be used unless the value of σ is known. It is convenient to continue the analysis, just for the moment, on the assumption that the correct value can be assigned to σ, but, in practice, there is no reason why one should know the variance or the standard deviation of the disturbance distributions.

We now have sufficient information to be able to say that there is a probability of 0·95 attached to the event that an individual slope estimate will fall in the range

$$\beta - 1·96\,\sigma/\sqrt{\Sigma x_t^2} \text{ to } \beta + 1·96\,\sigma/\sqrt{\Sigma x_t^2}$$

The range could also be written, more compactly, as

$$\beta \pm 1·96\,\sigma/\sqrt{\Sigma x_t^2} \qquad (2.4.2)$$

or as

$$\beta \pm 1·96\,se(\hat{\beta}) \qquad (2.4.3)$$

It is very important to understand exactly what is being said here. We know very well that, given a set of data, one would calculate a *single* estimate of the slope, so that $\hat{\beta}$ would take one particular value. That value either falls in the range defined by (2.4.3) or it does not and the probability statement merely says something about the chances. If it is helpful to think of the estimation being repeated, for many different sets of disturbances and hence for many different sets of observations on the dependent variable, then one can think of 95 per cent of all the slope estimates which could arise as falling within the range (2.4.3). But this is an aid to understanding rather than an accurate description of what the probability statement means. It is not necessary, either in theory or in practice, to be able to replicate the estimation.

The range defined in (2.4.3) is fixed and the random variable $\hat{\beta}$ falls within this range with a probability of 0·95. This implies that there is a probability of 0·95 attached to the event that $\hat{\beta}$ is no further than 1·96 standard errors from the true value. Exactly the same information can be conveyed by constructing a *variable* range

$$\hat{\beta} \pm 1 \cdot 96 \, se(\hat{\beta}) \tag{2.4.4}$$

which would include the *fixed* true value with a probability of 0·95. The range defined in (2.4.4) is described as a *95 per cent confidence interval* for the true value β and it is a variable interval because the centre point, $\hat{\beta}$, is a random variable. Notice, however, that the *width* of the interval is fixed, if σ is known. The confidence interval is a more useful form of probability statement than (2.4.3), because if σ is known, it is possible to replace the remaining terms by numerical values computed from the data. Although the fixed range in (2.4.3) does provide useful information, it involves the unknown true parameter β and so does not form the basis of an interval to which numerical values can be assigned.

The probability associated with the confidence interval can always be increased, but only at the cost of increasing the *critical value,* which in the interval above is the number 1·96. If the critical value is increased, the interval becomes wider and so there is a trade-off between the probability level and the width of the interval. A 95 per cent confidence interval is simply a convenient compromise between the level of probability and the width of the interval.

So far, it has been assumed that the disturbance variance, σ^2, is known, but this is seldom the case in practice. The obvious strategy is to try to form an estimate of σ^2 and then to ask whether this has any effect on the confidence interval. If a parameter of a probability distribution is unknown, it is natural to think in terms of using a corresponding sample quantity as an estimator, but we also know that there could be several possible estimators for any parameter and that the chosen estimator should satisfy certain criteria. In the case of a parameter of the distur-

bance process, there is an additional difficulty, because the *true* disturbances $(u_t; t = 1, 2, \ldots, n)$ cannot be observed. All that one has is the
set of *residuals*, defined as

$$e_t = Y_t - \hat{\alpha} - \hat{\beta}X_t; \quad t = 1, 2, \ldots, n \tag{2.4.5}$$

A sample variance based on these quantities would be

$$\Sigma(e_t - \bar{e})^2/n \tag{2.4.6}$$

but this expression has to be modified in two ways. It so happens that
the *sum* of the residuals defined in (2.4.5) is always zero: this follows
directly from the first normal equation in (2.1.7) and, if the sum of
residuals is zero, the sample mean is always zero. The term $\bar{e}$ in (2.4.6)
is thus redundant. The second modification is necessary because (2.4.6)
does *not* define an *unbiased* estimator of σ^2. To achieve the property of
unbiasedness, the divisor should be $(n - 2)$ rather than n and so the
appropriate estimator is

$$\hat{\sigma}^2 = \Sigma e_t^2/(n - 2) \tag{2.4.7}$$

The quantity $(n - 2)$ is known as the *degrees of freedom* and,
although this is defined as a purely mathematical concept, it is possible
to give an intuitive interpretation or, at least, a rule of thumb, to be
used in deciding what the degrees of freedom should be. If one were
to specify a two variable model based on just *two* fixed X_t values, it
would be quite possible to have two non-zero disturbance values, so
that the *true* line need not go through either of the (X_t, Y_t) points.
But if there are just two observations and the line has to be *estimated*,
it is possible to choose a line passing through both points, giving
residuals which are equal to zero and a sum of squared residuals, Σe_t^2,
equal to zero. As this is obviously the minimum possible values of the
sum of squares, the estimates obtained are least squares estimates. In
this case the two degrees of freedom provided by the observations are
used in estimating the parameters α and β and the parameter estimates
have to be obtained before the residuals can be found. Extending this
idea to more than two observations it would be argued that, of the n
degrees of freedom provided by the data, two are used in the estimation
of α and β, leaving $(n - 2)$ degrees of freedom to be associated with the
sum of squared residuals.

At this point, we must consider a question of terminology, which
relates to the standard error. In any practical situation, the standard
error would have to be constructed from an estimate of the disturbance
variance and, from now on, the term standard error will be taken to
imply that such an estimate is made. Indeed, some authors only use

standard error in the context of an *estimate* of the standard deviation of the distribution of an estimator. So $\text{se}(\hat{\beta})$ is *redefined* as

$$\text{se}(\hat{\beta}) = \hat{\sigma}/\sqrt{\sum x_t^2} \qquad (2.4.8)$$

and a confidence interval, based on this standard error, would be

$$\hat{\beta} \pm 1 \cdot 96 \; \hat{\sigma}/\sqrt{\sum x_t^2} \qquad (2.4.9)$$

The interval can still be written as

$$\hat{\beta} \pm 1 \cdot 96 \; \text{se}(\hat{\beta})$$

but it must be remembered that $\text{se}(\hat{\beta})$ is now based on an estimator of the disturbance variance and not on the true value.

In the previous formulation of the confidence interval, given in (2.4.4), the bounds of the interval were random variables, but the distance between the bounds was fixed. Since $\text{se}(\hat{\beta})$ is now derived from an *estimator* of the disturbance variance, it is a random variable and this means that the *width* of the interval is now a random variable. One would expect this to have some effect on the probability of finding that the interval does contain the true value and this is indeed the case. The interval defined by (2.4.9), making use of an estimated disturbance variance, is now associated with a probability of rather *less* than 0·95 and, to maintain the level of probability, it is necessary to have a wider interval. This is achieved by replacing 1·96 by an alternative critical value, taken from the *t distribution* rather than the normal distribution. The critical values from the t distribution depend on the number of observations, or, to be precise, on the number of degrees of freedom and, in this respect, the t distribution is different from the normal distribution. But, unless the number of observations is small, a 95 per cent confidence interval based on the t distribution is not very different from that which one would obtain from the normal distribution, ignoring the fact that the disturbance variance is actually an estimate. To give some idea of the differences involved, the following are 95 per cent confidence intervals, based on the t distribution, for various numbers of observations

$$n = 7, \quad n - 2 = 5 \quad : \hat{\beta} \pm 2 \cdot 57 \; \text{se}(\hat{\beta})$$
$$n = 12, n - 2 = 10 : \hat{\beta} \pm 2 \cdot 23 \; \text{se}(\hat{\beta})$$
$$n = 17, n - 2 = 15 : \hat{\beta} \pm 2 \cdot 13 \; \text{se}(\hat{\beta})$$
$$n = 32, n - 2 = 30 : \hat{\beta} \pm 2 \cdot 04 \; \text{se}(\hat{\beta})$$
$$n = 62, n - 2 = 60 : \hat{\beta} \pm 2 \cdot 00 \; \text{se}(\hat{\beta})$$

The critical values in these examples are taken from tables of the t distribution. But one could avoid the explicit use of the tables by having a fixed critical value of 2 and recognizing that this would give a rather lower confidence level when the number of observations is small. For $n = 7$, the confidence level would be 90 per cent, for $n = 22$, approximately 94 per cent and for larger numbers of observations, a critical value of 2 would provide a close approximation to a 95 per cent interval.

2.5 Testing a Simple Hypothesis

The two variable model states that Y is linked to X by means of the relationship

$$Y_t = \alpha + \beta X_t + u_t; t = 1, 2, \ldots, n \qquad (2.5.1)$$

but if the true value of β is zero, the model reduces to

$$Y_t = \alpha + u_t; t = 1, 2, \ldots, n \qquad (2.5.2)$$

in which case Y varies randomly around a fixed value α, but has no connection with X. The decision as to whether or not β is zero is therefore of fundamental importance in deciding whether the two variable model is appropriate. It can be assumed that the investigator does not *know* that $\beta = 0$, for he would not make use of (2.5.1) unless he believed that Y could be related to X. So it is only by observation of the real system that one could obtain information on the value of β, but the information is not complete: even if $\beta = 0$, it is highly unlikely that estimation based on (2.5.1) would produce a slope *estimate* exactly equal to zero and it is necessary to devise a test procedure to attempt to distinguish between a non-zero value of $\hat{\beta}$ that arises purely by chance and a non-zero value that arises because the true parameter is also non-zero.

All we have to go on, in constructing a test, is a single value of the estimator, $\hat{\beta}$, and the information that the probability of finding an estimate within 2 standard errors of the true value is approximately 0·95. But there is a value which, to the best of our knowledge, *could* be the true value and which is of particular interest, namely $\beta = 0$ and it *is* possible to say something about the probabilities that *would* hold if this were actually the true value. This is the key to the test procedure. Suppose that we do obtain a value of $\hat{\beta}$ which is more than two standard errors away from zero. This could happen because β is zero and we have actually observed an unlikely event, but although we have an interest in the possibility that β is zero, we have no reason to believe that this is the true value and, instead of concluding that we have observed an unlikely event, we could conclude that what has been observed is not necessarily unlikely, because β is *not* in fact zero. This rather complicated logic is the basis of the test procedure and it is hardened into a definite decision rule, which states that if $\hat{\beta}$ lies *outside* the range

$$0 \pm 2 \; \text{se}(\hat{\beta})$$

the conclusion drawn is that β is *not* zero, whereas if $\hat{\beta}$ lies *inside* the range, there is no evidence to suggest that β is not zero. For all practical purposes, one can treat the latter conclusion as saying that β is zero.

The rule suggested above is an example of a *statistical test* and there exists a formal framework for statistical testing which can be used in a number of different contexts. It is generally convenient to express the test procedure in terms of the calculation of a *test statistic*, which is then compared with the appropriate critical value to enable a decision to be made. In order to compute the test statistic, it is necessary to have a working value of the parameter of interest. Then, after the calculation has been performed, the decision is made as to whether the working value is reasonable, in the light of the observable evidence. The working value is called the *null hypothesis* and, in the example above, the null hypothesis is $\beta = 0$. It may well be that the investigator fully expects the null hypothesis to be rejected, but the test calculation can only be performed on the basis of some such working value.

The decision rule used in testing the null hypothesis that $\beta = 0$ is based on the knowledge that there is a probability of approximately 0·95 attached to the event that $\hat{\beta}$ lies inside the range

$$\beta \pm 2 \; \text{se}(\hat{\beta})$$

Under the conditions of the null hypothesis, this range becomes

$$0 \pm 2 \; \text{se}(\hat{\beta}) \tag{2.5.3}$$

The event defined by $\hat{\beta}$ falling in the range (2.5.3) can only occur if the *ratio* $\hat{\beta}/\text{se}(\hat{\beta})$ falls in the range -2 to $+2$ and this ratio defines the test statistic

$$t = \hat{\beta}/\text{se}(\hat{\beta}) \tag{2.5.4}$$

So long as β *is* zero, the test statistic lies in the range -2 to $+2$ with a probability of approximately 0·95 and this implies that the probability of the statistic being *outside* the range is approximately 0·05. The decision rule can therefore be expressed as saying that if the value obtained for t lies outside the range -2 to $+2$, the null hypothesis is rejected and we conclude that β is different from zero. Otherwise the null hypothesis is not rejected. The critical value here is 2, but it must be remembered that the null hypothesis is rejected if t is *either* greater than 2 *or* less than −2. If we wished the probabilities under the null hypothesis to be exact, it would be necessary to use the appropriate critical value taken from the t distribution and this explains the notation used for the test statistic. But, unless the number of observations is small, using the correct critical value would make very little difference.

It is useful to restate the argument leading to the use of (2.5.4) in a slightly different way. Since $\hat{\beta}$ has a normal distribution, with mean β and *true* variance $\sigma^2/\Sigma x_t^2$, there is a probability of *exactly* 0·95 attached to the event that $\hat{\beta}$ lies in the range

$$\beta \pm 1{\cdot}96\ \sigma/\sqrt{\Sigma x_t^2}$$

The following alternative descriptions specify exactly the same event

1. $(\hat{\beta} - \beta)$ lies in the range $0 \pm 1{\cdot}96\ \sigma/\sqrt{\Sigma x_t^2}$
2. the ratio $(\hat{\beta} - \beta)/(\sigma/\sqrt{\Sigma x_t^2})$ lies in the range $0 \pm 1{\cdot}96$

For economy of notation, let the ratio in 2 be represented by z

$$z = (\hat{\beta} - \beta)/(\sigma/\sqrt{\Sigma x_t^2}) \qquad (2.5.5)$$

The quantity z must be a random variable, since it involves the random variable $\hat{\beta}$: it is also a random variable that lies between −1·96 and +1·96 with a probability of 0·95. This does not prove anything, but it is certainly suggestive. A random variable having a normal distribution, with mean 0 and standard deviation 1 would lie between −1·96 and +1·96 with a probability of 0·95, and, in fact, z is just such a variable, having what is described as a *standard* normal distribution. Any variable having a normal distribution can be converted to a standard normal variable, by subtracting the mean and dividing by the standard deviation and is the standard form of normal distribution for which probabilities are tabulated.

If the disturbance variance, σ^2, were known, the ratio z could be used to test the null hypothesis $\beta = 0$. Under the null hypothesis, the ratio would reduce to

$$z = \hat{\beta}/(\sigma/\sqrt{\Sigma x_t^2}) \qquad (2.5.6)$$

and this would lie between −1·96 and 1·96 with a probability of 0·95. Consequently, if a value of z were found to lie *outside* this range, we would conclude that β is *not* zero. But σ^2 is not known and if the *estimated* disturbance variance $\hat{\sigma}^2$ is used, a ratio equivalent to (2.5.5) has a t distribution rather than a normal distribution. In this case the ratio is denoted by t rather than by z and, under the null hypothesis, the ratio would be

$$t = \hat{\beta}/(\hat{\sigma}/\sqrt{\Sigma x_t^2})$$

or

$$t = \hat{\beta}/\text{se}(\hat{\beta})$$

which is the test statistic (2.5.4). The critical value should now be taken from tables of the t distribution, but if an approximation is used, it should be 2 rather than 1·96, since the latter number implies a spurious accuracy.

There are two ways in which the wrong conclusion can be drawn from any test. Type I error is the rejection of a null hypothesis which is actually true and type II error is the failure to reject a null hypothesis which is false. Type I error can only occur if the null hypothesis is true which, in the test described here, would mean that $\beta = 0$. This makes it very simple to calculate the probability of type I error, since, if β *is* equal to zero, we know that the probability of rejection is approximately 0·05. If type II error occurs, it is because β is *not* zero and the probability of type II error depends on what the true value actually is. If the true value is well within 2 standard errors of zero, it is very likely that one would fail to reject the hypothesis that β is zero and the probability of type II error would be high. If, on the other hand, the true value is well away from zero, the probability of type II error would be low. Fortunately, when the probability of type II error is high, it is unlikely to matter very much that the error occurs, at least in the context of a two variable model. The investigator would conclude that there is no relationship between Y and X when, in fact, a relationship does exist, but under the conditions that would give a high probability of type II error, the relationship is likely to be very weak, dominated by the random disturbances and of little real value as an economic model.

If an investigator uses the two variable model and, as a result of the t test, fails to reject the hypothesis that $\beta = 0$, there is no longer any reason to use X as an explanatory variable and the evidence suggests that

$$Y = \alpha + u_t; t = 1, 2, \ldots, n$$

is the appropriate model. In practice, it is unlikely that an economist would be satisfied with a form of model which suggests that Y varies randomly around a fixed value and he would probably search for alternative explanatory variables. It may be necessary to try a number of different models before an acceptable form is found. There is no escaping the fact that such experimentation does take place, but the statistical theory that we have used does not allow for a situation in which a given model may be chosen after a sequence of experiments. Such a sequence can be difficult to analyse from a statistical viewpoint and the best that we can do is to say that, in such a situation, the results given in this chapter are likely to overstate the precision attached to estimation and hypothesis testing.

2.6   Prediction

If the parameters of the two variable model have been estimated and if this form of model is found to be acceptable, the *estimated* line can be found by substituting the particular values obtained for $\hat{\alpha}$ and $\hat{\beta}$ into

$$\hat{Y}_t = \hat{\alpha} + \hat{\beta}X_t; t = 1, 2, \ldots, n \qquad (2.6.1)$$

Suppose now that one wished to predict a value of the dependent variable which, for some reason, could not be observed. The usual context for this problem is when the data consists of a time series of observations, representing the recent past and the object of prediction is a value of the dependent variable which has not yet been observed, either because the relevant time period is still in the future or perhaps because that period has occurred so recently that no information is yet available. But this is not very different from a situation in which the data is taken from different units in a cross-section: the prediction would then concern a *unit* for which the dependent variable value was unknown. It is convenient to use time as the context for discussion, but the possibility of using similar ideas in a cross-section must not be overlooked.

We shall assume that the prediction is to be made for period $n + 1$. This naturally suggests the period immediately following the sequence $t = 1, 2, \ldots, n$ and this may be the period for which the prediction is required, but, in the discussion which follows, $n + 1$ can be taken to refer to *any* period not included in $t = 1, 2, \ldots, n$. The value of the dependent variable in period $n + 1$ would be Y_{n+1} and the obvious method for making a prediction is to apply the estimated equation to this period. If X_{n+1} represents the corresponding value of the explanatory variable, the formula for the prediction would be

$$\hat{Y}_{n+1} = \hat{\alpha} + \hat{\beta}X_{n+1} \qquad (2.6.2)$$

Clearly, one has to have a value for X_{n+1} before (2.6.2) can be used and the prediction is therefore *conditional* on the value chosen for X_{n+1}. If X_{n+1} is known, perhaps because it can be fixed by policy decision, well and good, but the more usual situation is one in which some uncertainty is attached to the value of X_{n+1}. In this case, the best strategy is to assume a set of *possible* values for X_{n+1} and to obtain a conditional prediction for the dependent variable corresponding to each possible value of the explanatory variable. Although this does not predict the future in a pure sense, it does at least provide some idea of the range of possibilities that *could* result from different values of the explanatory variable.

The original specification of the two variable model is

$$Y_t = \alpha + \beta X_t + u_t; \ t = 1, 2, \ldots, n \qquad (2.6.3)$$

which refers specifically to the data period. Before this can be used as a basis for the prediction of Y_{n+1}, it must also be assumed that

$$Y_{n+1} = \alpha + \beta X_{n+1} + u_{n+1} \qquad (2.6.4)$$

which states that the same form of model is valid in period $n + 1$ and moreover, that the values of α and β which make the model valid are exactly the same as those for the data period. It is possible that the model could be valid for period $n + 1$, but for *different* values of α and β. What we require is that it is valid for the *same* values of α and β, for otherwise the estimates obtained from the data period would not apply to the forecast period.

It is important to understand the nature of a prediction obtained from a model of this kind. According to (2.6.4), Y_{n+1} has a random component, u_{n+1}, and since there is no way of knowing the value that u_{n+1} will take, the best that one can do is to set that value to zero. One could not then expect a perfectly accurate prediction of the value of Y_{n+1}. But there is also another source of error, because the method of prediction is based on estimates of the parameters. Equation (2.6.2) states that

$$\hat{Y}_{n+1} = \hat{\alpha} + \hat{\beta} X_{n+1}$$

and, since $\hat{\alpha}$ and $\hat{\beta}$ are random variables, $\hat{Y}_{n+1}$ is also a random variable, known as the *predictor*. If particular values of $\hat{\alpha}$ and $\hat{\beta}$ are used in (2.6.2), a point *prediction* is obtained, but since the predictor is a random variable, the point prediction is only one of the values that the random variable could take. So, even if all the assumptions made are valid, it is highly unlikely that a point prediction would be exactly correct.

It is possible to go a little further in the analysis by looking at the probability distribution associated with the prediction. To do this, consider the random variable which defines the *prediction error,* the difference $(\hat{Y}_{n+1} - Y_{n+1})$. Equation (2.6.4) states that the random component of Y_{n+1} is u_{n+1} and, since $\hat{Y}_{n+1}$ depends on $\hat{\alpha}$ and $\hat{\beta}$, which in turn depend on the disturbances in the data period, the prediction error depends on the disturbances u_t; $t = 1, 2, \ldots, n$ and u_{n+1}. Although we shall not follow the analysis through, it can be shown that the prediction error is based on a linear combination of these disturbances and if, in addition to the assumptions already made, it is now assumed that u_{n+1} is generated from a normal distribution, it follows that the prediction error also has a normal distribution. Under the assumptions, the mean of the distribution is zero, so that 'on average', the prediction is correct. Finally, to obtain the variance of the prediction error, we assume that the distribution for u_{n+1} has a variance σ^2, the same as that for the other disturbances and that u_{n+1} is independent of the other disturbances. The variance of the prediction error can then be shown to be

$$\text{var}\,(\hat{Y}_{n+1} - Y_{n+1}) = \sigma^2 \left[1 + \frac{1}{n} + \frac{(X_{n+1} - \overline{X})^2}{\Sigma x_t^2} \right] \tag{2.6.5}$$

In this context, the standard deviation is again referred to as a standard error, but since 'standard error of the prediction error' is a rather awkward description, the phrase 'standard error of prediction' is often used instead. We also have the now familiar problem of lack of knowledge of the disturbance variance, σ^2, and this has to be replaced by the estimator $\hat{\sigma}^2$, defined in (2.4.7). The appropriate critical values should then be taken from the t distribution and the probability attached to the event that the prediction error lies within 2 standard errors of zero is only *approximately* 0·95.

The information on the distribution of the prediction error can also be used as a test of the predictive power of the model, but one can only compare prediction with reality in an ex-post sense, when the true value of Y_{n+1} is known. Even so, such a test can provide useful information and, for this reason, it is worth keeping one or two of the most recent observations out of the data set used for estimation, at least until the test has been made. The null hypothesis for the test is contained in (2.6.4), which states that the values of α and β appropriate to the prediction period are those which hold in the data period. It is only when this null hypothesis is true that the mean prediction error is zero. So it is only under the null hypothesis that the statistic

$$z = \frac{(\hat{Y}_{n+1} - Y_{n+1}) - 0}{\sigma \sqrt{1 + \dfrac{1}{n} + \dfrac{(X_{n+1} - \bar{X})^2}{\Sigma x_t^2}}} \tag{2.6.6}$$

has a standard normal distribution. If σ^2 is unknown and the estimator $\hat{\sigma}^2$ is used, this statistic becomes

$$t = \frac{(\hat{Y}_{n+1} - Y_{n+1})}{\hat{\sigma} \sqrt{1 + \dfrac{1}{n} + \dfrac{(X_{n+1} - \bar{X})^2}{\Sigma x_t^2}}} \tag{2.6.7}$$

which has a t distribution, with $(n - 2)$ degrees of freedom, under the null hypothesis. Again, we can use 2 as an *approximation* to the critical value, so that a result for the test statistic lying outside the range -2 to $+2$ would lead to the rejection of the null hypothesis and the conclusion that, even if the model holds in the prediction period, it does so with *different* true values of α and β.

There are various ways in which one could interpret rejection of the null hypothesis. It may mean that a given relationship has held in the past, but is now breaking down altogether, so that the model itself is not appropriate outside the data period. It might even mean that the apparently good fit in the data period is a statistical accident, since a 'good' model should really survive beyond the period for which the parameters are estimated. On the other hand, it may mean that the form of model is appropriate, but that the parameter values have changed. Whatever the reason for the rejection of the null hypothesis, it is serious from the point of view of using the model to forecast outside the data period, but it may also raise more fundamental questions about the nature of the model itself. It is perhaps unlikely that α and β remain stable through the data period and then change suddenly. A more satisfactory representation might be one in which the model parameters evolve slowly through time and, if this is the case, observations at the extremes of the data period may well show the accumulated effects of this evolution. All of this is rather speculative, because rejection of a specific null hypothesis cannot indicate directly what the 'true' situation actually is, but it is useful to be aware of the possibilities and, in this sense, the test does provide some general indications as to the stability of the model parameters and it could well be included in the battery of checks to be applied to any proposed model.

2.7 Asymptotic Properties

When the model satisfies the various assumptions laid out in this chapter, the least squares estimators have a set of properties which apply for any number of observations on the variables. But the estimates should improve as the number of observations is increased, in the sense that the true variance of $\hat{\beta}$ decreases. This variance is given by equation (2.3.14), which states that

$$\text{var}(\hat{\beta}) = \sigma^2/\Sigma x_t^2 \tag{2.7.1}$$

and, as the number of observations is increased, Σx_t^2 cannot decrease and will almost invariably increase, which leads to a reduction in the variance of $\hat{\beta}$. Of course, this depends on the assumption that the model continues to hold for the additional observations. Incidentally, it is not quite as simple as it may seem, to prove that Σx_t^2 cannot decrease: each x_t is defined as $X_t - \overline{X}$ and, as new observations are added, $\overline{X}$ would change. So it is not just a case of adding new squared terms to an existing sum of squares. Nevertheless, the result is true.

If the variance of $\hat{\beta}$ does decrease as the number of observations becomes larger, it is reasonable to suppose that, at some stage, the variance might become zero, in which case $\hat{\beta}$ would be equal to the true value, β. Such a result would hold as the *limit* of a process of adding successively more observations and a property based on this type of argument is known as an *asymptotic* property. There is no way of knowing how many observations would be necessary for the variance to become very close to zero, but it is likely to be a number greater than that which could be used in practice. In this sense, an asymptotic result is a rather weak property, but it may tell us something about *tendencies*, when the actual number of observations is relatively large and we should not be unduly discouraged by the thought that the limiting case cannot occur in practice. It would not be the first time that we have constructed a theoretical argument on the basis of a conceptual experiment, knowing full well that the experiment could not be performed in the real world.

Any argument concerning the asymptotic properties of an estimator tends to be qualified by a number of conditions and formal derivation is seldom a straightforward matter. Even the definition of an asymptotic result has to be chosen with some care. Thus, whilst it is correct to say that the variance of $\hat{\beta}$ might approach a certain limit it would *not* be correct to say that the estimator itself approaches a limit. A sequence of values of the variance, based on a progressively larger number of observations, is a sequence of non-random quantities, whereas a sequence of slope estimators is a sequence of random variables. So one cannot really say what happens to *the* value of $\hat{\beta}$, but one can say what happens to the distribution of *possible* values of $\hat{\beta}$. If $\hat{\beta}$ is unbiased and var $(\hat{\beta})$ has a limiting value equal to zero, it does follow that $\hat{\beta}$ has a *probability limit* equal to the true parameter value. This says that the probability of $\hat{\beta}$ being different from β approaches a limit of zero, which is not quite the same thing as saying that there is a limit to a sequence of *values* of the difference between $\hat{\beta}$ and β. It may seem to be hair-splitting, but this is typical of the logical distinctions that have to be made in the presentation of asymptotic results.

If the probability limit of an estimator is equal to the true parameter value, the estimator is said to be *consistent*. The probability limit is represented by the notation plim ( ) and so the result that $\hat{\beta}$ is a consistent estimator would be stated as

$$\text{plim} \, (\hat{\beta}) = \beta \qquad (2.7.2)$$

Consistency is often considered to be a weak alternative to the unbiasedness property and, if the assumptions made so far are satisfied, there is really no need to use an asymptotic result. In the example discussed above, unbiasedness was used as a condition for consistency, but it is not a necessary condition and this is the real significance of asymptotic properties. Although the properties are weaker, so are the necessary assumptions and, when the model is modified, there are situations in which *no* estimator has properties such as unbiasedness and it may then be necessary to choose the method of estimation on asymptotic criteria. There are two possibilities. The existing method may no longer be the best available, in which case an alternative should be chosen. On the other hand, the existing method may still be acceptable, so that essentially the same procedures are used, even though the properties of the estimator and the choice criteria are weaker than before.

To illustrate these ideas, consider the conditions under which the least squares estimators would no longer be unbiased. In the standard least squares method, a systematic distortion will arise when there is some definite connection between each observation on the explanatory variable and the *corresponding* disturbance. To take an extreme case, there may be some characteristic of the model which makes it highly unlikely, or even impossible, that certain values of X_t and u_t could occur together. An example is shown in Fig. 2.2. The explanatory

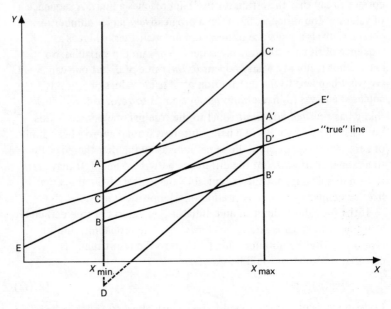

Figure 2.2

variable is assumed to take values between X_{min} and X_{max} and the
lines AA$'$ and BB$'$ are intended to indicate that, *without* any connection between X_t and u_t, disturbance values giving points outside these
bounds are unlikely, though not impossible. But it is also assumed that,
because of a connection between the X_t and u_t values, the observations
have to lie between the lines CC$'$ and DD$'$. This suggests that low values
of X_t tend to occur only with *negative* values of the disturbances and
high values of X_t with *positive* values of the disturbances. Obviously,
there must be some characteristic of the real system that causes the
model to have such a constraint and, in Chapter 6, we shall come across
exactly this situation, but whatever the reason, the outcome is that
the disturbances cannot now form a 'proper' spread of points and
minimizing the sum of squared residuals would tend to produce a line
such as EE$'$. In this case the least squares estimator would be biased and
it would also be inconsistent. If, on the other hand, there is no connection between each observation on the explanatory variable and the
corresponding disturbance, the scatter of points could be represented
by the area AA$'$B$'$B. In this case, there is no reason why the least squares
method should not tend to reproduce the true line, but the sense in

which this result would hold does need clarification. If the minimization of squared residuals is to give a line which, with a high probability, is close to the true line, there would have to be enough observations to produce a density of observed points that would approximate to that suggested by the disturbance distributions. So, when there is no connection between X_t and the corresponding disturbance, u_t, the diagram indicates the asymptotic property of consistency, but on the basis of the diagram alone, one could not necessarily draw the conclusion that the estimators are unbiased.

In the model used earlier in this chapter, the possibility of a connection between the explanatory variable observations and the disturbances is ruled out by the assumption that the explanatory variable is non-random. If each value of X_t is considered to be fixed and the values of the disturbances are determined from probability distributions, which have no connection with the X_t values, there is no way in which the explanatory variable can influence the disturbances or be influenced by the disturbances. In this case, it is possible to prove that the least squares estimators are both consistent *and* unbiased.

At this point, it is useful to recall the arguments used to demonstrate the unbiasedness of the slope estimator. Equation (2.3.5) states that

$$\hat{\beta} = \beta + \Sigma w_t u_t \tag{2.7.3}$$

where the weights are defined as

$$w_t = x_t / \Sigma x_t^2; t = 1, 2, \ldots, n \tag{2.7.4}$$

If the explanatory variable is non-random, then so are the weights and it is possible to argue that, if each disturbance, u_t, has a zero expectation, so does each term $w_t u_t$. If, on the other hand, the explanatory variable observations are to be random, the weights would also be random and, to find the expectation of a single term $w_t u_t$, one would have to average across all possible values of u_t *and* all possible values of w_t. This process can be envisaged as consisting of two steps: (1) for each value of w_t, find the *conditional* expectation of $w_t u_t$, which is the expectation that holds for that particular value of w_t, (2) then average the conditional expectations over all possible values of w_t, to obtain the overal expectation of $w_t u_t$. If each weight, w_t, is *independent* of the corresponding disturbance, u_t, a particular value taken by w_t has no influence on the probabilities attached to each range of values that u_t can assume and taking the *conditional* expectation of $w_t u_t$, for any value of w_t, is exactly like taking the expectation when w_t is non-random. Each conditional expectation would be zero and averaging the set of zeros over all possible values of w_t would produce an overall expectation of zero. So, for random weights which are independent of the disturbances, it can be shown that the expectation of each term $w_t u_t$ is zero and the remainder of the argument leading to the unbiasedness of $\hat{\beta}$ still holds. But if the weights are *not* independent of the disturbances, the conditional probability distribution of each u_t could alter, as the value of w_t is changed and there is no reason to believe that the conditional expectations would be zero. The argument leading to the unbiasedness property would then break down.

Although allowing the explanatory variables to be random is a relaxation of the assumptions, a restriction which states that the weights must be independent of the disturbances is still very strong. Equation (2.7.4) shows that each weight depends on *all* the explanatory variable observations and if each X_t; $t = 1, 2, \ldots, n$, is considered to be a random variable, the independence of w_t and u_t would require that *each* X_t is independent of *all* the disturbances, u_t; $t = 1, 2, \ldots, n$. So one could have a model in which X_t is independent of the *corresponding* disturbance, u_t, which, in terms of the argument based on Fig. 2.2 would suggest consistency and yet, if X_t depends on any of the *other* disturbances, it would not be possible to prove unbiasedness. To emphasize this point, we shall consider a specific example.

Suppose that X_t is independent of the corresponding disturbance, u_t, but that each explanatory variable observation does depend on the disturbance in the previous period. This could be expressed by saying that X_t depends on u_{t-1} or by saying that X_{t+1} depends on u_t. The lack of independence between w_t and u_t would then stem from the contribution that X_{t+1} makes to the determination of the weight, w_t. This weight is defined in terms of the deviation $x_t = X_t - \overline{X}$ and the sum of squared deviations, Σx_t^2 and X_{t+1} would influence both $\overline{X}$ and Σx_t^2. But as the number of observations is increased, the contribution made by X_{t+1} would become relatively less important and, in the limit, the contribution would be negligible. What this indicates is that there would be a bias when the number of observations is small, but the bias would tend to disappear as the number of observations is increased and this is roughly what is meant by saying that an estimator is consistent, even though it is biased. A formal proof would require one to show that the probability limit of $\Sigma w_t u_t$ is zero, but as we said at the beginning of this section, there are always various conditions to be satisfied and the proofs tend to be specific to particular types of model. We can, however, use the informal arguments of this section in the context of the particular cases that arise in later chapters.

Before leaving this topic, it should be noted that consistency is not the only asymptotic property of interest. If all the assumptions in Section 2.3 are satisfied, *except* for the normality of disturbances, the least squares slope estimator would still be best linear unbiased, but it would not be possible to prove that the estimator has an exact normal distribution. In this case, one would have to fall back on an asymptotic result, which suggests that the distribution is *approximately* normal, so long as the number of observations is large. This may seem to be at odds with the consistency property: in the limit, the distribution of $\hat{\beta}$ collapses entirely. But asymptotic normality is not proved directly in terms of the distribution of $\hat{\beta}$ and it is only indicative of the approximate behaviour of the distribution when the number of observations is large.

We now appear to have moved a long way from the problems of practical model building, but there is a reason for the digression. It is very convenient when the economic model does fit into the standard linear form and all the assumptions are satisfied, but the model should not be forced into this framework, when some of the assumptions are at odds with reality. So we are certainly not losing sight of the economic objectives. On the contrary, we want to be able to build models which are as realistic as possible and, if this can only be achieved at the cost of weaker statistical properties, then this is a cost that must be accepted.

In the next chapter, the format of the model is extended to allow for further explanatory variables and, to start with, the full list of assumptions is restored. Conducting the analysis under strong conditions may seem now to be at odds with the objectives of economic realism, but a further lesson of the asymptotic analysis is that the relaxation of assumptions does not always destroy the estimator properties completely and, although the results may eventually have to be modified, there is still a great deal to be learnt from a discussion of the basic model.

Exercises (solutions on page 230)

2.1   The outcomes of a game consisting of two tosses of a coin are represented in terms of two random variables, V_1 and V_2. Numerical values are assigned to these random variables by the code: head = 1, tail = 0. It is assumed that, on each throw, the outcomes 1 and 0 are equiprobable. A new random variable, L, is then defined as

$$L = 0 \cdot 2 V_1 + 0 \cdot 8 V_2$$

List the possible values of L. Given that each value of L is associated with a probability of 1/4, show that

$$E(L) = 0 \cdot 2E(V_1) + 0 \cdot 8E(V_2)$$

Explain the significance of this result.

2.2 Using the data given in exercise 1.4, find point estimates for the parameters of the model

$$C_t = \alpha + \beta D_t + u_t; t = 1, 2, \ldots, n$$

To avoid tedious calculation, you may wish to use the following information

$$\Sigma C_t = 224\ 453 \qquad\qquad \Sigma D_t = 244\ 918$$
$$\Sigma (D_t - \bar{D})^2 = 32\ 188\ 511 \cdot 6 \quad \Sigma (D_t - \bar{D})(C_t - \bar{C}) = 27\ 734\ 597 \cdot$$

2.3 A problem requiring a knowledge of calculus: show that minimizing the sum of squared residuals does lead to the normal equations (2.1.7).

2.4 Demonstrate the equivalence of the following expressions for $\hat{\beta}$, the least squares slope estimator

$$\hat{\beta} = \Sigma x_t y_t / \Sigma x_t^2$$
$$\hat{\beta} = [\Sigma X_t Y_t - (\Sigma X_t / n) \Sigma Y_t] / [\Sigma X_t^2 - (\Sigma X_t / n) \Sigma X_t]$$

2.5 Prove that $\hat{\beta}$ can be expressed as in equation (2.3.4)

$$\hat{\beta} = \beta + \Sigma x_t u_t / \Sigma x_t^2$$

2.6 Calculate the standard error for the slope estimate obtained in exercise 2.2. Then test the null hypothesis that $\beta = 0$. A convenient formula for computing the residual sum of squares is

$$\Sigma e_t^2 = \Sigma y_t^2 - \hat{\beta} \Sigma x_t y_t$$

Note that $\Sigma (C_t - \bar{C})^2 = 24\ 007\ 482 \cdot 1$ (exercise 1.4)

3 The Linear Model with Further Explanatory Variables

3.1 Interpretation

A dependent variable that represents measurements taken from an economic system is unlikely to be related only to a single explanatory variable and it is necessary to consider a more general version of the linear model, which allows the list of explanatory variables to be extended. We shall continue to use Y to represent the dependent variable and X as a general representation for the explanatory variables, but now individual explanatory variables have to be distinguished in some way. A single observation on one explanatory variable is therefore written as X_{jt}, where j represents a numbering to identify the *variable* and t represents the *observation* number, as before. Using k to denote the total number of explanatory variables, the complete set of observations would be

$$Y_t; \; t = 1, 2, \ldots, n$$

and

$$X_{jt}; j = 1, 2, \ldots, k; t = 1, 2, \ldots, n$$

It is also necessary to distinguish the parameters associated with the different explanatory variables and so the parameters become

$$\beta_j; j = 1, 2, \ldots, k$$

Within this framework, one can allow for an intercept by saying that X_1 is a 'variable' which can only assume a single value, $X_{1t} = 1$, for all values of t. If this is done, β_1 becomes the intercept and the k *variable linear model* can be written as

$$Y_t = \beta_1 + \beta_2 X_{2t} + \ldots + \beta_j X_{jt} + \ldots + \beta_k X_{kt} + u_t$$
$$t = 1, 2, \ldots, n \tag{3.1.1}$$

The model now looks rather complicated, but it is simply the

57

natural extension of the two variable case. From the way in which the model is written, it is clear that the values taken by the explanatory variables do have an effect on the dependent variable. The role of the disturbance, u_t, is again to allow for the fact that the relationship is inexact. In order to examine the interpretation of the parameters of the model, we shall temporarily ignore the effect of the disturbance term and also the fact that the observations relate to discrete periods of time, or to different units in a cross-section and we shall consider only the underlying linear relationship between the variables, which is

$$Y = \beta_1 + \beta_2 X_2 + \ldots + \beta_j X_j + \ldots + \beta_k X_k \qquad (3.1.2)$$

Equation (3.1.2) is described as a linear relationship, because it has the same essential characteristics as a linear relationship in the two variable case, namely that a change of one unit in a single explanatory variable, X_j, would lead to a change, equal to β_j, in the dependent variable and this would be true over the whole range of possible values of X_j. Each β_j (apart from β_1) represents a slope and the characteristic of a linear relationship is that the slopes are parameters, which are constant and which do not depend on the values taken by the variables. But there is now an important qualification on the interpretation of individual slopes. The parameter β_j measures the effect of a unit change in X_j, *with all the other variables held constant.* An easy way to see this is to note that if there is no change in any variable *except X_j*, all the terms except $\beta_j X_j$ would be constant and could be thought of as being part of the intercept in an artificially constructed 'two variable' relationship of the form

$$Y = \text{intercept} + \beta_j X_j$$

We know that, in such a relationship, β_j would represent the slope, but this interpretation holds only so long as the other variables are held constant and so the qualification on the meaning of β_j is important. In economics, the type of change that is envisaged here would often be described as a change in X_j, *ceteris paribus.*

With this in mind, we now consider the use of the full model, complete with random disturbances.

Throughout this chapter, the explanatory variable observations are considered to be non-random and, as before, there are various possible interpretations that could be used. In some contexts, it might be reasonable to assume that the explanatory variables can be fixed by policy decision, in which case the purpose of the model would be to explain the impact of policy on the dependent variable. One would then want to isolate the influence of each of the possible policy measures and so it would be effects of *ceteris paribus* changes that one would want to find. It is implicit in the formulation of the model that the *dependent* variable cannot be *exactly* determined by policy: if this could be done, there would be no point in having the model and it would be quite inappropriate to suggest that the variable in question has a random component.

An alternative interpretation of non-random explanatory variables is that the values are determined by other relationships in the system and we shall now present an example in which this interpretation would have to be used. The example is based, once again, on a version of the consumption function. Suppose that, in addition to disposable income (D), the level of liquid assets held by households (L) is thought to be an important determinant of consumption (C). The complete model would then be

$$C_t = \beta_1 + \beta_2 D_t + \beta_3 L_t + u_t; t = 1, 2, \ldots, n \qquad (3.1.3)$$

It would be unrealistic to regard disposable income and liquid asset holdings as being fixed by policy decision and the interpretation that would have to be used is that both quantities are determined by other variables in the system, perhaps including more legitimate instruments of fiscal and monetary control. Ideally, these other relationships should be built into the model, but we are not yet ready for the complexities of the multiple equation case and, for the time being, the use of $(3.1.3)$ must be considered as a *partial* analysis, conditional on the income and liquid asset values generated elsewhere. *Within the confines of the partial model*, it would be possible to treat the explanatory variable observations as non-random.

Now consider the meaning of the parameters of the model, taking β_2 as an example. This parameter measures the effect, on consumption, of a unit change in disposable income, with liquid assets held constant. It may well be that, in the history of the economic system in question, there has never been a change in disposable income that has not been accompanied by some change in liquid asset holdings and, given the way in which we have now interpreted the explanatory variables, it is easy to explain why this could be so. The two variables may be directly linked or they may have at least some explanatory factors in common. Although these additional relationships cannot yet be included in the model, the fact that such relationships can exist does help us to understand that there is usually a difference between the *direct* effect of income changes on consumption and the *total* effect, which would include any indirect linkages from income to liquid assets and thence to consumption. The indirect effect would only arise when income influences liquid asset holdings and liquid asset holdings influence consumption. The partial model cannot be used to analyse the relationship between income and liquid assets, but it does attempt to show the factors influencing consumption. Although the indirect effect may be *initiated* by a change in income, the change in consumption caused by the indirect effect is observed only because liquid assets influence consumption. So, in the partial model, a change in consumption arising from the indirect effect should be attributed to liquid assets and *not* to income and we would want the income parameter to include only the *direct* income effect. This is exactly what is measured by β_2. Even though *ceteris paribus* changes may never be observed, the model specification does suggest that one should attempt to isolate the 'pure' effects of the individual explanatory variables. Before we consider the estimation procedure that allows this to be done, we consider the concept of a 'true' model once again.

Suppose that (3.1.3) is 'true', in the sense that it includes the major determinants of consumption, with all other influences sufficiently well represented by the disturbance term. Then suppose that an investigator specifies the relationship

$$C_t = \alpha + \beta D_t + u_t; t = 1, 2, \ldots, n \tag{3.1.4}$$

One could argue that (3.1.4) is a perfectly legitimate model, so long as it is realized that β would include the effect of any indirect linkages between income, liquid assets and consumption and so would measure the *total* income effect. But, if it is possible to estimate the parameters of the correct version of the model, there is no advantage in using (3.1.4) and if the investigator uses (3.1.4) in ignorance of the 'truth', he would expect β to measure a pure income effect and he would interpret his results accordingly. We shall show, in Section 3.8, that the estimator, $\hat{\beta}$, obtained from (3.1.4), is not an appropriate estimator for the parameter β_2. This is hardly surprising, since, if (3.1.3) is the true model, β and β_2 are conceptually different.

3.2 Estimation and the Use of a Computer

The estimation of the parameters of the k variable model involves no new principle, but merely requires the application of the least squares method in the context of a larger number of unknowns. Instead of two linear equations in two unknowns, the minimization of the sum of squared residuals now leads to k linear equations in k unknowns. Even for quite modest values of k, the solution of the equations represents a lengthy calculation and, in practice, a computer would have to be used to obtain the parameter estimates. This adds a new dimension to our discussion. There are very few applications of econometric technique which would not involve computer usage at some stage and this means that it is essential to have some basic knowledge of what a computer actually does.

At the nucleus of any computer system, there is a unit which is capable of doing simple arithmetic at great speed. The information that has to be supplied to this unit falls into two categories. A *program* consists of a set of instructions, which break down a complex calculation into a series of steps. The *data* consists of the numbers that are to be used in the calculation. Because of the speed of operation of the arithmetic unit, it is necessary to have an elaborate control system, to ensure that work is supplied at a rate compatible with the speed of execution. Thus the other essential component of a computer system is some method of *storage*, in which both program and data are held before and during the calculation and to which results can be sent afterwards.

In a modern computer installation, the user is several stages removed from the central function of the machine. A program would not usually be written in the lengthy numerical code in which instructions are supplied to the arithmetic unit. Instead, one would use a *high-level* language, such as *Algol* or *Fortran*: these are somewhat similar in form to ordinary algebra. Translation into the basic machine code would then be performed automatically, under the control of a 'master' program, known as a *compiler*.

For most users, it is not even necessary to understand a high-level language. There are programs already written for standard econometric calculations and these will often be permanently available for use on the machine. In this case, the user has only to supply the data for his calculation and a small number of instructions to identify the program that is to be used. The data would usually have to be arranged in a definite form, specified by the user manual for that particular program. The medium for supplying information to the machine may be punched cards or, alternatively, it may be possible to obtain access via a console, which has a keyboard like a typewriter, enabling information to be transmitted directly to the computer. The medium for receiving the results is usually the printed page, referred to as the output or 'print-out'.

The knowledge that calculations would seldom be performed by hand does influence our presentation. Although it is still important to understand the principles which underlie the methods used and vital to know of any limitations, it is not necessary to describe each calculation in the minute detail that would be required for hand calculation. So, in dealing with the estimation of parameters in the k variable model, we do need to know something about the *form* of the equations to be solved, but all that we really need to know about the solution procedure is that the parameter estimates could be obtained by a generalization of the method used in the two variable case. The equations look rather complicated, which is why we have made a point of saying that the solution would not be obtained by hand, but inspection will reveal a regular pattern to the individual terms and the form of the equations is not really too difficult to understand. The equations are

$$\hat{\beta}_1 n \qquad + \hat{\beta}_2 \Sigma X_{2t} \qquad + \ldots + \hat{\beta}_j \Sigma X_{jt} \qquad + \ldots + \hat{\beta}_k \Sigma X_{kt} \quad = \Sigma Y_t$$

$$\hat{\beta}_1 \Sigma X_{2t} + \hat{\beta}_2 \Sigma X_{2t}^2 \qquad + \ldots + \hat{\beta}_j \Sigma X_{2t} X_{jt} + \ldots + \hat{\beta}_k \Sigma X_{2t} X_{kt} = \Sigma X_{2t} Y_t$$

$$\hat{\beta}_1 \Sigma X_{jt} + \hat{\beta}_2 \Sigma X_{jt} X_{2t} + \ldots + \hat{\beta}_j \Sigma X_{jt}^2 \qquad + \ldots + \hat{\beta}_k \Sigma X_{jt} X_{kt} = \Sigma X_{jt} Y_t$$

$$\hat{\beta}_1 \Sigma X_{kt} + \hat{\beta}_2 \Sigma X_{kt} X_{2t} + \ldots + \hat{\beta}_j \Sigma X_{kt} X_{jt} + \ldots + \hat{\beta}_k \Sigma X_{kt}^2 \quad = \Sigma X_{kt} Y_t$$

$$(3.2.1)$$

All the sums, sums of squares and sums of products represent quantities that could be calculated from a particular set of data, consisting of observations on the dependent variable and all the explanatory variables, from X_2 to X_k. The first equation looks different from the rest, but this is because X_1 is not made explicit. Remember that

$$X_{1t} = 1; t = 1, 2, \ldots, n$$

and so

$$\Sigma X_{1t}^2 = n, \Sigma X_{1t} Y_t = \Sigma Y_t \text{ and } \Sigma X_{1t} X_{jt} = \Sigma X_{jt}; j = 2, 3, \ldots, k$$

It would be possible to express the steps in the solution of the equations in algebraic terms, thereby providing a formula for each parameter estimator, expressed in terms of the sums, sums of squares and sums of products, but when k is greater than 2 or 3, the formulae do become complicated. Since it has been assumed that a computer would be used to obtain the estimates, it is not necessary to have these formulae. But the numbers provided on the computer print-out must mean something to the user and it is worth putting some effort into trying to understand how the estimation procedure works in the general case. What we shall do is to look at the estimators obtained from some very simple models and we shall use these results to suggest a general form for the least squares estimators, a form which holds for any value of k. The interpretation of this general form will show how the estimation procedure attempts to measure the effects of *ceteris paribus* changes in the explanatory variables and the interpretation will also provide a useful basis for explaining some of the problems that can arise in practice. With these objectives in mind, I would ask the reader to spend some time in careful study of the discussion which follows.

In Chapter 2, we made use of the two variable model ($k = 2$) to explain the nature of the least squares calculation. This is the simplest form of model that is likely to be of practical value, but there is an even simpler case, from which we can learn something of importance. If $k = 1$ and the only explanatory 'variable' is the artificial variable, X_1, the model would be

$$Y_t = \beta_1 X_{1t} + u_t = \beta_1 + u_t; t = 1, 2, \ldots, n \qquad (3.2.2)$$

The equations given in (3.2.1) are completely general and they can be applied to give the estimators corresponding to any value of k. If $k = 1$, there would only be a single equation

$$\hat{\beta}_1 n = \Sigma Y_t$$

and so the estimator for β_1 *based on the model (3.2.2)*, would be

$$\hat{\beta}_1 = \Sigma Y_t/n = \overline{Y} \qquad (3.2.3)$$

This represents a sample mean calculated from the dependent variable observations. For future reference, notice that if X_1 is made explicit, the estimator would be written as

$$\hat{\beta}_1 = \Sigma X_{1t} Y_t/\Sigma X_{1t}^2 \qquad (3.2.4)$$

If (3.2.2) is used, the values of the dependent variable *predicted* by the estimated equation would be

$$\hat{Y}_t = \hat{\beta}_1 X_1 = \hat{\beta}_1 = \overline{Y}; t = 1, 2, \ldots, n \qquad (3.2.5)$$

and the *residuals*, measuring the differences between the observed and predicted values of the dependent variable, would be

$$Y_t - \hat{Y}_t = Y_t - \overline{Y} = y_t; t = 1, 2, \ldots, n \qquad (3.2.6)$$

So this model can only account for the behaviour of the dependent variable to the extent that it explains a constant component of the Y_t observations, a component estimated as $\overline{Y}$. The remaining part of the observed behaviour cannot be explained by the deterministic part of the model and this component is estimated by the residuals defined in (3.2.6): these are equivalent to deviations of the dependent variable observations from the sample mean.

Now consider the case in which the model contains a single genuine explanatory variable, but no intercept term. The model is written as

$$Y_t = \beta_2 X_{2t} + u_t; t = 1, 2, \ldots, n \qquad (3.2.7)$$

where X_2 is used to distinguish the genuine variable from the artificial variable X_1. The only equation in (3.2.1) would now be

$$\hat{\beta}_2 \Sigma X_{2t}^2 = \Sigma X_{2t} Y_t$$

and the estimator for β_2 would be

$$\hat{\beta}_2 = \Sigma X_{2t} Y_t / \Sigma X_{2t}^2 \qquad (3.2.8)$$

It should be noted that this has the same general form as (3.2.4), the only difference being that X_1 is replaced by X_2.

When the model contains *both* an intercept term *and* a genuine explanatory variable, it is the standard two variable model of the previous chapter, albeit expressed here in a slightly different notation

$$Y_t = \beta_1 + \beta_2 X_{2t} + u_t; t = 1, 2, \ldots, n \qquad (3.2.9)$$

In this case the application of (3.2.1) would give two equations

$$\hat{\beta}_1 n + \hat{\beta}_2 \Sigma X_{2t} = \Sigma Y_t$$

$$\hat{\beta}_1 \Sigma X_{2t} + \hat{\beta}_2 \Sigma X_{2t}^2 = \Sigma X_{2t} Y_t$$

But we already know that it is possible to eliminate $\hat{\beta}_1$, to give a single equation in the slope estimator, β_2. In this equation

$$\hat{\beta}_2 \Sigma x_{2t}^2 = \Sigma x_{2t} y_t$$

the data is expressed in the form of deviations from the mean

$$y_t = Y_t - \overline{Y} \text{ and } x_{2t} = X_{2t} - \overline{X}_2$$

So the estimator corresponding to X_2 is now given by

$$\hat{\beta}_2 = \Sigma x_{2t} y_t / \Sigma x_{2t}^2 \qquad (3.2.10)$$

Finally, consider the estimation of the best fitting relationship *between* X_2 and X_1. In this case it cannot be assumed that there is an underlying *true* relationship, involving a random disturbance. Within our present framework, all the X variables are considered to be non-random. But there is no reason why the least squares calculation cannot be performed and this will be described as the *regression* of X_2 on X_1. In this context it is not really appropriate to talk of parameter estimates and we shall use the term *regression coefficients*, or simply *coefficients*, as an alternative. This terminology serves for the estimation of all types of relationship, those which involve an underlying model and those that do not. By analogy with the regression of Y on X_1, the regression of X_2 on X_1 gives residuals which are the deviations $x_{2t} = X_{2t} - \overline{X}_2$; $t = 1, 2, \ldots, n$. We shall shortly need to make use of this result.

In these simple examples, we have taken steps to avoid an unduly complicated system of notation. Thus the coefficients based on regressions *between* the X variables are not given a specific symbolic representation: all that we are interested in is the nature of the residuals. And, for regressions in which Y *is* the dependent variable, the symbol $\hat{\beta}_2$ is used for the estimator corresponding to the variable X_2, irrespective of the other explanatory variables in the model. When there is any possibility of confusion, the particular regression on which the estimation is based must be stated.

The examples illustrate a very important point. The estimator corresponding to the variable X_2 *does* change when X_1 is added to the model. In (3.2.8), the observations on the variables are used in original form whereas, in (3.2.10), the observations are expressed as deviations from the means. A similar result holds in the general case. The estimator corresponding to *any* variable depends on all the *other* explanatory variables in the model. And if the definition of the estimator is changed as variables are added to or removed from the model, it naturally follows that the estimates, obtained from a given set of data, would also change. In particular, the estimates obtained from a single regression of Y on several explanatory variables are *not* generally the same as those obtained from several regressions, each relating Y to *one* of the explanatory variables. The only exceptions are when the data has very special (and highly unlikely) properties. Thus (3.2.8) and (3.2.10) would give the same result if it happened to be true that $\overline{X}_2$ was *exactly* zero. Obviously, such accidents of the data are rare.

Now consider what the difference between (3.2.8) and (3.2.10) really amounts to. The estimator corresponding to X_2, obtained from the regression of Y on X_1 *and* X_2, is exactly that which would be obtained from the following procedure: (1) regress Y on X_1 and take the residuals, y_t; $t = 1, 2, \ldots, n$. (2) regress X_2 on X_1 and take the residuals, x_{2t}; $t = 1, 2, \ldots, n$. (3) regress y on x_2. The *form* of the estimator obtained from this last step would be that of (3.2.8), but the data used would be the residuals from steps (1) and (2), namely the deviations y_t and x_{2t}; $t = 1, 2, \ldots, n$. So the estimator would be

$$\hat{\beta}_2 = \Sigma x_{2t} y_t / \Sigma x_{2t}^2$$

But this *is* the estimator, corresponding to X_2, that is obtained from the regression of Y on X_1 *and* X_2.

The deviations y_t and x_{2t}; $t = 1, 2, \ldots, n$, contain all the available information concerning the *variation* in the observations on Y and X_2. The deterministic part of a model containing only the artificial variable, X_1, cannot explain the variation in the dependent variable and this is left to be explained by any genuine variables that may be added to the model. Consequently, it is only a part of the observed behaviour of Y that is used to establish the estimator, $\hat{\beta}_2$. That part is the variation in Y, the component not already explained by X_1, represented by the deviations y_t; $t = 1, 2, \ldots, n$. But we can also see that only a part of the observed behaviour of X_2 is used. That part again corresponds to the variation in X_2, as represented by the deviations x_{2t}; $t = 1, 2, \ldots, n$ and these deviations can also be interpreted as that part of the observed behaviour of X_2 that cannot be 'explained' by X_1.

The results that we have obtained can be generalized as follows. The estimator of the parameter corresponding to the variable X_j can always be expressed in a standard form

$$\hat{\beta}_j = \Sigma \tilde{X}_{jt} \tilde{Y}_t / \Sigma \tilde{X}_{jt}^2 \tag{3.2.11}$$

where $\tilde{X}_j$ is a variable defined by the *residuals* from the regression of X_j on all the *other* explanatory variables in the model and $\tilde{Y}$ is a variable defined by the residuals from a regression of Y on all the explanatory variables *except* X_j. Naturally, the special cases do fit the general form. If X_1 is the only explanatory 'variable', there would be no other variables with which to adjust Y and X_1, so $\tilde{Y} = Y$ and $\tilde{X}_1 = X_1$. The general form applied to the estimator $\hat{\beta}_1$ would then specialize to (3.2.4). If X_2 is the only explanatory variable, then $\tilde{Y} = Y$ and $\tilde{X}_2 = X_2$ and the general form, applied to $\hat{\beta}_2$, would specialize to (3.2.8). And, in the standard two variable model, the only explanatory 'variable', apart from X_2, is the artificial variable X_1, so $\tilde{Y} = y$ and $\tilde{X}_2 = x_2$.

To see what the general form means in a more realistic case, consider again the example of a consumption function based on the three variable model

$$C_t = \beta_1 + \beta_2 D_t + \beta_3 L_t + u_t; t = 1, 2, \ldots, n \qquad (3.2.12)$$

It has been argued that, in this model, the parameter β_2 represents the effect of a unit change in income (D) on consumers' expenditure (C), *ceteris paribus*. This effect is identified as the *direct* income effect, which leaves out the indirect effects caused by any linkage between income and liquid asset holdings (L). According to the general form (3.2.11), the estimator for β_2, obtained from the regression of C on D *and* L, is exactly that which *would* be obtained by the following procedure: (1) regress C on L (with an intercept term) and take the residuals, denoted as $\tilde{C}_t; t = 1, 2, \ldots, n$. (2) regress D on L (with an intercept term) and take the residuals, denoted as $\tilde{D}_t; t = 1, 2, \ldots, n$. (3) regress $\tilde{C}$ on $\tilde{D}$ (without an intercept term), giving an estimator

$$\hat{\beta}_2 = \Sigma \tilde{D}_t \tilde{C}_t / \Sigma \tilde{D}_t^2 \qquad (3.2.13)$$

The residuals from the regression of C on L represent a component of the observations on consumers' expenditure that is *not* already explained by the variation in liquid asset holdings and the residuals from the regression of D on L represent a component of the observations on disposable income that cannot be 'explained by' the behaviour of liquid asset holdings. This last statement does not depend on any direction of causality, between D and L, that we may subsequently want to consider *outside* the partial model represented by (3.2.12). Indeed, it does not depend on there being any *true* underlying relationship between D and L. The use of the residuals, $\tilde{D}_t; t = 1, 2, \ldots, n$, merely represents an attempt to measure a component of the observations on disposable income which is not associated with corresponding changes in liquid asset holdings. In other words, it is an attempt to measure a part of the observed behaviour of disposable income that can be interpreted as consisting entirely of *ceteris paribus* changes. It is by using only this 'pure' component of disposable income that the estimation procedure attempts to isolate the effects of a *ceteris paribus* change in income.

The general form (3.2.11) holds for any parameter estimator, based on any linear model, irrespective of the value of k, but it must be understood that it does not define the estimator in terms of sums, sums of squares and sums of products of the original data, at least not directly. Instead, it expresses a single coefficient, obtained from a k

variable regression, in terms of residuals from *other* regressions, each involving $(k-1)$ variables. The general form also holds for these other regressions, or rather, it holds for any regression involving Y as the dependent variable and an equivalent form holds for regressions *between* the X variables. The specific meaning to be attached to $\widetilde{Y}$ and $\widetilde{X}_j$ changes from case to case, but using the same general forms, one could express the coefficients of the $(k-1)$ variable regressions in terms of residuals from $(k-2)$ variable regressions, and so on. The definition of the estimator contained in the general form is *not* circular, because eventually one would get to the stage at which the substitutions involve the coefficients of regressions on only one or two variables and we do have explicit formulae for these simple cases. But if k is greater than 3, this procedure would be very tedious and the explicit formulae obtained would be rather complicated. This is precisely why we have avoided making use of the explicit formulae for the estimators in the general case. In practice, a computer is used to solve the equations for a given set of data, thereby providing the estimates required. We do not need the explicit formulae: the general form tells us how the estimation procedure works and what the estimates mean. It is the *nature* of the estimation method that must be understood.

We now summarize the results of this section. The problem to hand is that of establishing the effect on a dependent variable, Y, of a unit change in a single explanatory variable, X_j, *ceteris paribus*. If there are no other explanatory variables (except for the artificial variable, X_1) there is no problem, but if there *are* other genuine explanatory variables, the method used to establish an estimate of the parameter, β_j, is that of *multiple* regression, that is, a regression of Y on *all* the explanatory variables. The estimate obtained is *not* generally the same as that obtained from a two variable regression of Y on X_j (and X_1). In terms of the actual calculation, we now know the difference between the two approaches. In the multiple regression, the observations on X_j are 'corrected for' the effects of the other explanatory variables. By using only the residuals from the regression of X_j on all *other* explanatory variables, one attempts to isolate the component of X_j that corresponds to *ceteris paribus* changes. In the two variable regression, no such adjustment is made to the observations on X_j (except for the effect of X_1). It is therefore likely that the estimates of the parameter corresponding to X_j will be different in the two cases. This depends on the proposition that the adjustment of X_j for the effects of the other genuine explanatory variables does have some effect and we now give reasons why

this should be so. One possibility is that there are 'true' economic
relationships *between* the explanatory variables. If this is the case, the
true parameter attached to X_j in the two variable model is conceptually
different from that in the k variable model and only the latter represents
a *ceteris paribus* effect. Although such relationships cannot be analysed
within the confines of a partial single equation model, one would
certainly observe a tendency for some of the explanatory variables to
move together. But even when there are *no* true relationships between
the explanatory variables, one still does not observe *ceteris paribus*
variation directly. Virtually any regression run between the explanatory
variables would give coefficients that are not *exactly* zero and so the
adjustment of X_j, for the effects of other explanatory variables, will
invariably make *some* difference to the estimate obtained. It is
theoretically possible for the two variable regression and the multiple
regression to give the same estimates, but the type of observations that
would give rise to this could only be obtained under laboratory
conditions and economics is not an experimental science. So, in
practice, multiple regression has to be used to obtain the estimates.

One final comment is necessary. We have not yet considered
the possibility that there is no unique solution to the equations which
define the estimators. In such a case, one would not be able to obtain
the estimates. Our interpretation of the estimation procedure will
explain why this situation might arise. If the behaviour of a single
explanatory variable, X_j, can be predicted *exactly* by means of a
regression of X_j on one or more of the *other* explanatory variables, the
residuals, $\tilde{X}_{jt}; t = 1, 2, \ldots, n$ would all take the value zero. There is
then no 'pure' variation in X_j on which to base an estimate of the
parameter β_j: trying to solve the equations (3.2.1) is equivalent to
trying to base an estimate on data which does not exist and it is not
surprising that the estimate does not exist either. What would actually
happen is that the computer solution would simply stop at some point
and, depending on the particular program that is used, some form of
error message would usually be printed. Equation (3.2.11) is equivalent
to the calculation that is attempted and, if $\tilde{X}_{jt} = 0; t = 1, 2, \ldots, n$, it
follows that

$$\hat{\beta}_j = \Sigma \tilde{X}_{jt} \tilde{Y}_t / \Sigma \tilde{X}_{jt}^2 = 0/0$$

The division of zero by zero is an undefined operation and there is no
meaningful numerical result. The precise step at which the computer
solution would fail depends on the design of the program used, but the
outcome would be that *none* of the parameter estimates would be found.

Fortunately, the complete breakdown of the estimation procedure is rare, with a properly specified model, but there can be problems when there is very little 'pure' variation in X_j. We shall consider these problems in Section 3.9. There is one case in which the estimation procedure will definitely fail. At least two observations on the variables are needed to estimate the parameters of the two variable model and, in the general case, at least k observations are required. If n is less than k, the estimation procedure will fail and, in practice, n should be considerably greater than k, if satisfactory estimates are to be obtained.

3.3 Goodness of Fit

In Section 2.2, the simple correlation coefficient was used as a measure of the extent to which the behaviour of the dependent variable is explained by the deterministic part of the model, but this is specific to the two variable case and we shall now take a slightly different approach, in an attempt to find a measure that can be used with any linear model, irrespective of the number of explanatory variables.

The predicted values of the dependent variable, based a k variable regression, would be

$$\hat{Y}_t = \hat{\beta}_1 + \hat{\beta}_2 X_{2t} + \ldots + \hat{\beta}_j X_{jt} + \ldots + \hat{\beta}_k X_{kt}; t = 1, 2, \ldots, n \quad (3.3.1)$$

and the residuals, showing the differences between the observed and predicted values of the dependent variable, would be

$$e_t = Y_t - \hat{\beta}_1 - \hat{\beta}_2 X_{2t} - \ldots - \hat{\beta}_j X_{jt} - \ldots - \hat{\beta}_k X_{kt}; t = 1, 2, \ldots, n \quad (3.3.2)$$

These residuals represent the component of each observation on the dependent variable that is *not* explained by the deterministic part of the k variable model. In the *true* model, the unexplained components are the disturbances, but these cannot be observed and the residuals act as estimators for the disturbances. If estimated relationship does fit the observed data points exactly, the residuals would be zero, but this is an extreme case and, in practice, there would be non-zero residuals, some positive and some negative. A single quantity which can act as a measure of the extent to which the estimated relationship *fails* to explain the behaviour of the dependent variable is therefore provided by Σe_t^2, the residual sum of squares. A high value would indicate a low degree of explanation and a low value would indicate a good explanation.

When a particular regression calculation is performed, the value of residual sum of squares should be included in the information provided on the computer output, but this quantity cannot, in isolation, act as a measure of goodness of fit. It is very difficult to judge whether a given value is 'high' or 'low' without some form of scaling. To find an appropriate scale factor, we need to consider a particularly useful property of the residual sum of squares: whenever a variable is added to a given model and the estimation is repeated for the modified relationship, the residual sum of squares *decreases* or, strictly speaking, it does not increase. It is quite easy to see why this should be so.

If a variable is *omitted* from the model, the parameter *estimate* corresponding to that variable is implicitly set to zero. If it were not so, the variable would be included in the estimated relationship. Now consider what would happen when the variable *is* put into the model and the relationship is re-estimated. The least squares principle states that the parameter estimate is now set to the value that minimizes the residual sum of squares. It is no longer set automatically to the value zero. Even when the variable ought not to be included, because it has a *true* parameter equal to zero, it is highly unlikely that the *estimate* would be exactly zero. But, if the estimate is *not* exactly zero, it is some *other* value of the estimate that minimizes the residual sum of squares. By adding the variable in question, the residual sum of squares is permitted to find a new lower value. Thus we have a result which states that *adding* a variable *reduces* the residual sum of squares, except in the special (and highly unlikely) case in which there is no change. Obviously, adding a *set* of variables has the same effect and *removing* one or more variables has the opposite effect, namely to *increase* the residual sum of squares.

We already know something about the residual sum of squares from one particular type of regression. When Y is regressed on X_1, the residuals are the deviations, y_t; $t = 1, 2, \ldots, n$. Hence, the residual sum of squares, *from this regression*, is given by Σy_t^2. We now know that adding the variables $X_2, X_3, \ldots, X_k$ will reduce this quantity, to give the residual sum of squares from the k variable regression. In general, the residual sum of squares is represented by Σe_t^2. So we have a result which says that Σe_t^2 is *less than* Σy_t^2, except in the special case in which they are equal. It must also be true that both quantities are non-negative, since both are sums of squares and, for any realistic form of model, both will actually be positive.

We now have an appropriate scaling for Σe_t^2. Since Σe_t^2 is less than (or equal to) Σy_t^2 and since both quantities are positive (or zero), the *ratio* $\Sigma e_t^2 / \Sigma y_t^2$ must lie between 0 and 1 (except in the meaningless special case in which $\Sigma y_t^2 = 0$). The interpretation of the ratio is as follows. The quantity Σy_t^2 summarizes, in a single measure, the extent to which the behaviour of the dependent variables is *not* explained by the artificial variable X_1. It also acts as a measure of the total variation in the dependent variable observations. It is this variation that must be explained, as far as possible, by the addition of the genuine explanatory variables, X_2 to X_k. When these variables are added, the measure of variation that cannot be explained is reduced to Σe_t^2. So the ratio, $\Sigma e_t^2/\Sigma y_t^2$, expresses the variation that is *not* explained by the addition of X_2 to X_k as a *proportion* of the total variation that could possibly be explained by X_2 to X_k. The proportion that *is* explained by the addition of X_2 to X_k acts as a measure of goodness of fit

$$R^2 = 1 - \Sigma e_t^2/\Sigma y_t^2 \qquad (3.3.3)$$

The notation, R^2, is conventional and the measure is often described literally as 'R squared'; an alternative description is the *coefficient of determination*. If the estimated relationship did explain the behaviour of the dependent variable exactly, there would be no residual error and Σe_t^2 would be zero. R^2 would then be equal to 1. At the opposite extreme, R^2 would take the value zero if Σe_t^2 and Σy_t^2 were equal. This can only happen if the *estimates* of the parameters corresponding to $X_2, X_3, \ldots, X_k$ turn out to be *exactly* zero. Now it could happen that one had somehow managed to specify a model in which the *true* slope parameters were equal to zero, indicating that $X_2, X_3, \ldots, X_k$ have no real influence on the dependent variable, but even in this situation, it is highly unlikely that the parameter *estimates* would be exactly zero. As in the two variable case, the estimators are random variables, so the estimates are unlikely to take exactly the same values as the corresponding true parameters. It is also unlikely that one would find a perfect fit to the observed data and so, in practice, the value of R^2 will always tend to lie between 0 and 1, without reaching either of the extreme values.

The notation, R^2, does perhaps suggest that the measure is the square of a correlation coefficient. Obviously, one could compute a value for R^2 in the two variable case and the value obtained would in fact be the square of the simple (or *zero-order*) correlation coefficient defined in (2.2.1). In the general case, R^2 is still the square of a correlation coefficient, but the coefficient in question is no longer of a simple kind. There are actually many different types of correlation coefficient. These types differ according to the number of variables to which Y is related and they also differ in respect of what is assumed about the underlying relationship. To illustrate this last point, it should be noted that R^2 is a measure which is based on the assumption that there is an intercept term in the model, but it is also a measure which gives no 'credit' for the explanation achieved by the artificial variable X_1. If, in the k variable regression, the intercept estimate was different from zero, but the slope estimates were exactly zero, R^2 would take the value 0. In such a case, the artificial variable would have explained something about the behaviour of the dependent variable, but addition of the genuine variables, $X_2, X_3, \ldots, X_k$, would have achieved no further explanation. One would usually use R^2 as a measure of goodness of fit because it does have this characteristic. The explanation achieved by X_1 adds nothing to our understanding of the economic forces which help to determine the value of the dependent variable: and R^2 is a measure which reflects this, since it takes a value greater than zero only when the genuine explanatory variables appear to add something to the explanation.

Now consider what is meant by saying that R^2 is used on the assumption that there is an intercept in the model. The result which states that R^2 lies between 0 and 1 is based on this assumption and, if R^2 is used when there is *no* intercept, it *is* possible to obtain a value which is negative. This can only happen when there is a poor fit to the observed data, which would be discouraging in itself: but to obtain a negative value for R^2 could make one think that something has gone disastrously wrong with the calculation and perhaps, that the computer program is incorrect. In fact, although R^2 must still be less than (or equal to) 1, a negative value *is* possible when there is no intercept in the model.

The correct procedure to adopt, in the absence of an intercept term, is to use a measure which neither assumes nor 'allows for' the presence of the artificial variable. If X_1 is not included in the list of explanatory variables, the genuine variables, X_2 to X_k, are required to explain more than the variation of the dependent variable observations around the mean: they have also to explain the constant component which would otherwise be explained by X_1. The deterministic part of the model must then account, as far as possible, for all departures of the dependent variable observations from *zero* and not just departures from the mean. Although variation is usually taken to imply variation around the mean, one could also talk of variation around zero and, in the case of the dependent variable observations, this would be measured by ΣY_t^2 rather than Σy_t^2. So if there is no intercept term in the model, the variation available for explanation by the genuine explanatory variables is represented by

ΣY_t^2 and this should be used as a scale factor, giving a measure of goodness of fit which, for want of a better notation, can be represented as R_0^2 and which is defined by

$$R_0^2 = 1 - \Sigma e_t^2 / \Sigma Y_t^2 \qquad (3.3.4)$$

It is possible to interpret ΣY_t^2 as the residual sum of squares from a regression on nothing at all. This may seem to be a frivolous point, but it does enable us to use our existing results to state that Σe_t^2 is less than (or equal to) ΣY_t^2 and, as this conclusion does not depend on the presence of an intercept term, R_0^2 is a measure of goodness of fit which *always* lies between 0 and 1. It can therefore be used for models which do not contain an intercept term and the only reason for not using it when there *is* an intercept term is that it *does* give credit for any explanation achieved by the artificial variable X_1. So R_0^2 does not assume an intercept, but does give credit for explanation due to X_1 and R^2 does assume an intercept but does not give credit for explanation due to X_1. We have argued that, because of this, R^2 is the better measure when X_1 is included and R_0^2 is the better measure when X_1 is not included. Both measures are squared correlation coefficients, but the coefficients are of different types.

This discussion suggests that there are indeed many different types of correlation measure and, from now on, when we talk of correlation, it should be understood that we use the term in a general sense and that we do not necessarily imply correlation of a type that would be adequately measured by a simple correlation coefficient. The use of correlation measures is not confined to those involving the dependent variable: one could also compute coefficients measuring the association between the explanatory variables. But there is one important difference between measures involving the dependent variable and those that do not. Under the assumptions of our underlying model, the observations on the dependent variable have a random component, whereas those on the explanatory variables are considered to be non-random. So a coefficient involving Y is a random variable: a coefficient involving only the X variables is non-random and is a purely numerical measure of the extent to which the X variables move together.

One final comment on the use of R^2. It can happen that one is faced with two alternative explanations of the behaviour of the dependent variable. Subject to certain qualifications, it is reasonable to chose the relationship with the highest value of R^2. An important requirement is that both alternatives must be equally acceptable in terms of economic interpretation. Statistical criteria alone cannot identify a valid economic model. Next, it must be remembered that R^2 is a measure based on the dependent variable observations and so it is a random variable: small differences in the value of R^2 may be due entirely to random variation. Finally, there is a problem caused by the fact that R^2 will always increase (strictly, cannot decrease) as variables are added to the model and so it is always possible to achieve an apparent improvement by expanding the list of explanatory variables, even when the added variables do not seem to be particularly relevant. The reason for this can be seen by recalling the definition of R^2. As variables are added to the model, Σe_t^2 will almost always decrease and certainly cannot increase. But Σy_t^2 will remain the same, so $\Sigma e_t^2 / \Sigma y_t^2$ is reduced and R^2 is increased. Because R^2 has this property, an alternative measure is sometimes used. This measure, denoted as $\bar{R}^2$, involves a penalty weighting for the number of explanatory variables

$$\bar{R}^2 = 1 - [(1 - R^2)(n - 1)/(n - k)] \tag{3.3.5}$$

For given values of R^2 and n, the higher the value of k, the number of explanatory variables, the lower is the value of $\bar{R}^2$. Although $\bar{R}^2$ is less than 1, it is not necessarily greater than zero and, for very poor fits, negative values can be observed.

3.4 Nonlinear Relationships

We have described a method of estimation, for linear models, without a detailed consideration of the characteristic of a linear model that enables the method to be used. The crucial point is that it must be possible to write the model in the standard form

$$Y_t = \beta_1 + \beta_2 X_{2t} + \ldots + \beta_j X_{jt} + \ldots + \beta_k X_{kt} + u_t; t = 1, 2, \ldots, n.$$

But there is no reason whatsoever why Y and X_j; $j = 2, 3, \ldots, k$ should represent economic variables in exactly the form in which they are originally observed. One could, for example, specify a consumption function in which the underlying relationship is

$$C = \beta_1 + \beta_2 \sqrt{D} \tag{3.4.1}$$

This is not a linear relationship between C and D: the graph, assuming positive values for β_1 and β_2, is shown in Fig. 3.1 and the equation is seen to represent a curve rather than a straight line. As income is increased, the marginal propensity to consume (the slope of the curve) is decreased. Obviously, the reason for choosing this relationship would be that we want to impose this particular characteristic on the model.

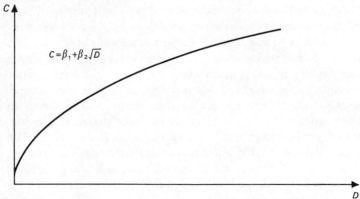

Figure 3.1

Despite the fact that (3.4.1) is a nonlinear relationship between the variables C and D, it *is* a linear relationship between C and $\sqrt{D}$ and, by setting $Y = C$ and $X = \sqrt{D}$, it would be possible to estimate the parameters of a model based on (3.4.1), using the standard least squares technique. The observations used would be consumption and the *square root* of income and X does not represent an economic variable as originally observed. Instead, X is now a *transformation* of the original income variable. The crucial point is that (3.4.1) *can* be written into the standard form for the deterministic part of a linear model and, so long as this can be done, the linear least squares method can still be used. The formal requirement is that the normal equations should still be linear in the parameter estimators, $\hat{\beta}_j$; $j = 1, 2, \ldots, k$.

A second example is a case in which there are only two basic variables, consumption and income, but in which income enters *both* as D and as D^2

$$C = \beta_1 + \beta_2 D + \beta_3 D^2 \qquad (3.4.2)$$

Once again, the graph (Fig. 3.2) shows that the relationship between C and D is nonlinear. The graph is drawn on the assumption that β_1 and β_2 are positive and that β_3 is negative (it is also assumed that β_2 is considerably greater than $-\beta_3$). If β_3 was zero, (3.4.2) would represent a linear relationship between C and D, but if β_3 is negative, the marginal propensity to consume decreases as income increases. We might base a model on this relationship if we wished to test whether the marginal propensity to consume varies with income: if β_3 turned out to be significantly different from zero, this would indeed be the case.

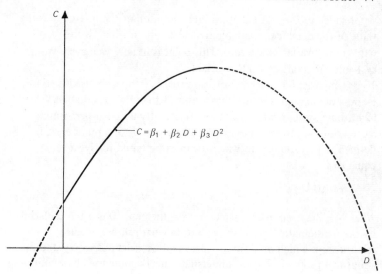

Figure 3.2

Equation (3.4.2) can be fitted into the standard form for the
deterministic part of the *three* variable model. To do this, we would
set $Y = C$, $X_2 = D$ and $X_3 = D^2$. So the parameters can again be found
by the linear least squares method, applied to a set of data formed by
transformation of the original economic variables. In this case, the
necessary transformation is the formation of D^2 from observations on
D.

In Fig. 3.2, some portions of the curve are shown by dotted lines.
This is intended to signify that there are ranges of the variables for which
the relationship is defined in mathematical terms, but for which there is
no real economic meaning (negative values for consumption or income)
or for which the approximation to economic behaviour is no longer
appropriate (the downward sloping part of the curve). It is perfectly
reasonable to use a portion of the curve, corresponding to points that
can actually be observed, as the basis of a model, so long as one does
not attempt to draw conclusions by extrapolating well away from
observed points. Similar reasoning applies to the use of a linear
relationship. A linear approximation may be reasonable for values
of the variables close to those observed in practice, but it can be
dangerous to extrapolate too far from this part of the estimated line.
This is one reason why the intercept estimate in a linear model is
often of limited interest. It can be misleading to attach any real

significance to the mathematical interpretation of the intercept as the value of the dependent variable that would hold when all the explanatory variables are zero. This point is usually well away from available observations on the variables.

One method of transformation that is frequently used is to express the data in terms of *logarithms* of the original variables. The logarithms, or logs, which are most frequently used for performing calculations are to *base* 10, in which case the log of a number, a, is defined as that 'power' to which 10 must be raised to give a value equal to a

$$a = 10^{\{\log(a)\}}$$

When logs are used in economic models, the base 10 is often replaced by the mathematical constant, e, but, in what follows, we use relationships which hold for any base and we need not worry unduly about this problem. But, to understand the example used below, it is necessary to be aware of three properties of logarithms

1. $\log(a)$ is not defined when a is negative

2. for any positive number, a, and any number, b
    $\log(a^b) = b\log(a)$

3. for any two positive numbers, a and c
    $\log(ac) = \log(a) + \log(c)$.

Now consider the example of the relationship between the demand for real money balances (M) and the rate of interest (r). To simplify, other relevant variables are ignored. In the Keynesian model, a shape similar to that in Fig. 3.3 is usually assumed for this relationship. The change in M associated with a given change in r is not thought of as constant over the range of r and, in particular, it is argued that as the interest rate approaches a given low level, the demand for money rises sharply and becomes very large. To capture this behaviour, the equation of the curve shown in Fig. 3.3 is

$$M = a(r - 2)^b \qquad (3.4.3)$$

where a is positive and b is negative. This relationship is certainly non-linear in the variables, but now we also have nonlinearity in the way in which the *parameters* enter the relationship and it is not possible to use (3.4.3), as it stands, as the basis for a model in which the parameters are to be estimated by the linear least squares method.

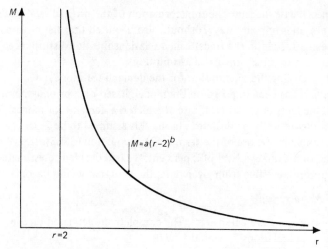

Figure 3.3

However, by applying the log transformation to both sides of the equation and adding a disturbance term, it *is* possible to obtain a model in the standard linear form. The steps are as follows

$$\log(M) = \log[a(r-2)^b]$$
$$= \log a + \log[(r-2)^b]$$

so that

$$\log(M) = \log a + b\log(r-2) \qquad (3.4.4)$$

If $Y = \log(M)$, $X_2 = \log(r-2)$, $\beta_1 = \log a$ and $\beta_2 = b$ and if a disturbance term is added, the transformed model can be written as

$$Y_t = \beta_1 + \beta_2 X_{2t} + u_t \; ; t = 1, 2, \ldots, n$$

The linear estimation method, applied to the transformed model, will produce estimators for β_1 and β_2, which can then be used to produce estimators for a and b, using the relationships

$$\log(\hat{a}) = \hat{\beta}_1 \text{ and } \hat{b} = \hat{\beta}_2 \qquad (3.4.5)$$

It should be made clear that, in this case, the linear form of model has been obtained by transformation of both variables and parameters and any properties that may be obtained for the estimators from a linear model would apply to the *transformed* parameters and not necessarily to the original parameters. The parameter b in (3.4.3) is a special case, because the transformation of the original relationship does not alter b in any way. It should also be noted that the disturbance has been attached to the transformed relationship: this disturbance would have to satisfy the usual assumptions.

In specifying the relationship for the demand for money, a *restriction* has been imposed on the model, based on a prior assumption about the level of the interest rate at which the demand for money would theoretically be infinite. This level is assumed to be 2 per cent, which explains the use of the term $(r-2)$ in equation (3.4.3). If, instead of assuming a level of 2 per cent, we had decided to estimate the appropriate value from given data, the equation would become

$$M = a(r - c)^b \qquad (3.4.6)$$

where a, b and c are parameters, The complete model based on the transformed relationship would now be

$$\log(M_t) = \log a + b \log (r_t - c) + u_t; t = 1, 2, \ldots, n \qquad (3.4.7)$$

and it would no longer be possible to define $\log(r-c)$ as an observable variable, to be denoted by X_2, because this term depends on the unknown quantity c. There is now no way in which the transformed relationship can be written so as to correspond to the standard form for a linear model and, although one could still try to find the estimates which minimize the sum of squared residuals, this criterion would no longer lead to a set of equations which are linear in the parameter estimates. There are methods for searching for solutions in the truly nonlinear case, but such methods are beyond the scope of this book. The only way in which we could proceed, within our present framework is to perform a whole series of regressions corresponding to (3.4.7), for different values of the parameter c, finally choosing that set of estimates for a and b which correspond to the *regression* having the smallest residual sum of squares.

It can now be seen that the basic least squares method is rather more powerful than it might appear, at first sight, to be. Some, but not all nonlinear relationships can be transformed to give an equation for estimation which is in standard linear form. Since it is often necessary to transform the observed economic variables, it is very useful if the computer program used for estimation has the facility for performing simple transformations, such as squaring, forming the square root and taking logs. This saves a great deal of time and may also avoid mistakes, which are easily made if large amounts of data have to be adjusted by hand. But it must be remembered that, when the calculation is performed on a transformed relationship, it is this relationship which is treated as though it were a linear model. Thus, in the example of the demand for money function, the value of R^2 that would be computed would represent the proportion of variation in the dependent variable that is explained by the relationship. But the dependent variable is $\log(M)$ and so R^2 measures the proportion of variation in $\log(M)$ that is explained and *not* the proportion of variation in M. It is very important to remember this in comparing the fit between two versions of a model in which the dependent variable enters in different forms. If, in one case, the dependent variable is $\log(M)$ and, in a different version, the dependent variable is M, the R^2 values are *not* comparable. Although the method of transformation is very convenient, one does have to pay attention to the implications of using the transformed relationship as the basis for estimation.

3.5 Properties of the Estimators

We now consider the statistical properties of the parameter estimators in the context of the k variable linear model. The disturbances are assumed to behave exactly as in the two variable case and the only additional assumption that is necessary is that it must actually be possible to solve the equations which define the estimators. It can be shown that each parameter estimator, $\hat{\beta}_j; j = 1, 2, \ldots, k$, has the following properties

1. it is an unbiased estimator
2. it is a best linear unbiased estimator
3. the estimator has a normal distribution

We did not prove all the corresponding properties in the two variable case, but it was possible to write explicit expressions for the estimators and for the variance of each estimator and to base a partial explanation on these expressions. It does seem reasonable to assert that similar properties will hold in the general case, without repeating the analysis, because any single estimator derived on the basis of the k variable model does have the same general form as the estimators used in the two variable case. The general form is

$$\hat{\beta}_j = \Sigma \tilde{X}_{jt} \tilde{Y}_t / \Sigma \tilde{X}_{jt}^2 \qquad (3.5.1)$$

where $\tilde{X}_j$ and $\tilde{Y}$ represent variables defined as residuals from the regressions of X_j and Y, respectively, on the *other* explanatory variables. The statistical properties can be derived by expressing $\hat{\beta}_j$

in terms of the disturbances. The general form for this expression is

$$\hat{\beta}_j = \beta_j + \Sigma \tilde{X}_{jt} u_t / \Sigma \tilde{X}_{jt}^2 \tag{3.5.2}$$

and, using (3.5.2), it can be shown that there is also a general form for the true variance of a single parameter estimator

$$\text{var}(\hat{\beta}_j) = \sigma^2 / \Sigma \tilde{X}_{jt}^2 \tag{3.5.3}$$

As before, σ^2 represents the true variance of the disturbance distributions. So we see that the arguments used in Section 2.3 are based on a special case of the general forms and we shall be content with having specified the statistical properties of the estimators by analogy with this special case.

Before moving on, it is useful to restate, in a more general form, the check list of assumptions and properties, given originally in Section 2.3. The assumptions are as follows

(A) $Y_t = \beta_1 X_{1t} + \beta_2 X_{2t} + \ldots + \beta_j X_{jt} + \ldots + \beta_k X_{kt}; t = 1, 2, \ldots, n$
where $X_{1t} = 1; t = 1, 2, \ldots, n$, if β_1 represents an intercept
(B) X_{jt} is non-random; $j = 1, 2, \ldots, k$ and $t = 1, 2, \ldots, n$
(C) $E(u_t) = 0; t = 1, 2, \ldots, n$
(D) $\text{var}(u_t) = \sigma^2; t = 1, 2, \ldots, n$
(E) The disturbance distributions are independent`
(F) The disturbance distributions are normal

For completeness, we should add a seventh assumption

(G) The equations defining the estimators can actually be solved.

The properties, with the assumptions used to obtain each property, are then as follows

1. $E(\hat{\beta}_j) = \beta_j$, indicating unbiasedness (A, B, C, G)
2. $\text{var}(\hat{\beta}_j) = \sigma^2 / \Sigma \tilde{X}_{jt}^2$ (A, B, D, E, G)
3. best linear unbiasedness (A, B, C, D, E, G)
4. best unbiasedness (A, B, C, D, E, F, G)
5. normality (A, B, F, G)

Now remember how the properties are applied when the two variable model is used. The slope estimator, $\hat{\beta}_2$, has a normal distribution and a standard error which, when based on an *estimated* disturbance variance, is given by

$$\text{se}(\hat{\beta}_2) = \hat{\sigma} / \sqrt{\Sigma x_t^2}$$

where

$$\hat{\sigma}^2 = \Sigma e_t^2 / (n - 2)$$

A confidence interval for the true parameter is then given by

$$\hat{\beta}_2 \pm 2\mathrm{se}(\hat{\beta}_2)$$

When the number of observations is relatively small, this interval will contain the true parameter with a probability of rather less than 0·95. The reason for this concerns the use of an estimated standard error. Although it is still true that $\hat{\beta}_2$ has a normal distribution, an exact confidence interval based on the normal distribution would require the *true* standard error, which is not known. When the estimated standard error is used, the critical value should be taken from tables of the t distribution, using the entry for $(n - 2)$ degrees of freedom. The value 2, used in the interval above, is an approximation. In the general case, a single parameter estimator, $\hat{\beta}_j$, also has a normal distribution and one can obtain a confidence interval for the true parameter, β_j, as

$$\hat{\beta}_j \pm 2\mathrm{se}(\hat{\beta}_j) \tag{3.5.4}$$

Again, if the number of observations is small, the probability that this interval will contain the true value is rather less than 0·95. It must now be assumed that the standard error would be obtained as part of the computer output, but there is one important point to be made. When the k variable model is used, the estimator for the disturbance variance is

$$\hat{\sigma}^2 = \Sigma e_t^2 / (n - k) \tag{3.5.5}$$

where $(n - k)$ is the number of degrees of freedom associated with Σe_t^2. Although the degrees of freedom is a purely mathematical concept, it was rationalized, in the two variable case, by saying that two parameters would have to be estimated before the residuals could be computed. In the general case, the residuals would be

$$e_t = Y_t - \hat{\beta}_1 - \hat{\beta}_2 X_{2t} - \ldots - \hat{\beta}_j X_{jt} - \ldots - \hat{\beta}_k X_{kt}; t = 1, 2, \ldots, n \tag{3.5.6}$$

and so k parameters have now to be estimated before the residuals can be obtained. The residual sum of squares is now associated with $(n - k)$ degrees of freedom. This would be important if an exact confidence interval is to be constructed, as the tables for the t distribution depend on the number of degrees of freedom involved. It is also important for the additional tests considered in the next section.

The explicit confidence interval formulation is not generally used in reporting on the results of econometric work. Instead, the estimated equation is written down, with the standard errors given in brackets underneath each coefficient. Any other useful information, such as the value of R^2, or $\bar{R}^2$, is also given. The example which follows is based on annual data for the U K economy, for the years 1963–72. It shows an estimated relationship between consumers expenditure (C), personal disposable income (D) and liquid assets held by households (L) and, since all the observations are expressed in terms of 1963 prices, they represent real rather than current price magnitudes. The estimated equation is

$$C_t = 1791 \quad + 0.58D_t + 0.32L_t; \quad \bar{R}^2 = 0.997$$
$$(42.24) \quad (0.11) \quad (0.12)$$

The value of $\bar{R}^2$ looks very high, but it is not unusual to find extremely good fits when one is trying to predict the *level* of an aggregate variable such as consumers expenditure. The standard errors, given in brackets, would enable one to construct the confidence interval for any true parameter. Thus, in the case of the income parameter, the confidence interval would be

$$0.58 \pm 2\,(0.11)$$

or

$$0.36 \text{ to } 0.80$$

If all the usual assumptions are satisfied, one would be almost '95 per cent confident' that the true parameter value lies in this interval. The actual confidence level is a little under 95 per cent because there are only 10 observations on the variables. The way in which the equation is reported would also enable one to test hypotheses concerning the individual parameters and we now consider how this is done.

The problem to hand is that of deciding whether an individual parameter, β_j, is really zero, given that the corresponding *estimate* is unlikely to reflect this condition exactly. By analogy with the two variable case, one would set up the null hypothesis that β_j *is* zero and, using the parameter estimate and standard error given on the computer output, one would calculate a value for the t test statistic

$$t_j = \hat{\beta}_j / \text{se}(\hat{\beta}_j) \tag{3.5.7}$$

The decision rule states that if t_j lies *outside* the range -2 to $+2$, the null hypothesis is *rejected* and β_j is assumed to be different from zero.

If t_j lies *between* -2 and $+2$, the evidence is compatible with β_j having a true value equal to zero. The interpretation of this latter conclusion is very important. It should be remembered that the meaning of an individual parameter and the estimate that is obtained can both depend on the other variables in the model. If β_j is zero, X_j does not have any influence on the dependent variable, *given* the list of other variables that do enter the relationship. This does not mean that the same conclusion would hold if some of the other variables had been omitted. If one is prepared to change the model, in the light of the observed evidence, it is tempting to delete *all* the variables for which the value of the t test statistic lies between -2 and $+2$, but this would be quite incorrect. Once you have decided to delete a single variable, you have implicitly accepted that the original model is *not* correct and, before any further analysis can be performed, it is necessary to re-estimate the parameters associated with the remaining variables and the corresponding standard errors. It is quite possible that this will alter the conclusions to be drawn from the t tests relating to the remaining variables. So, after the estimation of a given relationship, one can only delete a *single* variable on the basis of the associated t statistic. If there is a problem of choice as to which variable should be deleted, one could remove the variable associated with that t value which is closest to zero.

Suppose now that one variable has been removed, that the new relationship has been estimated and that one of the newly computed t statistics still lies between -2 and $+2$. Should the model now be modified again, to remove the second variable? There is a problem associated with such a procedure, because the deletion of the first variable could, with a non-zero probability, have been the wrong thing to do. As a result of this, the probabilities of drawing the wrong conclusion in a *two* step procedure are not exactly those suggested by our analysis. There is an alternative way of testing hypotheses concerning two or more parameters and it is to this that we now turn.

3.6 Tests Involving Several Parameters

Instead of testing a series of hypotheses, each concerning one parameter, it is possible to set up a *single* null hypothesis under which several parameters are *simultaneously* set to zero. Suppose that we had a model in the form

$$Y_t = \beta_1 + \beta_2 X_{2t} + \beta_3 X_{3t} + \beta_4 X_{4t} + u_t \quad ; t = 1, 2, \ldots, n \qquad (3.6.1)$$

and suppose that we wished to test the null hypothesis

$$\beta_2 = 0 \ and \ \beta_4 = 0 \qquad (3.6.2)$$

Before an appropriate test statistic can be constructed, it is necessary to compute two sets of estimates, the first based on the model (3.6.1) and the second based on the model as it *would* appear, under the conditions of the null hypothesis

$$Y_t = \beta_1 + 0 \cdot X_{2t} + \beta_3 X_{3t} + 0 \cdot X_{4t} + u_t$$

or

$$Y_t = \beta_1 + \beta_3 X_{3t} + u_t; t = 1, 2, \ldots, n \qquad (3.6.3)$$

Even when the null hypothesis is true, the estimates obtained from the two versions of the model will tend to be different and we now need a notation for the estimators which reflects this fact. Since the second set of estimates is obtained subject to the *restrictions* that $\beta_2 = 0$ and $\beta_4 = 0$, the estimators obtained from (3.6.3) are described as *restricted* estimators, which are denoted generally as $\hat{\beta}_{Rj}; j = 1,$ $2, \ldots, k$. The usual notation, $\hat{\beta}_j; j = 1, 2, \ldots, k$, is now reserved for the estimators obtained without explicit restrictions. By running the regression defined in (3.6.3), one can obtain estimates corresponding to $\hat{\beta}_{R1}$ and $\hat{\beta}_{R3}$ and these will almost always be different from the values taken by $\hat{\beta}_1$ and $\hat{\beta}_3$, the estimators based on (3.6.1). At the risk of being somewhat pedantic, it could also be said that the restricted estimators corresponding to β_2 and β_4 are given implicitly as $\hat{\beta}_{R2} = 0$ and $\hat{\beta}_{R4} = 0$. The unrestricted estimators, $\hat{\beta}_2$ and $\hat{\beta}_4$, will generally take nonzero values.

The test statistic that is required can now be constructed from the sums of squares of the residuals associated with the two sets of estimators. In the unrestricted case, the relevant quantity would be

$$\Sigma e_t^2 = \Sigma (Y_t - \hat{\beta}_1 - \hat{\beta}_2 X_{2t} - \hat{\beta}_3 X_{3t} - \hat{\beta}_4 X_{4t})^2 \qquad (3.6.4)$$

Since we shall make considerable use of residual sums of squares, the notation is simplified by means of the definition

$$S = \Sigma e_t^2 \qquad (3.6.5)$$

The corresponding quantity for the restricted case is written as S_R, which, in this example, would be defined by

$$S_R = \Sigma (Y_t - \hat{\beta}_{1R} - \hat{\beta}_{3R} X_{3t})^2 \qquad (3.6.6)$$

It is also necessary to know the number of parameters to which the value zero is assigned under the null hypothesis. This is the number of restrictions and this number is represented as g. In the example, the null hypothesis states that β_2 and β_4 are zero and, as this involves *two* restrictions, $g = 2$. Finally, we need to know the number of degrees of freedom associated with the residual sum of squares in the *unrestricted* estimation, given generally by $(n - k)$. In the example, $k = 4$ and so $(n - k) = (n - 4)$. Given all this information, the test statistic for any particular null hypothesis can be found by application of the formula

$$F = \frac{(S_R - S)/g}{S/(n - k)} \tag{3.6.7}$$

The notation F is used because, if the null hypothesis is true, the statistic has a distribution known as the F distribution.

Before we show how to conduct the formal test, we shall try to interpret the information that is used in constructing the test statistic. Equation (3.6.7) is based primarily on two residual sums of squares and we already know that such a quantity acts as a measure of the variation in the dependent variable that is *not* explained by a particular set of explanatory variables. We also know, from the discussion in Section 3.3, that *adding* variables to any existing estimated relationship will *decrease*, or at least cannot increase the residual sum of squares. Conversely, *removing* variables, by setting the corresponding parameter values to zero, will generally *increase* and cannot decrease the residual sum of squares. It follows that the residual sum of squares subject to the restriction imposed by the null hypothesis must be *greater* than the residual sum of squares of the original fit, without the restrictions, except in the special case in which the two are equal. So S_R is greater than (or equal to) S and $(S_R - S)$ will be positive (or zero).

If, in the example above, β_2 and β_4 *are* zero, the variables X_2 and X_4 should have very little measured effect on the explanation of the dependent variable. Consequently, there should be very little difference between the residual sum of squares *without* X_2 and X_4, given by S_R and the residual sum of squares *with* X_2 and X_4, given by S. Even when β_2 and β_4 do have *true* values equal to zero, the *estimates* corresponding to $\hat{\beta}_2$ and $\hat{\beta}_4$ are unlikely to be exactly zero and this is why there is usually *some* difference between S_R and S. The case in which the unrestricted estimates do happen to be exactly zero is the special case referred to above, in which S_R is equal to S, instead of being greater than S. In practice, one would invariably find that $(S_R - S)$ is positive rather than zero.

It has now been established that $(S_R - S)$ tends to be 'small' when β_2 and β_4 *are* zero, that is, when the null hypothesis is true. Conversely, $(S_R - S)$ would tend to be 'large' when β_2 and β_4 are *not* zero and X_2 and X_4 do add significantly to the explanation of the behaviour of the dependent variable. In the F test statistic, $(S_R - S)$ is divided by S: this gives a quantity that does not depend on the units of measurement and, since S is a sum of squares, $(S_R - S)/S$ is still positive (or zero). The statistic is also adjusted for the values g and $(n - k)$: once again, these are positive, so F is always greater than (or equal to) zero. This is as far as we can get with an intuitive interpretation of the information contained in F and we must now consider how the formal test is carried out.

Since large values of the test statistic indicate rejection of the null hypothesis and small values indicate acceptance, it is not surprising to find that there is a critical value below which the null hypothesis is accepted and above which the null hypothesis is rejected. The critical value is taken from tables of the F distribution. Like the t distribution, this depends on the number of degrees of freedom, but there are now *two* distinct quantities involved. In the unrestricted case, k degrees of freedom are used in the estimation of the parameters and S is associated with $(n - k)$ degrees of freedom. In the restricted case, g parameters are *not* estimated: instead the values of these parameters are specified by the restrictions. So S_R is associated with $[n - (k - g)] = (n - k + g)$ degrees of freedom and the difference, $(S_R - S)$, is associated with g degrees of freedom. The critical values in the F test depend on the values of g and $(n - k)$.

The difference between tables of the F distribution and tables of the t distribution can now be explained. The t tables give critical values for selected probabilities of rejecting a true hypothesis and also, for different values of $(n - k)$. By choosing to work with a standard probability of 0·05, one can use a rule of thumb which says that the critical value is approximately 2, except when $(n - k)$ takes a very small value. Unfortunately, it is not possible to do this in the case of the F distribution, because the critical values have to be given for different values of g and $(n - k)$ and, even if one is prepared to work only with a probability of 0·05, there is still some difference between the critical values appropriate to the various values that g and $(n - k)$ may assume.

There are published tables of the F distribution but, for our purposes, the following examples will serve to give some idea of the critical values involved, when the probability of rejecting a true hypothesis is set at 0·05. When there is just one restriction ($g = 1$), the critical values for $(n - k) = 10$ and $(n - k) = 60$ are 4·96 and 4·00 respectively. When there are two restrictions $(g = 2)$, the critical values are reduced to 4·10 and 3·15. When there are four restrictions $(g = 4)$, the critical values are 3·48 and 2·53. And when there are ten restrictions $(g = 10)$, the critical values are 2·98 and 1·99. So we see that the critical values decline as the number of restrictions is increased and, also, as the number $(n - k)$ is increased. In practice, one could use rough interpolation to obtain values that lie between those given in the examples: although there must be a formal decision rule, one would tend to be a little uneasy about the conclusions to be drawn when the calculated value of the test statistic is very close to the critical value. So undue precision in finding the critical values is not really necessary.

It is well worth mastering the technique of using the F test, because it does have a number of applications in econometrics and, despite the rather complicated nature of the distribution, the test is remarkably easy to apply. The calculation of the test statistic consists basically of finding the two sums of squares, S_R and S, and if the computer program provides the residual sum of squares for each regression that is run, one has only to compute two regressions and take the residual sum of squares from each. The test statistic can then be obtained from equation (3.6.7).

There are two special cases that should be noted. The F test could be used to test a hypothesis concerning a single parameter. If S is taken from a full k variable regression and S_R from a regression *excluding* X_j, then (3.6.7) would provide a test of the null hypothesis that $\beta_j = 0$. In this case, $g = 1$. But we already know that a t test can be used here and it turns out that the F test statistic is the square of the t test statistic. The critical value for F is also the square of the critical value for t. So, when $g = 1$, the tests are equivalent. The second case concerns a test of the null hypothesis that all the *slope* parameters are zero. Under the null hypothesis, the genuine variables $X_2, X_3, \ldots, X_k$ do not appear in the model and so the model offers no 'economic' explanation for the behaviour of the dependent variable. In this case, S_R would be the residual sum of squares from a regression involving only the artificial variable, X_1. From the discussion in Sections 3.2 and 3.3, we know that S_R would be given by Σy_t^2, the sum of squares about the mean of the dependent variable. So, for the null hypothesis that $\beta_j = 0; j = 2, 3, \ldots, k$, the test statistic could be expressed as

$$F = \frac{(\Sigma y_t^2 - \Sigma e_t^2)/(k - 1)}{\Sigma e_t^2/(n - k)} \tag{3.6.8}$$

It is interesting to note that (3.6.8) can be expressed in a slightly different form. Since R^2 is defined as

$$R^2 = 1 - (\Sigma e_t^2 / \Sigma y_t^2)$$

it follows that the F test statistic, for the null hypothesis that all the slope parameters are zero, can be written as

$$F = \frac{R^2 / (k-1)}{(1 - R^2)/(n - k)} \tag{3.6.9}$$

Even when the null hypothesis is true, the *estimates* corresponding to $\hat{\beta}_j; j = 2, 3, \ldots, k$ would tend to be somewhat different from zero and R^2 will take a small positive value. But, in such a case, any apparent explanation is due entirely to random variation and the small positive value of R^2 does not signify any *true* explanation of the behaviour of the dependent variable. In this sense, (3.6.9) provides a test to see whether the value of R^2 is *significantly* different from zero. Rejection of the null hypothesis would indicate that this is indeed the case, and that some real explanation has been achieved by the chosen model.

3.7 The Use of Restrictions

The type of null hypothesis used in the previous section involves the imposition of several *restrictions* or *constraints* on the parameters of the model. These are of a very simple type, known as *exclusion* restrictions, under which certain parameter estimates are constrained to take the value zero, thereby removing the corresponding variables from the model. As a result of changing the list of explanatory variables in this way, the estimates of the remaining parameters are altered. Both the way in which these restricted estimates are obtained and the way in which the restrictions themselves are tested will continue to work for *any* set of *linear* restrictions. A given restriction is linear if it can be written so as to fit the standard form

$$r_1 \beta_1 + r_2 \beta_2 + \ldots + r_j \beta_j + \ldots + r_k \beta_k = r_0 \tag{3.7.1}$$

where $r_j; j = 0, 1, \ldots, k$, are known constants. To illustrate the use of the standard form, consider two examples. If we have a restriction which states that $\beta_3 = \beta_4$, one could set $r_3 = 1, r_4 = -1$ and all other r_j values, including r_0, to zero. This would give

$$0 \cdot \beta_1 + 0 \cdot \beta_2 + 1 \cdot \beta_3 - 1 \cdot \beta_4 + \ldots + 0 \cdot \beta_k = \beta_3 - \beta_4 = 0$$

or $\quad \beta_3 = \beta_4$ $\hfill (3.7.2)$

Again, for a restriction which states that $\beta_2 = 1$, we would have $r_2 = 1$ and $r_0 = 1$, with all other r_j values equal to zero

$$0 \cdot \beta_1 + 1 \cdot \beta_2 + \ldots + 0 \cdot \beta_k = 1$$

or

$$\beta_2 = 1 \tag{3.7.3}$$

Suppose now that we wished to impose the restrictions (3.7.2) and (3.7.3) on the model

$$Y_t = \beta_1 + \beta_2 X_{2t} + \beta_3 X_{3t} + \beta_4 X_{4t} + u_t; t = 1, 2, \ldots, n \tag{3.7.4}$$

The first step would be to write the restrictions into the model

$$Y_t = \beta_1 + 1 \cdot X_{2t} + \beta_3 X_{3t} + \beta_3 X_{4t} + u_t; t = 1, 2, \ldots, n$$

The restriction $\beta_3 = \beta_4$ is imposed by actually writing the *same* parameter on X_3 and X_4 and the restriction $\beta_2 = 1$ is written in directly. Any terms involving the same parameter should be taken together

$$Y_t = \beta_1 + 1 \cdot X_{2t} + \beta_3 (X_{3t} + X_{4t}) + u_t; t = 1, 2, \ldots, n$$

and any terms involving a known parameter should be removed to the left hand side of the relationship and subtracted from the dependent variable

$$(Y_t - X_{2t}) = \beta_1 + \beta_3 (X_{3t} + X_{4t}) + u_t; t = 1, 2, \ldots, n \tag{3.7.5}$$

If $(Y - X_2)$ is treated as the dependent variable and $(X_3 + X_4)$ as a single explanatory variable, the resulting regression would give estimates corresponding to the restricted estimators, $\hat{\beta}_{R1}$ and $\hat{\beta}_{R3}$. The remaining restricted estimators are implicit: $\hat{\beta}_{R2} = 1$ and $\hat{\beta}_{R4} = \hat{\beta}_{R3}$.

What we have done is to impose the restrictions by substitution and it is then possible to write the restricted model into a form in which the parameters can be estimated by the standard least squares method. In doing this, some simple transformations of the original variables are used and it is a considerable advantage if the computer program allows for additions and subtractions of variables, as well as the square root, square and log transformations mentioned in Section 3.4. The substitution technique can be used for any set of linear restrictions and the estimates obtained are exactly the same as those from a formalized version of the method, described in more advanced texts as *restricted least squares*.

The restrictions can also be tested in exactly the same way as exclusion restrictions. A regression based on (3.7.4) would give an unrestricted residual sum of squares, S, and a regression based on (3.7.5) would give a restricted residual sum of squares, S_R. It is again true that S_R is greater than (or equal to) S. The null hypothesis would be that the restrictions are true, that is, $\beta_2 = 1$ and $\beta_3 = \beta_4$ and, under the null hypothesis, the test statistic

$$F = \frac{(S_R - S)/g}{S/(n - k)} \qquad (3.7.6)$$

would have an F distribution with g and $(n - k)$ degrees of freedom, where g is the number of restrictions, and $(n - k)$ is the number of degrees of freedom in the *unrestricted* estimation. In the example, $k = 4$ and $g = 2$. The calculation of the test statistic again requires only that two regressions are run, to give values for S and S_R and so the value of the test statistic is easily found. If it is greater than the critical value appropriate to g and $(n - k)$ degrees of freedom, the null hypothesis is rejected and the restrictions are not supported by the data. Otherwise, the null hypothesis is not rejected and the restrictions are consistent with the observations on the real system.

When a model contains several explanatory variables, there are many sets of restrictions that could be tested and one must obviously concentrate on those restrictions which have an economic interpretation of particular interest. An example is provided by the Cobb-Douglas production function, which is a simple form of relationship between output (Q) and labour and capital inputs (L and K)

$$Q = aL^bK^c \qquad (3.7.7)$$

As it stands, this cannot form the basis of a model in which the parameters are to be estimated by linear least squares, but the log transformation gives

$$\log(Q) = \log(aL^bK^c)$$
$$= \log(a) + b\log(L) + c\log(K) \qquad (3.7.8)$$

and, on adding a disturbance, the transformed model can be written as

$$Y_t = \beta_1 + \beta_2 X_{2t} + \beta_3 X_{3t} + u_t; t = 1, 2, \ldots, n \qquad (3.7.9)$$

where $Y = \log(Q)$, $X_2 = \log(L)$, $X_3 = \log(K)$, $\beta_1 = \log(a)$, $\beta_2 = b$ and $\beta_3 = c$. Now it happens to be true that if $b + c = 1$, equation (3.7.7) exhibits constant returns to scale. This means that if labour and capital inputs are increased by the same proportion, output also increases by that proportion. This is a condition of some interest and, if (3.7.9) is used as the basis for estimation, it is worth testing the equivalent hypothesis that $\beta_2 + \beta_3 = 1$. The estimator subject to this restriction can be obtained by writing the restriction into the model, as follows

$$Y_t = \beta_1 + \beta_2 X_{2t} + (1 - \beta_2) X_{3t} + u_t$$

or

$$(Y_t - X_{3t}) = \beta_1 + \beta_2 (X_{2t} - X_{3t}) + u_t \tag{3.7.10}$$

The regression of $(Y - X_3)$ on $(X_2 - X_3)$ would give the estimator $\hat{\beta}_{R2}$ and $\hat{\beta}_{R3}$ can be found as

$$\hat{\beta}_{R3} = 1 - \hat{\beta}_{R2} \tag{3.7.11}$$

One can then use the F statistic (3.7.6) to test for constant returns to scale. The restricted residual sum of squares, S_R, would be obtained from a regression based on (3.7.10) and the unrestricted quantity, S, from a regression based on (3.7.9). If the restriction is supported by the data, one might want to make use of the restricted estimates. There are certain advantages to this, discussed in the next section. If the restriction is rejected, one would simply conclude that it is not true that there are constant returns to scale in the economic system under investigation and the unrestricted estimates would be used. Notice that there is no suggestion that the entire model has to be discarded, simply because the restriction is found to be invalid. The null hypothesis does involve a condition of some interest, but it is not vital to the model that the null hypothesis should be satisfied.

We have given an example in which the decision as to whether or not the restriction is valid is answered by making use of the observed data and in which any prior beliefs concerning the likelihood of constant returns to scale are not enforced. A rather different approach is sometimes used, perhaps because the information contained in the data is considered, for some reason, to be unreliable or because the investigator has strong prior beliefs concerning the parameter values or, as a final possibility, because the existence of certain restrictions is an integral part of the economic theory contained in the model, without which the model is considered to be invalid. In each of these cases, the restrictions would be imposed as a matter of course and one would use only the restricted estimates. If the explanation of the behaviour of the dependent variable is then considered to be unsatisfactory, the entire model would have to be discarded. There is no question of testing the restrictions and making use of the unrestricted model as a possible alternative to the restricted version.

The balance between prior belief and empirical observation is a matter of considerable debate between economists and this is perhaps a question on which the individual must reach his own conclusions. There are methods which formalize the process of using the two types of information together, based on a rather different scheme of statistical inference to that which we have used. These methods, based on the *Bayesian* approach, are outside the scope of this book, but we can make some progress using our existing framework. It may be wrong to rely entirely on observed data but, on the other hand, economic theory is usually developed in the context of an ideal system and it may be equally wrong to expect the restrictions suggested by the theory to be exactly realized in practice. Instead, one might want to use *stochastic* restrictions, in which disturbance terms are added, to allow the restrictions to hold in an approximate rather than an exact sense.

A stochastic linear restriction can be written as

$$r_0 = \beta_1 r_1 + \beta_2 r_2 + \ldots + \beta_j r_j + \ldots + \beta_k r_k + v \tag{3.7.12}$$

where v is a random disturbance. The reason for writing the restriction in this way is that there is a striking parallel between (3.7.12) and the statement of the model for a single time period

$$Y_t = \beta_1 + \beta_2 X_{2t} + \ldots + \beta_j X_{jt} + \ldots + \beta_k X_{kt} + u_t \tag{3.7.13}$$

The terms Y_t and r_0 are both known 'left hand sides' and each X_{jt}; $j = 1, 2, \ldots, k$ is a known quantity, similar to the corresponding r_j; $j = 1, 2, \ldots, k$. The term $X_{1t} = 1$ is implicit in (3.7.13), but it is there nonetheless. Finally, u_t and v are both random disturbances. The similarity between (3.7.12) and (3.7.13) is very real. The model specification actually does consist of n stochastic restrictions, although, with the exception of X_1, the values of the Y and X variables are observed rather than specified 'a priori'. The crucial point is that the r, Y and X values are all known when the estimation is performed.

The analogy that has been drawn suggests a way in which a stochastic linear constraint can be imposed on the parameter estimates. If r_0 is added to the observations on Y and each r_j; $j = 1, 2, \ldots, k$ is added to the observations on the corresponding X_j, a regression run on this *augmented* data would actually impose the constraint upon the estimates. Moreover, several such restrictions can be handled the same way. But there are some practical difficulties: there is no reason why the disturbance v should have the same probability distribution as the disturbances u_t; $t = 1, 2, \ldots, n$ and, in particular, the variance attached to v is usually specified, by the investigator, as a measure of the confidence attached to the prior information contained in the restriction. Since this is unlikely to be the same as the unknown variance associated with each u_t, it is not true that the disturbances in the *augmented* model all have the same properties. It is possible to overcome this problem, using methods developed in the next chapter, but the realization that the restrictions are so similar to the statement of the model is the most important single step towards understanding the use of stochastic restrictions and, even though the practical difficulties remain, an important principle has been established.

There is one case which can be dealt with here. In Section 2.6, we introduced an *ex-post* test for the predictive performance of the two variable model. If the model parameters are estimated on the basis of data for the periods $t = 1, 2, \ldots, n$, the question is whether the same model holds in period $n + 1$. The null hypothesis is that the model *does* hold

$$Y_{n+1} = \alpha + \beta X_{n+1} + u_{n+1} \tag{3.7.14}$$

where α and β represent the same 'true' parameters that apply in periods $t = 1, 2, \ldots, n$. But this is simply a stochastic restriction on α and β and, moreover, it is assumed that the disturbance, u_{n+1}, has exactly the same properties as u_t; $t = 1, 2, \ldots, n$. If we wished to impose the restriction (3.7.14) on the parameter estimates, as well as the restrictions imposed by the statement of the model for the data period, it would seem natural to re-estimate the parameters on the basis of observations for $t = 1, 2, \ldots, n$ *and* $n + 1$. This is precisely what we have suggested for the imposition of *any* stochastic restriction.

The t test given in (2.6.7) is specific to the two variable model, but the test can be generalized and, at the same time, expressed in a form which is convenient for computer calculation. Once again, an F statistic replaces the t statistic and the generalization allows both for the extension to the k variable model and also, for the test to be applied to several additional time periods. A regression run only on the original data is an unrestricted regression, giving a residual sum of squares denoted as S. A regression run on the original data *and* the additional observations is a restricted regression, in which the estimates satisfy extra stochastic constraints and the residual sum of squares is denoted as S_R. Obviously, the additional observations have to be available, and this is why predictive power is tested only in an *ex-post* sense. The test statistic is given by

$$F = \frac{(S_R - S)/g}{S/(n - k)} \tag{3.7.15}$$

where g is now the number of stochastic constraints, that is the number of additional periods for which the model structure is to be tested. Note that n refers to the *original* number of observations. The critical value for the test is found from an F table entry corresponding to g and $(n-k)$ degrees of freedom and a calculated value of the test statistic which is greater than the critical value again leads to rejection. The interpretation of the conclusions to be drawn from the test is exactly parallel to that given for the t test in Section 2.6. In the special case of a two variable model and only one additional observation ($k = 2$ and $g = 1$), the F statistic is the square of the t statistic and the tests are identical.

3.8 Specification Error

The statistical properties of the least squares estimators have been obtained on the basis of an assumed 'true' model, but since we can never be sure whether we have a true model or not, it is as well to be aware of the effects of making a *specification* error, by inadvertently choosing the wrong version of the model. To conduct the analysis, it is still necessary to assume that there is a version of the model that is true and it is necessary to assume that some specific type of specification error is made. In any practical application, we would not know, with certainty, that such an error had occurred, but from the analysis in this section, it will be possible to obtain some idea of what is *likely* to happen, as a result of certain decisions that can be made in a practical context.

For the moment, our attention is confined to the situation in which the list of explanatory variables is incorrect and two special cases are considered. The first is where some of the variables that should be included are *omitted* and the second is where some variables that should be omitted are incorrectly *included*. The discussion is based on the comparison between a three variable model and a two variable model and, in the first case, the three variable model

$$Y_t = \beta_1 + \beta_2 X_{2t} + \beta_3 X_{3t} + u_t; t = 1, 2, \ldots, n \tag{3.8.1}$$

is assumed to be correct. The two variable model is written as

$$Y_t = \beta_1 + \beta_2 X_{2t} + v_t; t = 1, 2, \ldots, n \tag{3.8.2}$$

and we shall consider what would happen if (3.8.2) is used as the basis for estimation. The disturbances in (3.8.2) are written as v_t; $t = 1, 2, \ldots, n$, to distinguish from u_t; $t = 1, 2, \ldots, n$, which are the disturbances in the true model (3.8.1).

In the discussion in Section 3.1, it was suggested that one could use an incorrect model, so long as it is realized that the meaning of the parameters can be different from that in the true model. But, in taking this approach, it is illogical to use the same notation for the parameters which appear in both versions of the model: the reasoning behind the approach is that the omission of the term $\beta_3 X_{3t}$ can be taken up by *changing* the definition of the parameter attached to X_2. What we are now trying to do is to analyse the effect of using (3.8.2) in *ignorance* of the true model, a situation in which the investigator thinks that he can estimate the effect of a change in X_2, *ceteris paribus*, by using (3.8.2). What he does not know is that the parameter that he is trying to estimate is actually a parameter of (3.8.1). In this situation, it is helpful to use the same notation for both sets of parameters: the omission of X_3 from (3.8.2) is taken up by the resulting change in the disturbances. But the *estimators* obtained from the two versions of the model will be different and we need a notation for the estimators which reflects this fact. In this example only, the estimators obtained from the incorrect model are denoted as $\hat{\beta}*_1$ and $\hat{\beta}*_2$ ($\hat{\beta}*_3$ is implicitly set to zero). The usual notation, $\hat{\beta}_1$, $\hat{\beta}_2$ and $\hat{\beta}_3$, is reserved for the estimators based on the correct model.

Equation (3.8.2) represents a two variable model, so the slope estimator, $\hat{\beta}*_2$, is given by

$$\hat{\beta}*_2 = \Sigma x_{2t} y_t / \Sigma x_{2t}^2 \tag{3.8.3}$$

We know, from Section 2.3, that the estimator can also be written in terms of the disturbances which, in (3.8.2), are denoted by v_t; $t = 1, 2, \ldots, n$, rather than u_t; $t = 1, 2, \ldots, n$. The appropriate expression is therefore given by

$$\hat{\beta}*_2 = \beta_2 + \Sigma x_{2t} v_t / \Sigma x_{2t}^2$$

or

$$\hat{\beta}*_2 = \beta_2 + \Sigma w_t v_t \tag{3.8.4}$$

where

$$w_t = x_{2t} / \Sigma x_{2t}^2; \, t = 1, 2, \ldots, n$$

The argument leading to the unbiasedness of estimators which are based on a *true* model requires that the random component of an expression like (3.8.4) should have a zero expectation. But v_t does *not* represent a disturbance from a true model: if (3.8.1) is true, it follows that

$$v_t = \beta_3 X_{3t} + u_t; \, t = 1, 2, \ldots, n \tag{3.8.5}$$

The expectation of a single disturbance, v_t, would then be $\beta_3 X_{3t}$ and in general, the expectation of $\Sigma w_t v_t$ will be non-zero, so that $\hat{\beta}_{*2}$ would be a *biased* estimator. The only exceptions are: (1) when β_3 is really zero, in which case there is no specification error and, (2) when it so happens that $\Sigma w_t X_{3t}$ is exactly zero, for then $\Sigma w_t v_t$ would reduce to $\Sigma w_t u_t$, which does have a zero expectation. This last case corresponds to the situation in which the addition of X_3 to the model makes absolutely no difference to the estimator corresponding to X_2, which in turn requires that some particular correlation measure should take the value zero. In our example, the omission of X_3 would not cause bias in the estimation of the parameter corresponding to X_2 if the simple correlation coefficient between X_2 and X_3 is exactly zero. But we know that when economic data is used, such cases are extremely rare and so we can say that, in general, the incorrect omission of one or more variables *will* cause a bias in the estimation of the remaining parameters. It should be obvious that there is also a bias in the estimation of the parameters of the omitted variables: the estimates are implicitly set to zero but, if the variables are wrongly excluded, the true values are non-zero.

The omission of X_3 from (3.8.1) corresponds to the incorrect imposition of an exclusion restriction. The restriction states that $\beta_3 = 0$ when, in fact, this is not true. The conclusion that this will generally cause a bias in the estimation of the remaining parameters generalizes to *any* incorrectly imposed linear restriction.

Now consider the opposite situation which, in terms of our example, is that the two variable model is true. We should now rewrite (3.8.2) as

$$Y_t = \beta_1 + \beta_2 X_{2t} + u_t; t = 1, 2, \ldots, n \qquad (3.8.6)$$

where u_t is used in place of v_t to signify that the disturbances in the two variable model are now 'true' disturbances, which can be assumed to satisfy the usual conditions. The question to be asked is what will happen if the three variable model is used as the basis for estimation when, in fact, β_3 is really zero. It is not necessary to alter (3.8.1)

$$Y_t = \beta_1 + \beta_2 X_{2t} + \beta_3 X_{3t} + u_t; t = 1, 2, \ldots, n \qquad (3.8.7)$$

since, if β_3 *is* zero, (3.8.6) and (3.8.7) are actually identical *true* models, with identical disturbances. So there is no reason why the estimators based on a regression of Y on X_2 and X_3 should be biased. The effect of this type of mis-specification arises from the fact that, even when β_3 is zero, an *estimate* of β_3, based on the three variable regression, would generally be non-zero, simply because of random variation. In Section 3.5, it was stated that the true variance of a single parameter estimator can be expressed in the general form

$$\mathrm{var}(\hat{\beta}_j) = \sigma^2 / \Sigma \tilde{X}_{jt}^2 \qquad (3.8.8)$$

where $\tilde{X}_j$ represents the variable formed by the residuals from the regression of X_j on all the other explanatory variables in the model. This general form holds for all versions of the model, so long as the disturbances satisfy the assumptions of constant variance and independence. In particular, it holds for the estimator corresponding to β_2, irrespective of whether (3.8.6) or (3.8.7) is used as the basis for estimation. But the specific interpretation of the general form does differ in the two cases. If (3.8.7) is used, $\tilde{X}_2$ would represent the residuals from a regression of X_2 on X_1 *and* X_3. If (3.8.6) is used, $\tilde{X}_2$ would represent the residuals from a regression of X_2 on X_1 *alone*. We know that the addition of variables to a given regression decreases (or, at least, cannot increase) the residual sum of squares and this applies equally to the subsidiary regression of X_2 on the other explanatory variables. Hence, $\Sigma \tilde{X}_{2t}^2$ would take a *smaller* value when (3.8.7) is used, that is, when X_3 is *included* in the model, than would be the case when (3.8.6) is used, that is, when X_3 is *excluded* from the model. The only exception would be the special case in which X_2 and X_3 are completely uncorrelated, in which case the addition of X_3 would have no effect on $\Sigma \tilde{X}_{2t}^2$. The special case is highly unlikely and we can conclude that the addition of X_3 *would* generally *reduce* $\Sigma \tilde{X}_{2t}^2$. Given the form of (3.8.8), this means that the addition of X_3 *increases* the variance of the estimator for β_2. Generalizing this conclusion, we can say that the addition of *any* variable will tend to increase the variance of the estimators for *all* the parameters in the model.

A word of warning is in order here. The result established concerns the *true* variances, all of which involve σ^2, the true variance of the disturbance process. It does not *necessarily* apply to variances or standard errors which are based on an *estimated* disturbance variance. It is, however, the true variance of a given estimator that is the relevant property in evaluating the quality of that estimator.

The addition of X_3 to the model corresponds to a failure to impose the restriction that $\beta_3 = 0$ and, as we have seen, there is a cost in terms of increased variance of the parameter estimators. Conversely, the imposition of the restriction *reduces* the estimator variance and, as this conclusion is true of all exact linear restrictions, we can see why it is advantageous to use any restrictions that are available, so long as the restrictions are valid. As we have already shown, the use of invalid restrictions leads to bias in the estimation procedure. Since the variance measures the spread of individual estimates about the expected value of the estimator, it is of little use when there is a relatively small spread about an expected value which is some distance from the true parameter and this is what happens when there is a small variance, but a relatively large bias. On the other hand, there is little point in having an unbiased estimator if there is also a very high variance, since the probability of finding a single estimate well away from the true value would be relatively high. The most satisfactory estimators would be obtained in some compromise situation, in which there is a balance between bias and variance. The estimators based on the true model reflect one possibility, in which the variance is as small as possible, given that there is to be no bias at all: these are best linear *unbiased* estimators. But there are situations in which the lack of bias can only be achieved at the cost of some very high variances. In such a case, it may be preferable to delete one or two variables, thereby inducing bias, if, at the same time, one can achieve a significant reduction in the variances associated with the remaining parameter estimators. Despite the fact that this would amount to the deliberate use of an incorrect model, it is possible for the estimators attached to the remaining variables to be 'better' estimators of some of the parameters *of the true model*, as judged by a *combination* of bias and variance.

Obviously, one cannot take a conscious decision to use an incorrect model, since there is no way of identifying a true model with certainty. Even so, the analysis of this section is very valuable. It tells us that one can decrease the chance of bias in the estimation procedure by simply adding more explanatory variables that may conceivably be relevant. But it also tells us that there is a cost, possibly an unacceptable cost, in terms of higher variances of the estimators. In the next section, we shall see why the variances can sometimes be very large and why there is usually a limit to the number of variables that can be added in this way.

3.9 Multicollinearity

Observations on economic variables are not generated under controlled conditions, such as those used in experimental science and, as a result, there is always some general intercorrelation *between* the explanatory variables. The name given to this phenomenon is *multicollinearity*.

When we talk of correlation between the explanatory variables, we do not necessarily mean correlation of a kind that could be adequately represented by a simple correlation coefficient. We know that there are many different types of correlation measure and, in general, virtually any such measure applied to relationships between the explanatory variables will take a value which is somewhat different from zero. It is precisely because of this property of economic data that multiple regression is used to estimate the parameters of a k variable model. So long as none of the correlations between explanatory variables is particularly high, there is no difficulty associated with multicollinearity. The phenomenon exists and our estimation method is designed accordingly. What is usually referred to as the *problem* of multicollinearity arises from the effects on the estimators of very high correlations between the explanatory variables and we now consider what these effects are.

We already know how the estimation procedure attempts to deal with the lack of control in the generation of economic data. A single parameter, β_j, is estimated by using only that part of the variation in X_j that is *not* associated with the other explanatory variables in the model. This 'pure' component of X_j is represented by the residuals from the regression of X_j on the other explanatory variables and the residuals are denoted by $\tilde{X}_{jt}; t = 1, 2, \ldots, n$. The estimator, $\hat{\beta}_j$, is then given by

$$\hat{\beta}_j = \Sigma \tilde{X}_{jt} \tilde{Y}_t / \Sigma \tilde{X}_{jt}^2 \qquad (3.9.1)$$

where $\tilde{Y}$ is a variable defined by the residuals from the regression of Y on all the explanatory variables *except* X_j. The variance of β_j is given by

$$\mathrm{var}(\hat{\beta}_j) = \sigma^2 / \Sigma \tilde{X}_{jt}^2 \qquad (3.9.2)$$

If X_j is highly correlated with one or more of the other explanatory variables, there is very little pure variation on which to base an estimate of the effect of a change in X_j, *ceteris paribus*. A single measure of the pure variation is provided by the residual sum of squares from the regression of X_j on the other explanatory variables and this residual sum of squares is $\Sigma \tilde{X}_{jt}^2$. When X_j is highly correlated with the other variables, $\Sigma \tilde{X}_{jt}^2$ will tend to be small and, from (3.9.2), it can be seen that the effect of this will be to make the variance of $\hat{\beta}_j$ relatively large. There would thus be considerable uncertainty attached to the estimate of the parameter β_j. In the extreme case in which X_j is *perfectly* correlated with one or more of the other explanatory variables, there is *no* pure variation and the estimation procedure will fail. This is the situation described at the end of Section 3.2 and, from now on, we will refer the extreme case as perfect or complete multicollinearity.

There is a parallel in the analysis of the two variable model. If the single genuine explanatory variable exhibits very little variation around the mean, the variance of the slope estimator is high and the parameter estimate is thus imprecise. This situation was discussed in Section 2.3 and it does actually represent a type of 'correlation' between the 'variables'. If the genuine variable is nearly constant in the data period, it is 'correlated' with the artificial variable X_1, but the appropriate correlation measure would be defined in terms of the original observations, rather than deviations from the mean. In the extreme case in which the genuine variable does not actually vary at all, no solution would be obtained. The two normal equations which define the estimators would in fact represent the same straight line.

The implications of perfect multicollinearity are obvious: no solution is obtained and it is not possible to estimate the parameters of the chosen model on the basis of the data available. But, with a properly specified model, perfect multicollinearity is rare and, in the remainder of this section, we shall concentrate on the case in which multicollinearity is serious, but not complete. We know that some parameters estimators will be associated with high variances and therefore with high standard errors and, if the primary objective of building the model is to obtain reasonably precise estimates of certain key parameters, one need look no further to see the consequences of a high level of multicollinearity. But if the model is used as an experimental device, to try to discover which explanatory variables are really important, the implications of a high level of multicollinearity can be even more serious. Suppose that an individual variable, X_j, has a true parameter, β_j, which is different from zero and consider what would happen in two different situations: in the first case suppose that the level of multicollinearity is not unduly high and that the *true* value of the parameter is more than 2 standard errors different from zero. The t test statistic for the null hypothesis that $\beta_j = 0$ is given by

$$t_j = \hat{\beta}_j/\text{se}(\hat{\beta}_j) \tag{3.9.3}$$

Since β_j is more than two standard errors distant from zero, *at least* 50 per cent of all values taken by the *estimator*, $\hat{\beta}_j$, would be more than two standard errors distant from zero and so *at least* 50 per cent of possible values of t_j would be outside the range -2 to $+2$. All such values of t_j would lead to rejection of the null hypothesis. Now suppose that, in the second case, the level of multicollinearity is high and that the standard error is considerably greater than in the first case. This could mean that the (same) true value, β_j, now falls well within 2 standard errors of zero and the percentage of all possible values of the estimator falling in the rejection range would then be considerably less than 50 per cent. Although this argument is based on one specific example, it can be seen that increasing the level of multicollinearity makes it less likely that one is able to reject the false hypothesis $\beta_j = 0$, on the basis of the available data. Whereas rejection of the null hypothesis implies a definite decision, that β_j is not zero, with a known probability that the decision is incorrect, a failure to reject the null hypothesis does not necessarily imply a definite decision that β_j *is* zero. A failure to reject may occur because β_j *is* really zero, in which case no amount of extra evidence would lead to rejection: but our example illustrates a situation in which a failure to reject can arise because of a deficiency of the data, in this case due to serious multi-collinearity. If it were possible to observe more 'pure' variation in X_j, it would be possible to achieve a considerable increase in the probability of drawing the correct conclusion by rejecting the false null hypothesis. So, in using the model experimentally, one should perhaps be rather more cautious about the deletion of an explanatory variable, on the basis of the associated t value, than would be the case when the level of multicollinearity is not unduly high.

It should be emphasized that serious multicollinearity usually affects the precision with which *individual* parameters can be estimated. It is quite possible that one could obtain a relationship in which *no t* statistic takes a value outside the range -2 to $+2$, but in which the explanation of the behaviour of the dependent variable is good, as judged by the value of R^2. In such a case, it would be quite clear that the explanatory variables *do* jointly determine the behaviour of the dependent variable. The problem would be in isolating the individual effects. It is for this reason that it is often asserted that multicollinearity does not affect the use of a given relationship for forecasting. If one can assume that the pattern of intercorrelation between the explanatory variables will remain unchanged, the estimated relationship can be used for forecasting and it need not matter that it is difficult to isolate the effects of individual variables. But, in such a case, the forecasts are conditional on assumptions about the future behaviour of explanatory variables to an even greater extent than usual and the estimated relation-ship would certainly not be useful for predicting the effects of a policy decision that would break the pattern of intercorrelation, by changing only one of the explanatory variables.

There is one aspect of the probability distributions of the estimators obtained by multiple regression that has not yet been made explicit. It is true that, under standard assumptions, each individual estimator has a normal distribution, but the distributions are *not* independent. In particular, if two explanatory variables have a high *positive* correlation, the estimators would tend to have a *negative* correlation. It is perfectly correct to assert that there is a probability of approximately 0·95 attached to the event that an individual estimator takes a value within 2 standard errors of the true value, but this is an *unconditional* probability, calculated without reference to the behaviour of any other estimator. It is *not* true that the same probabilities would apply to particular ranges of values of $\hat{\beta}_j$, if the question concerns the probabilities *given* that some other coefficient takes some other specified range of values. To be rather more specific, we can say that if one coefficient happens to take a value well above the true value, there is a relatively greater *conditional* probability that the other coefficient will take a value which is lower than the true value. Of course this is only true if the correlation between the two estimators is negative; the reverse effect would apply for a positive correlation.

We can now see rather more clearly what is meant by saying that it is difficult to isolate individual effects under conditions of serious multicollinearity. Suppose that two parameters, attached to two similar explanatory variables, have the same true value. To fix ideas, let the variables be two interest rates attached to different financial assets. Interest rates do tend to move together over time, so the two variables are likely to have a high positive measured correlation. It is then likely that the two parameter estimators would have a strong negative correlation. Even though the common true parameter value may be quite different from zero, both estimators will have a high variance and it is quite possible for one of the estimators to be close to zero. Given the negative correlation between the estimates, there is then an increased conditional probability that the other estimate will lie beyond the common true value and well away from zero. The conventional *t* test procedure might then suggest that one interest rate is very important and that the other is not. But the observed result is due to random variation and an equally possible result would be a reversal, in which the parameter estimate attached to the *other* rate takes a value close to zero. The fact that one result is observed and the other is not has nothing to do with the underlying economic relationship: it is due entirely to the fact that one particular set of disturbances happen to arise in the one set of data actually observed.

We already know that a true parameter can be different from zero and yet the estimate may be close to zero. What is new, in the particular case chosen for our example, is that it is unlikely that *both* estimates would be close to zero. So, although there may be no difficulty in saying that interest rates in general do have an effect on the dependent variable (and an *F* test on both coefficients should support this conclusion), there is a difficulty in saying *which* rates are important and this reinforces our earlier conclusion that the real problem with serious multicollinearity is the rather arbitrary way in which estimates are assigned to the parameters corresponding to individual explanatory variables. The example also suggests that it is particularly dangerous to conclude that there are real differences between parameter values, on the basis of a casual inspection of the estimates obtained under conditions of high positive correlation between the explanatory variables. The individual standard errors tend to be high and in addition to this, if one estimate is much greater than the true value, the other tends to be less than the true value and so the probability of an *observed* difference, due entirely to random variation, is reinforced by the negative correlation between the estimators.

In Chapter 2, the origin of random variation in the estimators was explained by considering what would happen to the estimates if a different set of random disturbances could be generated. If the variances or standard errors of the estimators are high, a small change in the disturbances could have a relatively large effect on the estimates obtained. Equally, any *actual* change in the data could have a relatively great effect on the estimates. A change, in this context, could be an error in one observation on the variables, which is subsequently rectified. It could be a revision in the data: official statistics are often revised several times after the initial publication. It could also be the use of a different year as the price base, for expressing variables in real, as opposed to current price terms. Finally, it may be the addition or deletion of some observations. Whatever the cause, the instability of estimates in the face of such changes is a characteristic of estimation under conditions of severe multicollinearity.

There is one other manifestation of serious multicollinearity, which is closely related to the instability of estimates in response to small changes in the data. A computer does not perform arithmetic operations with complete accuracy, although the level of accuracy attained would put most hand calculations to shame. If a small error does occur, this is equivalent to a small change in the original data. Under conditions of serious multicollinearity, the effect is amplified and this can result in a relatively large change in the estimates. If this does happen, it is no longer true that one would obtain an answer which is numerically correct in relation to a *given* set of data. Unfortunately, it is also true that there are certain methods of performing the least squares calculation which involve operations that are particularly likely to *generate* small errors. It is therefore possible for the computer calculation to be both the source and the 'amplifier' of small errors, giving answers which are numerically inaccurate. The extent to which this can happen depends on the accuracy with which a particular type of computer can operate and, although it is not always true, it is likely that the least accurate results would be obtained from a small machine. Fortunately, the numerical problems of regression analysis are well known to those who design computer programs and, in any case, such problems tend to occur only when multicollinearity is very serious indeed. But it is as well to be aware of this aspect of multicollinearity and, before using a computer program for the first time, it may be useful to run a test problem, which is subject to multicollinearity and for which the results are already known or, failing this, to seek some professional advice on the adequacy of the program.

We now consider whether anything can be done to mitigate the effects of multicollinearity on the estimation of the parameters of a given model. It must be realized that multicollinearity does not constitute a breakdown of the assumptions, except in the extreme case in which the estimation fails. It may well be that the reason for a high correlation between explanatory variables is that there is a meaningful relationship between some of these variables and, in a *complete* model, it would no longer be appropriate to consider all such variables to be non-random. But the additional relationship cannot be analysed within the *partial* model and, in the partial model, it is usually quite legitimate to treat all the X variables as non-random. In any case, it does not necessarily follow that high correlations between the explanatory variables are due to an additional true relationship: the correlations may simply be an accident of the only data that is available.

If one takes the model and the data as given, with no possibility of change, there is really nothing that can be done about multicollinearity. It is simply a fact of life that the chosen data does not contain enough information to enable one to obtain satisfactory estimates of all the individual parameters. So, if one is concerned about the effects of serious multicollinearity, one must either use the data to estimate fewer parameters, thereby reducing the demands that are placed on the observed information, or one must change the data. We shall consider each of these possibilities in turn.

The obvious way to reduce the demands on the data is to base the estimation on a form of model in which some of the explanatory variables are deleted. It is true that, by doing this, one is actually throwing away some of the available information but, at the same time, there is a reduction in the number of parameters to be estimated from the data: the estimates corresponding to the excluded variables are implicitly set to zero, but this is not done on the basis of observed information, except in the sense that one might choose the variables to be deleted by performing statistical tests derived from a preliminary regression on the original form of the model. If some variables are excluded, we do not necessarily believe that the reduced model is the true model: on the contrary, we would presumably believe that the *original* model is the best approximation to the true model and, if it were not for serious multicollinearity, we would obviously prefer to use the original model. The discussion in the previous section would suggest that, by deleting some variables, biases will be introduced, but there will also be a reduction in the variances and it is possible that, by basing the estimation on a reduced version which is *not* the true model, we could actually get better estimates of at least some of the parameters of the true model.

If the decision as to which variable should be deleted is based on test statistics taken from a preliminary regression on the original form of the model then, as we have said, there is a sense in which the data *is* used to set a zero value on an estimate corresponding to a variable which is deleted, but this argument becomes rather complicated and we shall not pursue the point. It *is* often convenient to have some way of choosing the variable to be deleted and, in the absence of any available prior information, there is a rule of thumb that can be used: this states that one could delete any single variable for which the t statistic, based on the original regression, lies between -1 and $+1$. The corresponding statistic for a *set* of variables is the F test statistic. Here the null hypothesis is that several parameters are zero and we could apply a similar rule, which states that one could delete any *set* of variables corresponding to an F value in the range 0 to 1. Under normal conditions, if one was prepared to change the model at all, any variable or set of variables associated with such test values would be deleted anyway. But, with serious multicollinearity, one might be reluctant to use the usual test procedures and what we are now suggesting is a narrowing of the range of values which would lead to the deletion of a given variable or set of variables. In comparison with the usual test procedures, we would be *decreasing* the risk of bias due to the incorrect deletion of variables and this is a recognition of the high degree of multicollinearity in the data. But, in comparison with a strategy of no change to the model, irrespective of the nature of the data, one would be *increasing* the risk of bias, in an attempt to reduce the variances. As we have said, the result may well be 'better' estimators of the parameters of the true model, as judged by a combination of bias and variance.

The deletion of one or more variables corresponds to the use of restrictions that may not really be valid. There are also other types of restriction, not necessarily simple exclusions, which could be imposed. If there are any *valid* restrictions, perhaps suggested by the theory underlying the model, these should certainly be used and, as we know, the effect of imposing 'true' restrictions is to reduce the variances of the estimators, without causing bias. The only exception is the rather unlikely situation in which the restrictions are already satisfied *exactly* in the initial estimation, in which case there is no change in the variances when the restriction is formally imposed. Another approach which is sometimes used is to create artificial restrictions, which are almost satisfied, but which are *not* simple exclusions. One way of doing this is to make use of *principal components*. We are already familiar with the idea that the observations on a given variable can be divided into two components, a part which is 'explained' by other variables and a part which is not. When principal components are calculated from a given set of explanatory variables, the total 'information' contained in the variables is rearranged into a *new* set of variables, each consisting entirely of information which is *not* contained in the others. These new variables are the principal components and the other important characteristic is that it is possible to order the components in terms of their contribution to the explanation of the behaviour of the dependent variable. It is sometimes possible to identify individual components as containing specific types of information: thus one component may consist largely of the time trend in the data. But this identification is not essential. Once the components have been obtained, it is possible to run a regression in which the components are used in place of the original explanatory variables and then to convert the resulting coefficients back into estimates of the parameters of the original model. If *all* the components are used, the estimates obtained would be identical to those from a regression on the original variables but, because the components can be ordered in terms of importance, it is possible to exclude the least important components and, if this is done, the estimates obtained on converting back to the parameters of the original model are no longer the same. By deleting some of the components, one is imposing exclusion restrictions on the coefficients relating to the components, restrictions which are 'almost' valid. But these restrictions are equivalent to a set of restrictions on the *original* parameters, restrictions which are *not* simple exclusions. Instead of deleting some of the original variables completely, one is effectively removing 'bits' taken from many of the original variables. Although some marginally useful information is discarded, one is no longer basing the estimation entirely on the data. Some additional information is introduced in the form of the artificial restrictions. Again, since the restrictions are not exactly true, there will be some bias, but hopefully, the reduction in the variances will more than compensate for the biases that are introduced.

The extraction of principal components represents a somewhat lengthy calculation and we shall not attempt to describe how that calculation is performed. Obviously, a computer program would have to be available. The reason for mentioning the method is that it is used in econometric studies and it is therefore convenient to have some understanding of what is involved. The important point is that the technique represents a way of choosing some restrictions which are almost satisfied and which are used to reduce the high variances that are otherwise obtained under conditions of serious multicollinearity.

If the data does not contain enough information to allow the parameters of the original model to be estimated with sufficient precision, then one can only use the original model, without any additional restrictions, if it is possible to find more data. The new data must represent a significant addition to the available information. Extending a time series that is dominated by multicollinearity would not help very much if the new observations are also subject to serious multicollinearity, but a technique that is sometimes used is the *pooling* of time series and cross-section data. The standard example of this method is taken from the estimation of demand functions. Suppose that expenditure on a particular food item is related to disposable income, the price of the food item and the prices of close substitutes. If income and prices exhibit a strong time trend, time series data can be subject to fairly severe multicollinearity. But data taken from a cross-section of households, at a particular point in time, would not be subject to this problem. In the simplest case, in which all households face the same prices, there is *no* price variation in the cross-section sample, but there is income variation and so it should be possible to establish a reasonably precise estimate of the income parameter. This estimate could then be imposed, as a restriction, in a regression run on the time series data and this would mean that the time series data is used only to establish price effects. There are some problems of compatibility between the cross-section and time series estimates, but the principle underlying the method is clear. The effects of a high correlation between income and the prices can be mitigated by adding to the available data. Alternatively, in the context of the original time series sample, we can say that a restriction has been introduced, thereby decreasing the amount of information to be extracted from the given time series data. Before leaving this example, it should be noted that the pooling method would not be of much help in overcoming multicollinearity *within* the set of price variables. The method is designed to improve the estimation when the main problem is cor-relation between income, on the one hand, and prices on the other.

We have assumed, throughout this section, that one would have no difficulty in detecting the presence of serious multicollinearity and it is tempting to say that multicollinearity is only a problem insofar as one can detect the various effects. If one is able to obtain estimates of all the parameters of interest and if these estimates seem to be sufficiently precise, one would not be unduly worried by the fact that the standard errors could have been lower if the explanatory variables had not been so highly correlated. But, in practice, it can be difficult to decide on what is an unreasonably high value for a particular standard error and, in any case, multicollinearity is not the only reason for obtaining high standard errors. We have said that a particular estimate will be imprecise if there is very little pure variation in the corresponding explanatory variable, but you would get exactly the same effect if there is very little variation to start with, before adjusting for the effects of the other genuine explanatory variables. One obvious case is where the number of observations is limited. So lack of information in the data does not arise *only* because of high correlations between the explanatory variables and we really do need some way of finding whether high standard errors are due to multicollinearity.

To be sure of detecting the presence of serious multicollinearity and of identifying the variables involved, one would need a *complete* set of correlation coefficients relating to the explanatory variables. Some computer programs do provide this information: others may only give the simple or zero order coefficients between pairs of variables. If one or more of the simple coefficients is very close to 1, then serious multicollinearity does exist in the set of explanatory variables. Whether or not this matters depends largely on the objectives of model construction. But high values of the simple coefficients do not necessarily reveal the pattern of intercorrelation and the absence of any particularly high *simple* coefficients does not necessarily mean that other types of correlation are not at a high level. Again, there are various ways in which one could arrange for a computer program to provide some specific warning that there is serious multicollinearity, somewhere in the explanatory variable set, but there is no single measure which is universally accepted as an indicator, in the sense that all computer programs would provide such a measure as a matter of course. One cannot assume that the computer output will contain any information other than the usual parameter estimates, standard errors, etc., and the detection of serious multicollinearity may have to be a rather informal process, making use of whatever clues are available. A first and important source of information is prior knowledge: if one were to use a set of interest rates as explanatory variables and if it were known that the rates on various financial assets tend to move together, one would expect some multicollinearity and one would be alert to the possibility that it might be serious. Given this prior warning, it seems more reasonable to assert that one could examine the standard errors and make some judgement about whether they are high. And if they are very high, it is also reasonable to assert that it is the correlations between the interest rates that are responsible. A further clue would be provided by the sensitivity of the estimates to small changes in the data, including the deletion of one of the interest rates. Admittedly, these informal procedures are not entirely satisfactory, but, unless one is prepared to modify the program, to provide all the necessary information, there may be very little choice. So long as one is aware of the effects of serious multicollinearity, one *can* usually identify estimated equations in which the condition does cause real problems.

3.10 Dummy Variables

The final section of this chapter is concerned with the problems that arise when a given set of data divides naturally into two or more subsets, according to the categories of some *qualitative* variable. Thus one might have data for two or more regions, or a long time series containing pre-war and post-war observations, or data for the periods before and after a devaluation of the currency, or data relating to periods with and without an incomes policy, or quarterly data relating to different seasons of the year, and so on. We shall use region as a convenient example, but what is said would apply equally to any other qualitative influence. For simplicity, we base the discussion on the two variable model, in the original notation

$$Y_t = \alpha + \beta X_t + u_t; t = 1, 2, \ldots, n \qquad (3.10.1)$$

Now suppose that there are just two regions, labelled as regions 1 and 2. It may well be that the appropriate true parameters are different in the two regions and, if this is so, the model should be based on two distinct relationships between Y and X

$$Y_t = \alpha_1 + \beta_1 X_t + u_t; \text{ in region 1} \qquad (3.10.2)$$
$$Y_t = \alpha_2 + \beta_2 X_t + u_t; \text{ in region 2}$$

There are also some other possible specifications. If the intercept differs between regions, but the slope does not, the model would be

$$Y_t = \alpha_1 + \beta_1 X_t + u_t; \text{ in region 1} \qquad (3.10.3)$$
$$Y_t = \alpha_2 + \beta_1 X_t + u_t; \text{ in region 2}$$

where the subscript on β is now redundant. In this version of the model, a unit change in X has the same effect on Y, irrespective of region, but the observations on Y have an additional constant component, that is present is one region, but not in the other. It is also possible that the intercepts are the same, but the slopes are different

$$Y_t = \alpha_1 + \beta_1 X_t + u_t; \text{ in region 1} \qquad (3.10.4)$$
$$Y_t = \alpha_1 + \beta_2 X_t + u_t; \text{ in region 2}$$

Unless the intercept does have some specific economic meaning, this is unlikely to be a version of the model that is of interest. The final possibility is that both parameters are the same in both regions, which would give

$$Y_t = \alpha_1 + \beta_1 X_t + u_t; \text{ in region 1} \qquad (3.10.5)$$

$$Y_t = \alpha_1 + \beta_1 X_t + u_t; \text{ in region 2}$$

where the subscripts on α and β are now redundant. In this version of the model, the deterministic relationship is the same in both regions and there is no point in writing two separate relationships. So (3.10.5) can be written as

$$Y_t = \alpha + \beta X_t + u_t; \text{ in regions 1 and 2} \qquad (3.10.6)$$

where the subscripts on α and β have now been removed.

The various versions of the model are illustrated in Fig. 3.4. It is obvious that the number of possibilities increases with the number of explanatory variables and also, with the number of categories of the qualitative variable. With several explanatory variables and several regions, there would be many alternative specifications, only one of which could correspond to a 'true' model.

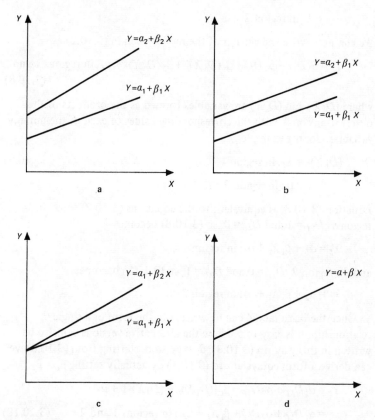

Figure 3.4

The introduction of models based on several relationships obviously raises some problems of estimation and testing that we have not encountered previously. But there is a very simple 'trick' which enables us to convert any of the models (3.10.2) to (3.10.5) into the form of a single relationship and, if this can be done, we can use our existing methods for estimation and testing.

Suppose that we create two *dummy variables*, denoted as

D_1 and D_2 and defined so that

$$D_{1t} = 1; \text{ in region 1} \tag{3.10.7}$$

$$= 0; \text{ in region 2}$$

$$D_{2t} = 0; \text{ in region 1}$$

$$= 1; \text{ in region 2}$$

We can now write the version of the model given in (3.10.2) as

$$Y_t = \alpha_1 D_{1t} + \alpha_2 D_{2t} + \beta_1 (D_1 X)_t + \beta_2 (D_2 X)_t + u_t; \text{ in regions 1 and 2} \tag{3.10.8}$$

where $(D_1 X)$ and $(D_2 X)$ are variables formed as the products of the observations on X with the corresponding values of each of the dummy variables. So, for example

$$(D_1 X)_t = X_t; \text{ in region 1} \tag{3.10.9}$$

$$= 0; \text{ in region 2}$$

Equation (3.10.8) is equivalent to the equations (3.10.2) since, in region 1, $D_{1t} = 1$ and $D_{2t} = 0$, so (3.10.8) becomes

$$Y_t = \alpha_1 + \beta_1 X_t + u_t; \text{ in region 1}$$

and, in region 2, $D_{1t} = 0$ and $D_{2t} = 1$, so (3.10.8) becomes

$$Y_t = \alpha_2 + \beta_2 X_t + u_t; \text{ in region 2}$$

Once the basic model can be written in the form of a single relationship, it is easy to see how the alternative versions can also be written in this way. In (3.10.3), $\beta_1 = \beta_2$, and, starting from (3.10.8) we can derive a form equivalent to (3.10.3) by actually setting $\beta_1 = \beta_2$

$$Y_t = \alpha_1 D_{1t} + \alpha_2 D_{2t} + \beta_1 [(D_1 X)_t + (D_2 X)_t] + u_t$$

$$= \alpha_1 D_{1t} + \alpha_2 D_{2t} + \beta_1 X_t + u_t \text{ ; in regions 1 and 2} \tag{3.10.10}$$

since

$$(D_1 X)_t + (D_2 X)_t = X_t, \text{ for all values of } t$$

Again, the subscript on β_1 is now redundant and could be dropped. It is clear that (3.10.10) is derived from (3.10.8) by imposing the *restriction* that $\beta_1 = \beta_2$. In the original formulation, this would be a *cross-equation* restriction, but in the dummy variable formulation, the restriction is a simple 'within-equation' equality, which can be imposed and tested by our existing methods.

Before we proceed further, it should be noted that (3.10.8) can
be expressed in a slightly more convenient form. It is not necessary to
make explicit use of both dummy variables. Since $D_{1t} + D_{2t} = 1$, for all
values of t, it is possible to eliminate D_1, giving

$$Y_t = \alpha_1(1 - D_{2t}) + \alpha_2 D_{2t} + \beta_1[(1 - D_2)X]_t + \beta_2(D_2 X)_t + u_t$$

$$= \alpha_1 + (\alpha_2 - \alpha_1)D_{2t} + \beta_1 X_t + (\beta_2 - \beta_1)(D_2 X)_t + u_t$$

or

$$Y_t = \alpha_1 + \delta_2 D_{2t} + \beta_1 X_t + \gamma_2(D_2 X)_t + u_t \text{ ; in regions 1 and 2}$$

$$(3.10.11)$$

where $\delta_2 = (\alpha_2 - \alpha_1)$ represents the *difference* between the intercepts
in the two regions and $\gamma_2 = (\beta_2 - \beta_1)$ represents the *difference* between
the slopes. This is more convenient than (3.10.8) for two reasons.
Firstly, the restrictions are now simple exclusions: if the intercepts are
equal, $\delta_2 = 0$ and if the slopes are equal, $\gamma_2 = 0$. Exclusion restrictions
can be imposed by simply omitting the corresponding variable. The
omission of $(D_2 X)$ gives a specification equivalent to (3.10.3), the
omission of D_2 gives a specification equivalent to (3.10.4) and the
omission of *both* D_2 and $(D_2 X)$ gives a specification equivalent to
(3.10.5) or (3.10.6). In all these versions of the model, there is a 'proper'
intercept term: the parameter α_1 is attached to a 'variable' which takes
the value 1 in *both* regions. Specifications based on (3.10.8) do not
have a proper intercept term. Many computer programs automatically
insert an intercept, unless the user takes specific steps to avoid this and,
if both dummy variables are used in addition to a 'variable' which is
always equal to 1, we would have complete multicollinearity, caused
by the fact that $D_{1t} + D_{2t} = 1$, for all values of t. These problems are
avoided by using (3.10.11), rather than (3.10.8), as the starting point
for the imposition of restrictions.

Suppose now that we wished to test the null hypothesis of no
difference between regions. Under the null hypothesis, region has no
influence on the relationship between Y and X and $\alpha_1 = \alpha_2$, $\beta_1 = \beta_2$.
The equivalent null hypothesis, in terms of δ_2 and γ_2, is that $\delta_2 = 0$
and $\gamma_2 = 0$. The general form for the test statistic for exact restrictions
is

$$F = \frac{(S_R - S)/g}{S/(n - k)}$$

$$(3.10.12)$$

where S_R is the residual sum of squares *with* restrictions imposed, S
is the residual sum of squares *without* restrictions, g is the number of

restrictions under test and k refers to the number of parameters to be estimated in the *unrestricted* form. A regression corresponding to (3.10.11) would give estimates corresponding to $\hat{\alpha}_1$, $\hat{\delta}_2$, $\hat{\beta}_1$ and $\hat{\gamma}_2$ and implicitly, $\hat{\alpha}_2 = \hat{\alpha}_1 + \hat{\delta}_2$ and $\hat{\beta}_2 = \hat{\beta}_1 + \hat{\gamma}_2$. It would also give a value for S and since *four* parameters are estimated, $k = 4$. It should be noted that n refers to the *total* number of observations, from both regions. To find the restricted sums of squares, the restrictions $\delta_2 = 0$ and $\gamma_2 = 0$ are imposed by deleting D_2 and $(D_2 X)$ and a regression based on

$$Y_t = \alpha_1 + \beta_1 X_t + u_t; \text{ in regions 1 and 2} \qquad (3.10.13)$$

would give restricted estimators $\hat{\alpha}_{1R}$ and $\hat{\beta}_{1R}$ and the restricted residual sum of squares, S_R. Note that the subscripts on α and β are now redundant and that, since there are two restrictions, $g = 2$. Assembling this information into the F test statistic (3.10.12) will give a value for the test statistic and, as usual, the null hypothesis would be rejected if the value obtained is greater than the critical value for g and $(n - k)$ degrees of freedom. Rejection means that there *is* a difference between the parameters in the two regions and so region *does* have some effect on the relationship between Y and X.

The advantage of the dummy variable formulation is that is shows how our existing methods can be used to test restrictions *between* the parameters of different relationships. The particular test described above attempts to discriminate between the totally unrestricted and totally restricted versions of the model. This special case is often described as the *Chow* test, particularly in the context of testing for the stability of parameters between two time periods. Although we have used the dummy variable formulation to explain how the test works, it is not necessary, in this special case, to make *explicit* use of dummy variables. The reason for this is that the parameters of the unrestricted version of the model can be estimated by fitting two *separate* regressions and this gives precisely the same estimates of α_1, β_1, α_2 and β_2 as those derived from (3.10.11): the unrestricted residual sum of squares can be obtained by adding the values obtained from the two individual regressions. Thus, if S_1 is the residual sum of squares from a regression on the data from the first region only and S_2 is the corresponding quantity from the second region, the sum of squares, S, is given by

$$S = S_1 + S_2 \qquad (3.10.14)$$

The totally restricted estimates are obtained by fitting a regression to (3.10.13) and this states directly that one should fit a single regression to the data from both regions. The residual sum of squares from this regression provides a value for S_R. Since the dummy variables are eliminated by the restrictions, S_R can be obtained without *actually* making use of the dummy variables. But, by using dummy variables to express the unrestricted model in the form of a single relationship, it is possible to see *why* the test works and also, it becomes clear how one should assign values to n, k and g.

In any situation in which one wants to estimate a version of the model which lies between the extremes of total restriction and total lack of restriction, the dummy variable method is used *explicitly*. Thus, to estimate the parameters in a specification in which the intercepts are different in each of *three* regions, but in which the slopes are the same, one would estimate a single relationship

$$Y_t = \alpha_1 + \delta_2 D_{2t} + \delta_3 D_{3t} + \beta X_t + u_t \ ; t = 1, 2, \ldots, n \qquad (3.10.15)$$

where

$D_{2t} = 1$; in region 2

$\quad\ \ = 0$; elsewhere

$D_{3t} = 1$; in region 3

$\quad\ \ = 0$; elsewhere

and

$$\delta_2 = \alpha_2 - \alpha_1 ; \delta_3 = \alpha_3 - \alpha_1$$

Obviously, as the number of explanatory variables is increased, one could form specifications which allow some slope parameters to differ between regions, while others do not. It is also possible to allow for differences between some regions and no difference between others. And one could introduce further dummy variables to allow for additional qualitative effects. The only limitation to the process of expansion of the model is that there must be enough observations to allow all the parameters to be estimated and it is possible to encounter problems of multicollinearity if the process of expansion is taken too far. Despite this, it is obvious that the dummy variable formulation does offer great flexibility in the specification of models which incorporate the effects of qualitative variables.

The method of testing is also quite general and can be used in an attempt to choose between any two versions of a given model, so long as one structure is a restricted version of the other. It must be understood, in this context, that 'unrestricted' and 'restricted' are relative descriptions. For the purpose of a particular test, the least restricted version of the model becomes the 'unrestricted' model, giving a residual sum of squares, S, and degrees of freedom $(n - k)$, where n refers to the total number of observations, in all regions, and k refers to the total number of parameters to be estimated in the (relatively) unrestricted version of the model. Similarly, S_R refers to the residual sum of squares in the more restricted version and g refers to the number of restrictions under test.

Before leaving this topic, we should note an important assumption that underlies our treatment so far. When a model is written in terms of a single relationship, it is assumed that the disturbances behave as in any single equation model and, throughout our discussion, we have assumed that the disturbances are independently distributed, with common variance, σ^2. In the next chapter, we shall see how this assumption can be modified, but for the moment, our assumptions imply that the disturbances in each region are independent of disturbances in all other regions and that the disturbances in all regions have a common variance.

When the methods of this section are used to allow for the effects of a qualitative variable, one is seldom interested in how well the qualitative variable explains the behaviour of the dependent variable. What we are really interested in is the way in which the qualitative variable affects the relationship between the economic variables in the underlying model. For this reason, the qualitative variables are often referred to as 'nuisance' variables, which have to be allowed for, in order to avoid distortion in the estimates of the parameters of the underlying economic relationship. The dummy variable formulation shows exactly what such distortions would imply. If the parameters of a given model do vary between regions, but the relevant dummy variables are omitted, there will be bias in the estimation of the parameters of the 'economic' variables. It is obvious that something must go wrong if the true parameters are different and the estimates are constrained to be the same. Our analysis tells us exactly how such an error of specification does affect the estimates obtained.

It is interesting to note that the artificial variable that allows for an intercept term is very similar to a dummy variable. Unless we have reason to believe that the intercept is zero, an intercept term must be included, but the intercept estimate is seldom of intrinsic interest. So the artificial 'variable' is really a nuisance effect.

A final comment on the use of qualitative variables relates to problem of seasonality in quarterly data. Season is a somewhat special case in that it is often possible to obtain data which has already been adjusted for any known effects which are specific to particular quarters of the year. In some cases, two sets of data are available, one *seasonally adjusted* and one set which is not adjusted and there is then a problem of choice as to which set of data should be used. The answer to this question depends heavily on the particular situation under investigation, but we can perhaps give some indication as to how the choice should be made and as to what difference this is likely to make. Consider a specific example in which the sales of a particular commodity are related to disposable income and in which sales reach a seasonal peak in the fourth quarter of the year. Suppose that the reason for this sales peak is that there is an additional demand for the commodity, caused by purchases prior to the Christmas period.

If the primary interest is the relationship between sales and income, the seasonal peak is a distortion. We would presumably not believe that the sales peak is due entirely to the behaviour of income and so we would set up a model which applies to all four quarters, but which includes a dummy variable, taking the value 1 in the fourth quarter and zero elsewhere. If season is not thought to affect the way in which sales react to income, the dummy variable would be used to allow the intercept to shift, but not the slope parameter. In this way, we would allow for a known seasonal effect and it should then be possible to obtain an estimate of the income parameter which is not distorted by seasonality.

This method would work if the data on sales and income level had not been seasonally adjusted: it would also work if the data on sales had not been adjusted and season had no effect on income. But, if the data had already been adjusted, the sales peak would already have been allowed for and the dummy variable would be redundant. So, when using seasonally adjusted data, there would be no dummy variable in the regression. The obvious question is whether there would be any difference between the estimates from the unadjusted data with a dummy variable and those from the seasonally adjusted data without a dummy variable. One way in which the seasonal adjustment of an individual series can be performed is by taking the residuals from a regression on the dummy variable and the discussion in Section 3.2 would suggest that, in this case, there is no difference between the estimates obtained by first adjusting the data and then running a regression on the adjusted data and those obtained by including the dummy variable in a regression on the unadjusted data. For any other method of seasonal adjustment, there will be some difference between the two sets of estimates obtained.

Although, as we have said, there are no hard and fast rules, it is worth mentioning that the use of dummy variables with unadjusted data does give the investigator considerable freedom of choice as to the way in which seasonality is handled in the model specification. For this reason, we can reach the tentative conclusion that, where possible, the unadjusted data should be used, providing of course that the appropriate dummy variables *are* added to allow for the seasonal effects.

Exercises (Solutions on page 233)

3.1 Consider the model

$$Y_t = \alpha_1 + \alpha_2 X_{2t} + \alpha_3 X_{3t} + u_t; \text{ in region 1}$$

$$Y_t = \beta_1 + \beta_2 X_{2t} + \beta_3 X_{3t} + u_t; \text{ in region 2}$$

$$Y_t = \gamma_1 + \gamma_2 X_{2t} + \gamma_3 X_{3t} + u_t; \text{ in region 3}$$

Show how one could test the null hypothesis that $\alpha_3 = \beta_3 = \gamma_3$. What is assumed about the disturbances?

3.2 A 'true' model is given by

$$Y_t = \alpha + \beta X_t + u_t; t = 1, 2, \ldots, n$$

$$E(u_t) = 0; t = 1, 2, \ldots, n$$

An investigator attempts to estimate β by running a regression of Y on X, without an intercept term. What can one say about the resulting estimator for β? Can you state your result algebraically?

Interlude

With the introduction of the k variable model, we have at our
disposal a method of considerable practical value. It is now possible to
explain the behaviour of a dependent variable in terms of several
explanatory variables and, subject only to the limitations imposed by
multicollinearity, to isolate the individual factors influencing the
dependent variable. It is also possible to test a variety of hypotheses, to
impose linear restrictions and to examine the effects of various qualitative influences on the model. Moreover, the model need not be based on
a linear relationship between the original economic variables: certain
types of nonlinear relationship can also be used.

We do know that the least squares estimators have certain desirable
properties, but these properties depend on a particular set of assumptions
and this is a limitation on the applicability of the methods described so
far. There are cases in which a particular assumption *cannot* be satisfied,
because of some specific feature of the chosen economic model and there
are other situations in which it is *unlikely* that an assumption will be
satisfied, in which case it is safer to relax that assumption. Whenever
this is done, there are two basic questions to be answered. The first
concerns the implications of the new situation for existing methods of
estimation and the second is concerned with the possibility that an
alternative estimator may be the optimal choice for the new situation.
It is important to be able to answer both questions. It is necessary to
be able to say *why* existing methods are deficient before we can look
for an alternative which is, in some sense, better. But we also need to
be able to state the likely consequences of using existing methods. The
existing methods may be used deliberately or, alternatively, they may
be used in ignorance of the fact that an assumption has been violated.

The remaining chapters of the book deal with the relaxation of
assumptions under three headings. Chapter 4 is concerned with the use
of different specifications for the behaviour of the disturbances in the
model. Chapter 5 examines some of the implications of making the
deterministic part of the model dynamic and Chapter 6 extends the

analysis to models containing several inter-related equations. We shall find that the methods introduced are not fundamentally different from those used so far. Indeed, many of the alternative estimators considered are extensions of the basic least squares method and, because of this, the detailed and rather lengthy analysis of the basic *k* variable model *does* provide a useful foundation for estimation and testing with more realistic forms of economic model.

To enable the appropriate distinctions to be drawn, we shall, in future, refer to the basic least squares estimators as *ordinary least squares* (OLS) estimators. Alternative estimators are then given different names, but it is important to note that these names refer to a *complete* estimation procedure. We shall often find that, *at one stage* of such a procedure, it is necessary to perform a regression calculation of the kind that we have already described. With reference to that one stage, such a calculation is indeed an OLS regression and it can be carried out by using a computer program designed for OLS. This is very convenient: it may enable us to describe an estimation procedure in terms of one or more OLS regression calculations, together with any additional transformations of the original model and it may not be necessary to write down explicit formulae for the modified estimators. Moreover, it may not be essential to have additional computer programs for all the new methods that are introduced. This is obviously an important consideration in deciding which of the various methods of estimation one can expect to be able to use in practice.

4 Alternative Disturbance Specifications

4.1 Introduction

So far, it has been assumed that a satisfactory form of model is one in which the disturbances are drawn from independent distributions with zero mean and constant variance. For some purposes, notably for the construction of test statistics, it has also been assumed that the distributions are normal. We already know that certain errors of specification of the deterministic part of the model might imply disturbances which do not have zero mean but, *in a properly specified model,* there can be little objection to the assumption that the means of the disturbance distributions are all zero: a non-zero mean would imply some systematic component of the disturbances, that ought to be included in the deterministic part of the model. So, for example, in the case in which each disturbance has the *same* non-zero mean, μ, this component could simply be added to the intercept. The model

$$Y_t = \alpha + \beta X_t + u_t; \, t = 1, 2, \ldots, n \tag{4.1.1}$$

$$E(u_t) = \mu; \, t = 1, 2, \ldots, n$$

could be transformed as

$$Y_t = (\alpha + \mu) + \beta X_t + (u_t - \mu); \, t = 1, 2, \ldots, n \tag{4.1.2}$$

The new disturbances, $(u_t - \mu)$, would have a zero mean for all values of t and $(\alpha + \mu)$ and β could be estimated under standard assumptions. Admittedly, it would not be possible to estimate α and μ separately, but the intercept is not usually a meaningful economic parameter and so this would seldom be a real problem. Similarly, the normality assumption is not unduly restrictive: although one can sometimes argue that it is not appropriate to assume normality of the disturbance distributions, there is no obvious alternative that is widely applicable and, in any case, the results which hold exactly when the disturbances are normal will often hold approximately, in large samples, when the disturbances are

not restricted to normality. This leaves the assumptions of constant
variance and independence and there certainly are occasions on which
one might object to the limitations imposed by these conditions. So,
in this chapter, we consider the removal of each of these assumptions.
To concentrate attention on the problem to hand, the simplest possible
forms of model are used to illustrate the discussion and it is implicit
that, when a particular assumption is removed, all other assumptions
continue to hold, unless this proves to be impossible.

We can make some progress without having to consider any of the
particular examples dealt with in this chapter. From the check-list of
assumptions, given in Section 3.5, it can be seen that the following
properties of the OLS estimators depend on constant variance and
independence of the disturbance distributions

1. the fact that the form of var $(\hat{\beta}_j)$ is

$$\text{var}(\hat{\beta}_j) = \sigma^2 / \Sigma \tilde{X}_{jt}^2 \qquad (4.1.3)$$

2. the minimum variance property that makes OLS a *best* linear
   unbiased estimator and a *best* unbiased estimator.

Now it may or may not be true that the removal of the assumptions
invalidates these properties, but it is certainly likely that this would
happen, for it seems pointless to make assumptions unless they are
needed. In fact, the consequence of removing the assumptions is precisely
what we would expect. Equation (4.1.3) is no longer valid and the
OLS estimators are no longer *best* unbiased. On the other hand, if all
other assumptions are satisfied, the OLS estimators are still unbiased
and the estimators still have normal distributions. This essentially
disposes of one of the questions that should be asked on introducing
new conditions for the disturbances. It is also suggestive as to the
answer to the other question, concerning alternative methods of
estimation. If the OLS estimators are unbiased, but no longer have the
minimum variance property that makes them best unbiased or best
linear unbiased, then we should look for alternative estimators that
have one or both of these properties. Best linear unbiasedness is the
criterion that is most commonly used in econometrics and, from
now on, we shall use this criterion. To see how best linear unbiased
estimators can be obtained, we consider the first special case, that
in which the disturbances do *not* have equal variances. The section
which follows is rather long, but there is a reason for this. The first
special case is used to establish general principles for dealing with
disturbance 'problems' and, having dealt with one case in some

detail, we will find it relatively easy to apply similar principles to alternative patterns of disturbance behaviour.

4.2 Heteroscedasticity and Generalized Least Squares

When the disturbances do not have constant variance, the model is said to be subject to *heteroscedasticity*: alternatively, we may say that the disturbances are heteroscedastic. To illustrate the nature of the problem, consider a simple model with a single 'genuine' explanatory variable, but no intercept term

$$Y_t = \beta X_t + u_t; t = 1, 2, \ldots, n \tag{4.2.1}$$

The variances of the disturbance terms are now written as

$$\text{var}(u_t) = \sigma_t^2; \ t = 1, 2, \ldots, n \tag{4.2.2}$$

where the subscript t signifies the fact that the individual variances may all be different. We shall, in due course, give several examples to show why heteroscedasticity may occur but, first, we shall concentrate on the implications for the estimation of the parameter β.

A simple regression run on (4.2.1) would provide an estimate of β, but this estimate would be a particular value taken by the OLS estimator. From the discussion in the previous section, we know that the OLS estimator is linear unbiased, but is no longer *best* linear unbiased. We should therefore try to find an alternative estimator which *is* a minimum variance estimator and there is a very useful trick which enables us to do this directly.

The model shown in (4.2.1) violates the original list of assumptions because the disturbance variances are not equal. If we can find a way to transform the model, so that the variances in the transformed model *are* equal then, so long as all the other assumptions continue to be satisfied, the use of OLS *on the transformed model* would provide a best linear unbiased estimator. We have already used this approach, in several different contexts: what is new here is that the transformation is required because of a particular property of the disturbance distributions.

Before we can show how the transformation works, it is necessary to note a result concerning the variance of a random variable. If a random variable, V, is multiplied by a constant, c, the variance of the new random variable is given by

$$\text{var}(cV) = c^2 \text{var}(V) \tag{4.2.3}$$

This result is stated and illustrated in the solution to exercise 1.1 and it should be noted that c can be any non-random quantity.

We can now apply (4.2.3) to the individual disturbance terms in (4.2.1), using a *different* non-random quantity with each u_t; $t = 1, 2, \ldots, n$. If a single disturbance, u_t, is multiplied by the corresponding value of $(1/\sigma_t)$, the transformed disturbance would have a variance given by

$$\text{var}(u_t/\sigma_t) = \text{var}(u_t)/\sigma_t^2 = \sigma_t^2/\sigma_t^2 = 1 \tag{4.2.4}$$

and this result holds for all values of t. To preserve the identity of the model, the same transformation must be applied to each term and so the transformed model would be

$$(Y_t/\sigma_t) = \beta(X_t/\sigma_t) + (u_t/\sigma_t); \quad t = 1, 2, \ldots, n \tag{4.2.5}$$

The transformation does not violate any of the other assumptions of the original model and (4.2.4) shows that the variances of the transformed disturbances are constant (in fact, a *known* constant, equal to 1). The application of OLS to (4.2.5), treating (Y_t/σ_t) as the dependent variable and (X_t/σ_t) as the explanatory variable, would therefore produce a best linear unbiased estimator for β. There is, however, a problem. To carry out the transformation shown in (4.2.5), it is necessary to know the value of each disturbance variance, σ_t^2; $t = 1, 2, \ldots, n$. If these variances are known then, as we have seen, it is possible to obtain a transformed model in which all the variances are equal to 1. But there is no reason to suppose that all the variances in the original model would be known and it is sufficient to find a transformation under which the transformed disturbances have a constant *unknown* variance. We can use such a transformation without complete knowledge of the disturbance variances in the original model.

The specification of the variances is therefore modified to read

$$\text{var}(u_t) = \sigma_t^2 = \sigma^2 \lambda_t^2; t = 1, 2, \ldots, n \tag{4.2.6}$$

where σ^2 is an *unknown* constant, the meaning of which will shortly become clear and where λ_t^2; $t = 1, 2, \ldots, n$, is a representation for a set of *known* values, each one specific to a particular disturbance. There is a reason for choosing to use squared values for the specific components: this too will shortly be clarified.

Now consider a transformation that will produce equal disturbance variances. All that we need to do is to use the square roots of the known components of each disturbance variance in the original model. Then

$$\text{var}(u_t/\lambda_t) = \text{var}(u_t)/\lambda_t^2 = \sigma^2 \lambda_t^2/\lambda_t^2 = \sigma^2; t = 1, 2, \ldots, n \qquad (4.2.7)$$

and the appropriate transformed model is

$$(Y_t/\lambda_t) = \beta(X_t/\lambda_t) + (u_t/\lambda_t); t = 1, 2, \ldots, n \qquad (4.2.8)$$

or

$$Y_t^* = \beta X_t^* + u_t^*; t = 1, 2, \ldots, n \qquad (4.2.9)$$

where

$$Y_t^* = (Y_t/\lambda_t); X_t^* = (X_t/\lambda_t); u_t^* = (u_t/\lambda_t); t = 1, 2, \ldots, n$$

It is now clear why we chose σ^2 as a representation for the unknown component in (4.2.6): this emerges as the unknown disturbance variance in the *transformed* model. It is also clear why we used squared values for the specific components. The transformation uses the square roots

$$\lambda_t = \sqrt{\lambda_t^2}; t = 1, 2, \ldots, n$$

Incidentally, both σ^2 and λ_t^2 have positive values and, by convention, we always use positive square roots.

Equation (4.2.9) is a standard form of linear model *in the variables* Y^* *and* X^* and (4.2.7) shows that the variances of the transformed disturbances are constant. The other assumptions of the original model remain valid, so a simple regression run on (4.2.9) would define a best linear unbiased estimator. The one remaining problem is what we should call the estimator that is obtained in this way. In terms of Y^* and X^*, the variables of the transformed model, we have an OLS estimator but, in terms of Y and X, the variables of the original model, we do *not* have an OLS estimator. Instead, we use the description *generalized least squares* (GLS) and the distinguishing notation $\hat{\beta}_G$

$$\hat{\beta}_G = \frac{\Sigma X_t^* Y_t^*}{\Sigma X_t^{*2}} = \frac{\Sigma[(X_t/\lambda_t)(Y_t/\lambda_t)]}{\Sigma[(X_t/\lambda_t)^2]} \qquad (4.2.10)$$

Before we go any further, we should ask whether this is the estimator that we would have obtained by using the original transformation, shown in (4.2.5). We shall anticipate the answer to this question by using the same notation for an estimator based on (4.2.5)

$$\hat{\beta}_G = \frac{\Sigma[(X_t/\sigma_t)(Y_t/\sigma_t)]}{\Sigma[(X_t/\sigma_t)^2]} \qquad (4.2.11)$$

Now replace σ_t by $\sigma\lambda_t$ and note that, since σ is a constant for all values in the summations, terms in σ can be taken outside the summation sign

$$\hat{\beta}_G = \frac{\Sigma[(X_t/\sigma\lambda_t)(Y_t/\sigma\lambda_t)]}{\Sigma[(X_t/\sigma\lambda_t)^2]} = \frac{(1/\sigma^2)\Sigma[(X_t/\lambda_t)(Y_t/\lambda_t)]}{(1/\sigma^2)\Sigma[(X_t/\lambda_t)^2]}$$

$$= \frac{\Sigma[(X_t/\lambda_t)(Y_t/\lambda_t)]}{\Sigma[(X_t/\lambda_t)^2]}$$

The algebra shows that we get exactly the same estimator for β, whichever version of the transformation we happen to use: any constant factor in the original variances cancels out of the expression for the GLS estimator. The difference between the two approaches lies lies in the treatment of the disturbance variance in the transformed model. If the transformation shown in (4.2.5) is used, the variances in the transformed model are known to be equal to 1. With the modified version, shown in (4.2.8), the variances of the transformed disturbances are equal to an unknown constant, σ^2. But the transformed model is treated exactly like any model which satisfies *all* the basic assumptions and so it is possible to estimate σ^2 as

$$\hat{\sigma}^2 = \Sigma e_t^2/(n-1) \tag{4.2.12}$$

where

$$e_t = Y_t^* - \hat{\beta}_G X_t^*; t = 1, 2, \ldots, n \tag{4.2.13}$$

Notice that the residuals are taken from the transformed model and *not* from the original model.

Heteroscedasticity is only one of the disturbance 'problems' that we shall consider in this chapter but, in each case, a similar method of estimation is used. The procedure is

1. to transform the model, so as to create independent disturbances with constant variance
2. to apply OLS to the transformed model.

Again, in each case, the estimator is described as a GLS estimator, with reference to the variables in the *original* model. The transformation required does vary from problem to problem and the GLS estimator does not always take the form shown in (4.2.10): apart from anything else, this expression applies only to a model with single explanatory variable and no intercept term. Even for this special case, the form of the estimator changes under different disturbance specifications. But we do not really need explicit expressions for the estimators. As well as showing what GLS estimation actually does, the method of transformation is a very convenient practical procedure. Once we know the appropriate transformation for a particular disturbance problem, all that we need to do is to run a standard regression calculation on the transformed model. We shall adopt the convention of always using Y^* and X^* to represent the variables of the transformed model and, although the method of generating Y^* and X^* varies from case to case, the appropriate estimators can always be found by using Y^* and X^* as input variables to a computer program for OLS regression. Whilst it may be convenient to have a program written especially for GLS, so that the *original* variables can be input directly, it is not *essential* to have such a program. It is worth pursuing the implications of this a little further.

First, it should be noted that we can use exactly the same procedure when there are several explanatory variables. The appropriate transformation follows from a property of the disturbances and the number of variables in the original model is irrelevant. All that we do is to apply the transformation to all the variables that are used. Once the computation is under way, the fact that the regression is based on a transformed model has no influence on the course of the calculation. The program would therefore produce standard errors, t statistics and measures of goodness of fit, in the same way as for any other regression. What we actually want are measures appropriate to GLS estimation of the parameters, rather than those for OLS estimation: but, *because the regression is run on the transformed model*, this is precisely what we would obtain. And we have already seen that we would, as a matter of course, obtain an estimate of σ^2, the unknown component of the original disturbance variances. The residuals generated would be those from the transformed model and these would be used to estimate the disturbance variance in the transformed model. This would be an estimate of σ^2.

There is, however, one problem that may cause some difficulty. The original model shown in (4.2.1) does not contain an intercept term and nor does the transformed model shown in (4.2.8). We have noted before that some computer programs will automatically insert an intercept, unless the user takes steps to avoid this happening. Even when the original model does have an intercept, the transformed model may not and the transformation for heteroscedasticity provides an example. Consider the model

$$Y_t = \alpha + \beta X_t + u_t; t = 1, 2, \ldots, n \qquad (4.2.14)$$

$$\text{var}(u_t) = \sigma^2 \lambda_t^2; t = 1, 2, \ldots, n$$

After transformation, this becomes

$$(Y_t/\lambda_t) = \alpha(1/\lambda_t) + \beta(X_t/\lambda_t) + (u_t/\lambda_t); t = 1, 2, \ldots, n \qquad (4.2.15)$$

The variable attached to the parameter α is now a genuine variable, $(1/\lambda)$, which would, by definition, take different values for different observations if heteroscedasticity is present in the original model. So, in estimating the parameters of (4.2.14), from a regression run on (4.2.15), there is an additional variable in place of an intercept term. The input variables would therefore be (Y/λ), (X/λ) *and* $(1/\lambda)$, but there is *no* additional intercept. Because of this, some care may be needed in the interpretation of the measure of goodness of fit. You may recall, from the discussion in Section 3.3, that the measure of goodness of fit appropriate to a regression with no intercept is the statistic R_0^2, defined in (3.3.4). In the computer calculation, a regression run on (4.2.15) is treated like a regression without an intercept and so the measure of goodness of fit may well be the equivalent of R_0^2, defined on the transformed model. If so, this will be a correct measure for GLS estimation of the parameters of the original model but it *will* include the 'explanation' achieved by the artificial variable which is implicitly attached to α in (4.2.14).

One final point concerning the computation. The ideal situation is obviously one in which there is a computer program for GLS estimation already available. It is likely that such a program would actually work by a variant of the transformation method, but the transformation would be carried out automatically and the input variables would be the variables of the *original* model. If a GLS program is not available, the next best solution would be to use an OLS program with the facility for performing transformations of the data, prior to the regression calculation proper. The minimum requirement for the transformations used to correct for heteroscedasticity would be a facility for multiplication or division of the input variables. It would then be possible to input the variables of the *original* model, together with the values λ_t; $t = 1, 2, \ldots, n$, treated as observations on an additional variable. The transformation facility could then be used to divide the observations on the original variables by the corresponding values of λ_t, prior to running the regression on the transformed variables. But none of this is essential: one could, if necessary, perform the transformations by hand and use the *transformed* variables as input to a basic OLS program, which has no transformation facilities. There is also one other possibility: the computer program may have an option for *weighted* regression and, in the case of the transformations for heteroscedasticity, one could use such a facility. To see how this would work, it is helpful to consider the GLS estimator, shown in (4.2.10), in a slightly different way.

The implication of unequal disturbance variances is that individual observations on the dependent variable are no longer of equal reliability. It is still assumed that the disturbance distributions have zero mean, but if the variance of one particular distribution is relatively high, there is a correspondingly greater probability of finding a value of that disturbance which is well away from zero. So the corresponding value of the dependent variable is more likely to contain a relatively large random error than is the case with other observations on the dependent variable. In this sense, an observation associated with a relatively *high* disturbance variance is likely to contain *less* information about the deterministic relationship between Y and X.

This argument would suggest that a suitable method of estimation would be one in which individual observations are *not* given equal weight in the choice of the estimated line. Those observations corre-sponding to relatively *high* disturbance variances should be given a relatively *low* weight, since a high variance implies low reliability; observations corresponding to relatively low disturbance variances should be given a high weighting. This is precisely what the estimator shown in (4.2.10) does. The estimator is

$$\hat{\beta}_G = \frac{\Sigma[(X_t/\lambda_t)(Y_t/\lambda_t)]}{\Sigma[(X_t/\lambda_t)^2]} = \frac{\Sigma[(1/\lambda_t^2)X_tY_t]}{\Sigma[(1/\lambda_t^2)X_t^2]}$$

or

$$\hat{\beta}_G = \Sigma(w_tX_tY_t)/\Sigma(w_tX_t^2) \qquad (4.2.16)$$

where

$$w_t = (1/\lambda_t^2); t = 1, 2, \ldots, n$$

When the variance of a particular disturbance is high, the weight, w_t, is low and vice-versa. An estimator in the form of (4.2.16) is sometimes called a *weighted* least squares estimator and this description holds for *any* set of non-random weights, w_t; $t = 1, 2, \ldots, n$. But it is only when the weights are those that make the estimator *best* linear unbiased that the weighted least squares estimator is also a GLS estimator. Some computer programs do have the facility for applying weights in the regression calculation and, if such a program is used to find the GLS estimates under heteroscedasticity, the values $(1/\lambda_t^2)$; $t = 1, 2, \ldots, n$, should be read in as weights. This is, of course, exactly equivalent to multiplying each observation on each variable by the corresponding value of $(1/\lambda_t)$. The weights used in the weighted regression formula are $(1/\lambda_t^2)$; $t = 1, 2, \ldots, n$, but the transformation used on individual observations involves the square roots, $(1/\lambda_t)$; $t = 1, 2, \ldots, n$.

We now look at some specific examples of models which are likely to have heteroscedastic disturbances and, in doing so, we consider whether it is reasonable to assume that the values λ_t^2; $t = 1, 2, \ldots, n$ would be known. The first example is based on a relationship between household expenditure on food (F) and household disposable income (D). Typical data would be that available from a household expenditure survey, giving expenditure and income, during a single time period, for each household in a cross-section sample. The theory underlying such a relationship has been extensively worked and there is also a considerable amount of empirical evidence on which one can draw but, to keep the illustration simple, suppose that we are satisfied with a linear form and that we ignore any other complications, such as household size. The model might then be

$$F_t = \beta D_t + u_t; t = 1, 2, \ldots, n \qquad (4.2.17)$$

where the subscript t identifies individual households. According to the model, household expenditure on food is a constant proportion (β) of household disposable income and all households tend to follow this rule. The only departures from the rule are assumed to consist of effects that can be adequately represented by random disturbance terms.

The deterministic part of this model is probably too simple to justify the assumption that the disturbances are purely random but, even with a more elaborate specification, it is likely that we would still be faced with the following problem. Although, in some average sense, food expenditure may be related to disposable income, high income households are not constrained to follow this rule as closely as those with lower levels of income. In giving reasons for this, we must be careful. One might cite differential holdings of liquid assets and different opportunities for bulk purchase as examples of the sort of influence that would allow high income households greater freedom in varying their pattern of food purchase from that suggested by disposable income in a given period. It is certainly true that both of these factors would tend to increase the disturbance variances of high income households, given the specification of the model shown in (4.2.17). On the other hand, it might be argued that influences of this kind, which can be identified, ought properly to belong in the deterministic part of the model and that it is the many small unidentified influences on the purchasing behaviour of households that make up the 'natural' disturbances to the expenditure–income relationship. In theory, there is a distinction between the omission of important, identifiable variables and the omission of factors which would make up the natural disturbances. In the first case, it is likely that estimates will be biased, whatever method of estimation is used: this is not so in the second case. In practice, such distinctions become very blurred. Whatever the reasons, it is likely that the disturbances to the expenditure–income relationship will be heteroscedastic and, having taken all reasonable precautions in the specification of the deterministic part of the model, all that we can do is to treat the symptoms of heteroscedasticity. There is very little that can be done about the causes. It is worth bearing this in mind when interpreting parameter estimates. At the theoretical level, we tend, for obvious reasons, to analyse pure problems. In practice, the results obtained are indicative of the behaviour of estimators, but the various properties may not hold as hard and fast rules.

In this example, we have replaced the specific information contained in the assumption of equal disturbance variances by the very vague information that the variances are not equal and we cannot make any progress without providing a more precise statement of exactly how the disturbance variances do behave. If all that we can say is that the variances are different, we have n unknown quantities σ_t^2; $t = 1, 2, \ldots, n$, and this does not help us at all. But there *is* some further information implicit in our statement of the problem. It was argued that high income households tend to be associated with relatively high disturbance variances and, if we assume that the disturbance variances are actually *proportional* to disposable income, we would have

$$\mathrm{var}(u_t) = \delta D_t; t = 1, 2, \ldots, n \qquad (4.2.18)$$

where δ is an unknown parameter. Once we have this additional hypothesis, the disturbance variances follow a specification equivalent to (4.2.6). The values D_t; $t = 1, 2, \ldots, n$, represent a set of known values which are equivalent to λ_t^2; $t = 1, 2, \ldots, n$, and δ is an unknown constant, equivalent to σ^2 in (4.2.6). The application of the transformation shown in (4.2.8) to this particular case would therefore give a transformed model

$$(F_t/\sqrt{D_t}) = \beta(D_t/\sqrt{D_t}) + (u_t/\sqrt{D_t}); t = 1, 2, \ldots, n. \qquad (4.2.19)$$

and a regression run on (4.2.19) would provide a best linear unbiased estimator for β.

The relationship between food expenditure and disposable income can be used to provide a second example of a model with heteroscedastic disturbances and the main purpose of this example is to show that heteroscedasticity may arise simply because of a data problem. Suppose that the only data available consists of *average* food expenditure and *average* disposable income for groups of households. The results of official expenditure surveys are often published in precisely this form, with households grouped according to the level of income. Now suppose that we have exactly the same hypothesis as before, namely that the behaviour *individual* households can be represented by

$$F_t = \beta D_t + u_t; \ t = 1, 2, \ldots, n \tag{4.2.20}$$

Ideally, we should use (4.2.20) as the basis for estimation but, because of the lack of suitable data, this is impossible. Instead, we have to derive a form of model which relates to the averages for each income group. Suppose that the first n_1 households belong to the first income group. The averaging process consists of adding over all observations within the first group and dividing by the number of households in the group. To preserve the identity of the model, the averaging operation has to be applied to both sides of (4.2.20)

$$\frac{\sum\limits_{t=1}^{t=n_1} F_t}{n_1} = \frac{\sum\limits_{t=1}^{t=n_1} (\beta D_t + u_t)}{n_1} = \beta \left[\frac{\sum\limits_{t=1}^{t=n_1} D_t}{n_1} \right] + \left[\frac{\sum\limits_{t=1}^{t=n_1} u_t}{n_1} \right]$$

or

$$\bar{F}_1 = \beta \bar{D}_1 + \bar{u}_1$$

where $\bar{F}_1, \bar{D}_1$ and $\bar{u}_1$ are all group averages for the first income group.

A similar operation applied to each group would produce a derived model

$$\bar{F}_i = \beta \bar{D}_i + \bar{u}_i; i = 1, 2, \ldots, m \tag{4.2.21}$$

where the subscript i identifies a particular income group, there being m such groups in total. Because (4.2.21) does not represent the origin model, the properties of the disturbances $\bar{u}_i; i = 1, 2, \ldots, m$, should really be derived from assumptions concerning the original disturbances, $u_t; t = 1, 2, \ldots, n$. To bring out the main point of the example, we shall assume that the original variances are constant. This is not a serious constraint: the more realistic assumption of heteroscedasticity in the original variances actually tends to reinforce the argument presented on the basis of the constant variance assumption. So let us assume that

$$\text{var}(u_t) = \sigma^2; t = 1, 2, \ldots, n \tag{4.2.22}$$

It then follows that the variances in the derived model would be

$$\text{var}(\bar{u}_i) = \sigma^2/n_i; i = 1, 2, \ldots, m \tag{4.2.23}$$

We shall not prove this last statement, but note that the result is entirely plausible. What it says is that the average of several identically distributed random variables shows considerably less variation than do the individual random variables and that the variance of the average will *decrease* as the number of variables over which the average is taken is *increased*. This follows because, in the averaging process, extreme values of the random variables tend to cancel out. It is obvious that this tendency is greater when the number of variables in the average is relatively large.

The implication of (4.2.23) is that there will be a problem of heteroscedasticity inherent in using the derived model as the basis for estimation, unless it happens that all the income groups are of the same size. This would not usually be the case: in particular, high income groups tend to contain a relatively small number of households. But the pattern of heteroscedasticity again corresponds to the general specification shown in (4.2.6), with σ^2 as an unknown constant and $(1/n_i); i = 1, 2, \ldots, m$ as a set of known specific components. The application of the transformation shown in (4.2.8) would therefore give

$$(\sqrt{n_i}\bar{F}_i) = \beta(\sqrt{n_i}\bar{D}_i) + \sqrt{n_i}\bar{u}_i; i = 1, 2, \ldots, m \tag{4.2.24}$$

and a regression run on (4.2.24) would provide a best linear unbiased estimator for β.

If it is also true that there is heteroscedasticity in the original model, with the disturbance variances increasing with income, this tends to reinforce the differences between the disturbance variances in the derived model, at least to the extent that high income groups tend to contain relatively few households. In this case two separate transformations would have to be applied to (4.2.21), to correct for heteroscedasticity arising from two different sources.

A final example of estimation with heteroscedastic disturbances is provided by a problem mentioned in the previous chapter. In Section 3.7, it was argued that a stochastic restriction in the form

$$r_0 = \beta_1 r_1 + \beta_2 r_2 + \ldots + \beta_j r_j + \ldots + \beta_k r_k + v \tag{4.2.25}$$

could be imposed on the parameters of the general model

$$Y_t = \beta_1 + \beta_2 X_{2t} + \ldots + \beta_j X_{jt} + \ldots + \beta_k X_{kt} + u_t; t = 1, 2, \ldots, n \tag{4.2.26}$$

by treating r_0 as an additional observation on the dependent variable and $r_j; j = 1, 2, \ldots, k$, as additional observations on each of the explanatory variables. There is no particular reason to suppose that the disturbances $u_t; t = 1, 2, \ldots, n$ would be heteroscedastic, but the variance of v would be specified by the investigator as a measure of the precision of the stochastic constraint and it is highly unlikely that this would be the same as the disturbance variances in (4.2.26). So there will be a problem in the estimation of the parameters of the *complete* model, consisting of (4.2.25) *and* (4.2.26). Taking both types of disturbance together, we have

$$\text{var}(u_t) = \sigma^2; t = 1, 2, \ldots, n \text{ and var } (v) = \delta^2 \qquad (4.2.27)$$

where δ^2 is a *known* constant. What is needed is a transformation that will equalize the variances in the transformed model. If σ^2 were known, all that we would do is to transform the *restriction* as

$$\left[\frac{\sigma r_0}{\delta} \right] = \beta_1 \left[\frac{\sigma r_1}{\delta} \right] + \beta_2 \left[\frac{\sigma r_2}{\delta} \right] + \cdots + \beta_j \left[\frac{\sigma r_j}{\delta} \right] + \cdots$$

$$+ \beta_k \left[\frac{\sigma r_k}{\delta} \right] + \left[\frac{v \sigma}{\delta} \right] \qquad (4.2.28)$$

for then

$$\text{var} \left[\frac{v \sigma}{\delta} \right] = \text{var } (v) \frac{\sigma^2}{\delta^2} = \frac{\delta^2 \sigma^2}{\delta^2} = \sigma^2$$

Unfortunately, σ^2 is not likely to be known and so the following strategy might be used. A regression run on (4.2.26), *without* the restriction, will provide a set of *unrestricted* estimates, $\hat{\beta}_j; j = 1, 2, \ldots, k$ and a set of residuals

$$e_t = Y_t - \hat{\beta}_1 - \hat{\beta}_2 X_{2t} - \ldots - \hat{\beta}_j X_{jt} - \ldots - \hat{\beta}_k X_{kt}; t = 1, 2, \ldots, n$$

From these residuals, it is possible to estimate σ^2 as

$$\hat{\sigma}^2 = \Sigma e_t^2 / (n - k)$$

We could then use the transformation shown in (4.2.28), with $\hat{\sigma}^2$ in place of the unknown true value σ^2 and, having transformed the restriction in this way, a second regression could be run on (4.2.26), *together with* the transformed restriction. Whilst this is quite a sensible strategy to adopt, there are certain difficulties caused by the fact that the transformation makes use of an estimate, rather than a known true value. We shall encounter similar problems in the later sections of this chapter and, in Section 4.5, we shall consider the implications of using estimated disturbance parameters in this way.

4.3   Serial Correlation of the Disturbances

We now consider what happens when the assumption of independence of the disturbances is removed. The usual context for this problem is that of a time series of observations and, in this case, the assumption would break down if the disturbance in one period does have an influence on the disturbance in the following period. It would be implausible to argue that successive disturbances are *exactly* determined by the value in the previous period. If this were true for all time periods, it would imply that, once the first period disturbance had taken a particular value, the future behaviour of the disturbances would be deterministic. This in turn would imply that the future behaviour of the *complete model* would be deterministic. It is more reasonable to suppose that successive disturbances are *partly* determined by previous values, but that there is also an additional random component to each disturbance. In other words, we could model the disturbance process in a way which is very similar to that previously used for relationships between economic variables, replacing the assumption of independence by a particular hypothesis about the way in which successive disturbances are linked. One novel feature is that such a hypothesis involves a linkage which extends over the divisions between different periods of time.

A simple form of relationship, applied to the disturbances, would be

$$u_t = \rho u_{t-1} + v_t; t = 1, 2, \ldots, n \tag{4.3.1}$$

where u_t is determined in part by the previous value u_{t-1}, and in part by a *new* random variable, v_t. The quantity ρ is a parameter of the relationship. Thus a particular disturbance, say u_2, is determined as

$$u_2 = \rho u_1 + v_2$$

But (4.3.1) also implies that u_1 is formed in a similar way

$$u_1 = \rho u_0 + v_1$$

where u_0 is a *starting value* for the process by which the disturbances are generated. The value, u_0, may, in turn, have been determined by earlier values, but this is outside the scope of our model. Continuing the analogy with the modelling of economic relationships, we assume that v_t has all the characteristics previously attributed to u_t. So

$v_t; t = 1, 2, \ldots, n$, represents a *new* set of disturbances, which *do* have independent distributions, with zero means and constant variance. Although $u_t; t = 1, 2, \ldots, n$ are no longer independent, the new disturbances *are* independent and, following the principle of examining one problem at a time, we rule out the possibility that the new disturbances are heteroscedastic.

The process shown in (4.3.1) is a particular example of a situation in which there is *serial correlation* or *autocorrelation* of the disturbances $u_t; t = 1, 2, \ldots, n$. There are two respects in which (4.3.1) is a specialized example. The first concerns the *form* of (4.3.1), in which u_t is linked to a past value, u_{t-1}, by means of a regression type relationship. This is known as an *autoregressive* process. Next, it is a first-order process, because u_t is explicitly related to u_{t-1} and not to earlier values such as u_{t-2}, u_{t-3}, etc. Of course u_t is *indirectly* related to earlier values. For a particular time period, say, $t = 3$, we have

$$u_3 = \rho u_2 + v_3$$

But it is also true that

$$u_2 = \rho u_1 + v_2$$

and that

$$u_1 = \rho u_0 + v_1$$

Putting these equations together, we have

$$u_3 = \rho(\rho u_1 + v_2) + v_3 = \rho^2 u_1 + \rho v_2 + v_3$$

or

$$u_3 = \rho^2(\rho u_0 + v_1) + \rho v_2 + v_3 = \rho^3 u_0 + \rho^2 v_1 + \rho v_2 + v_3$$

More generally, u_t is directly linked to u_{t-1}, but it can also be expressed in terms of any earlier value, as far back as the starting value u_0. The other terms in these expressions are past values of the *new* disturbances. By analogy with the example above, the relationship between u_t and u_0 is

$$u_t = \rho^t u_0 + \text{other terms}; t = 1, 2, \ldots, n \qquad (4.3.2)$$

Equations (4.3.1) and (4.3.2) are alternative expressions for the *dynamic* process by which the successive values $u_t; t = 1, 2, \ldots, n$ are determined. Whereas previously the disturbances in each time period could be treated quite separately, we now have a hypothesis concerning the evolution of disturbances through time and, as (4.3.2) shows, it is possible to establish a relationship between any single disturbance, u_t, and the starting value, u_0. Obviously, we would expect the starting value to have some influence on the process, but it does seem reasonable to assert that this influence should tend to diminish as we move forward in time. Ignoring the effect of the other terms in (4.3.2), this will only happen if ρ^t becomes progressively closer to 0 as t is increased and this in turn requires that ρ should lie between -1 and $+1$, without reaching either extreme value. If this condition is satisfied, ρ^2 is closer to 0 than ρ, ρ^3 is closer to 0 than ρ^2, and, in general, ρ^t does become closer to 0 as t is increased. Hence the term $\rho^t u_0$ diminishes in importance as we move forward in time. If (4.3.1) is to be an acceptable specification for the disturbance behaviour, this condition on the value of ρ must be satisfied.

Under ideal conditions, with a properly specified model, it is perhaps difficult to see why there should be serial correlation of the disturbances. At one level, the answer would be that independence of the disturbances is simply an assumption and that (4.3.1) is an alternative and less restrictive assumption. Perhaps more relevant is the argument that models are not constructed under ideal conditions and, in particular, the unit time period is largely determined by the frequency of observation of the data. There is no reason why relationships between variables should be fully worked through within the chosen time period. This may mean that the deterministic part of the model involves *lag* relationships, in which linkages between variables extend over the divisions between successive periods of time and we consider this possibility in the next chapter. But it should be remembered that the disturbances are a summary representation for all the variables that are not included in the deterministic part of the model and so it seems reasonable to assert that there can be factors contributing to the disturbances which could influence the behaviour of the model for more than one time period. What this would mean is that successive disturbance terms have common components and they cannot therefore be independent. One other point is that the form of equation used for estimation is not always the same as the original specification and there are transformations that can induce serial correlation. We shall see examples of this in due course.

There is no reason to suppose that (4.3.1) would always represent the correct pattern of serial correlation, but it is equally clear that the assumption of independence cannot always be maintained and, once this assumption is removed, it is necessary to introduce some specific alternative hypothesis. The first order autoregressive scheme is often used as an approximation. As in the case of heteroscedasticity, we have a form of disturbance behaviour that can arise for a variety of reasons and it is quite possible that this is not the only problem associated with a given model. Despite this fact, we have to proceed, at the theoretical level, as though it were true that serial correlation is a property of the 'natural' disturbances to a model in which all other assumptions are satisfied.

We now return to problems of estimation and, once again, we use the simple model

$$Y_t = \beta X_t + u_t; t = 1, 2, \ldots, n \tag{4.3.3}$$

where now

$$u_t = \rho u_{t-1} + v_t; t = 1, 2, \ldots, n$$

If OLS is used to estimate β then, as in the case of heteroscedastic disturbances, the estimator would be linear unbiased, but not *best* linear unbiased. It is therefore necessary to find a transformation of (4.3.3), chosen in such a way that the disturbances in the transformed model *are* independent. This, together with OLS estimation applied to the *transformed* model, would define a GLS estimator and, so long as the transformation does not violate any of the other assumptions of the model, the GLS estimator would be best linear unbiased.

If we choose a particular time period, say $t = 2$, then, from (4.3.3) it follows that

$$Y_2 = \beta X_2 + u_2 \tag{4.3.4}$$

But it is also true that

$$Y_1 = \beta X_1 + u_1 \tag{4.3.5}$$

and, on multiplying both sides of (4.3.5) by ρ, that

$$\rho Y_1 = \rho(\beta X_1 + u_1) = \beta(\rho X_1) + (\rho u_1) \tag{4.3.6}$$

Finally, subtracting (4.3.6) from (4.3.4) gives

$$(Y_2 - \rho Y_1) = \beta(X_2 - \rho X_1) + (u_2 - \rho u_1) \tag{4.3.7}$$

This last statement must be valid: because (4.3.6) holds, we are effectively subtracting the same quantity from both sides of (4.3.4). More generally, we have that

$$Y_t = \beta X_t + u_t; t = 1, 2, \ldots, n$$

so that

$$Y_{t-1} = \beta X_{t-1} + u_{t-1}; t = 2, 3, \ldots, n$$

and

$$\rho Y_{t-1} = \beta(\rho X_{t-1}) + (\rho u_{t-1}); t = 2, 3, \ldots, n$$

and finally

$$(Y_t - \rho Y_{t-1}) = \beta(X_t - \rho X_{t-1}) + (u_t - \rho u_{t-1}); t = 2, 3, \ldots, n$$

$$(4.3.8)$$

Notice that the last three statements are true for values of t from $t = 2$ to $t = n$. They may also be true for $t = 1$, but we are looking for an operational transformation, to be applied to a given set of data, Y_t, X_t; $t = 1, 2, \ldots, n$, and the equivalent statements for period $t = 1$ would involve values represented as Y_0 and X_0, which are not part of the given data.

Equation (4.3.8) does represent a transformed model in which the disturbances are independent. This follows directly from (4.3.1). If

$$u_t = \rho u_{t-1} + v_t; t = 1, 2, \ldots, n$$

then

$$u_t - \rho u_{t-1} = v_t; t = 1, 2, \ldots, n$$

The disturbances in (4.3.8) are therefore given by $v_2, v_3, \ldots, v_n$ and, by assumption, these are independent, with zero expectation and constant variance. The only problem with (4.3.8) is that, by carrying out the transformation, we have lost an observation. For this reason, the application of OLS to (4.3.8) does not produce the best linear unbiased estimator, although such a method is often used in practice. To be strictly correct, another observation should be added to the transformed model, based on a different transformation

$$(\rho^* Y_1) = \beta(\rho^* X_1) + (\rho^* u_1) \qquad (4.3.9)$$

where

$$\rho^* = \sqrt{(1 - \rho^2)}$$

The disturbance in (4.3.9) has a zero mean, the same variance as $v_2, v_3, \ldots, v_n$ and it is independent of $v_2, v_3, \ldots, v_n$. We can therefore define transformed variables, Y^* and X^*, where

$$Y_1^* = \rho^* Y_1 \text{ and } Y_t^* = (Y_t - \rho Y_{t-1}); t = 2, 3, \ldots, n \qquad (4.3.10)$$

$$X_1^* = \rho^* X_1 \text{ and } X_t^* = (X_t - \rho X_{t-1}); t = 2, 3, \ldots, n$$

and a *complete* transformed model

$$Y_t^* = \beta X_t^* + u_t^*, t = 1, 2, \ldots n \qquad (4.3.11)$$

where

$$u_1^* = \rho^* u_1 \text{ and } u_t^* = v_t; t = 2, 3, \ldots, n$$

The application of OLS to (4.3.11) *does* produce the best linear unbiased estimator of β and, in terms of the *original* variables, Y and X, this is a GLS estimator. Obviously, one must know the value of ρ before this method can be used and we shall have more to say about this in due course.

The procedure that we have described seems to be rather more complicated than that for heteroscedastic disturbances, although the basic approach is similar. In the simplified version, mentioned above, the additional transformed observations, Y_1^* and X_1^*, are ignored. This is obviously convenient, because it amounts to a regression run on (4.3.8) or, equivalently, on

$$Y_t^* = \beta X_t^* + u_t^*; t = 2, 3, \ldots, n \qquad (4.3.12)$$

where the $(n - 1)$ observations on Y^* and X^* are all generated in a similar fashion. In most cases, the omission of the first observation on the transformed model makes little difference to the final estimate of β, but one can always find counterexamples. The real reason for the widespread use of the simplified approach is that of convenience.

Now consider the use of a computer program for the calculation. The ideal situation is again one in which there is a program written especially for estimation with serial correlation of the disturbances, but this is not essential. The next best solution would be to have an OLS program with facilities for transformations of the variables, prior to the regression calculation proper. Computer programs do vary widely in design and it is difficult to decide on what might be available in a typical case. If the list of transformations includes those shown in (4.3.10), or at least those for the simplified method, so much the better. Alternatively, it may be possible to carry out the transformations in a series of steps, each consisting of a simpler transformation of the variables. The following table illustrates this procedure, applied to the generation of $Y_t^*, X_t^*; t = 2, 3, \ldots, n$

Observa-tion	Original Variables		Lagged Variables		Multiplication by a Constant		Subtraction of Variables	
t	Y_t	X_t	Y_{t-1}	X_{t-1}	ρY_{t-1}	ρX_{t-1}	Y_t^*	X_t^*
2	Y_2	X_2	Y_1	X_1	ρY_1	ρX_1	$Y_2 - \rho Y_1$	$X_2 - \rho X_1$
3	Y_3	X_3	Y_2	X_2	ρY_2	ρX_2	$Y_3 - \rho Y_2$	$X_3 - \rho X_2$
.	.	.	.	.	.	.	.	.
.	.	.	.	.	.	.	.	.
n	Y_n	X_n	Y_{n-1}	X_{n-1}	ρY_{n-1}	ρX_{n-1}	$Y_n - \rho Y_{n-1}$	$X_n - \rho X_{n-1}$

There is a problem of terminology here. In the context of the computer calculation, there is as much difference between the columns headed Y_t and Y_{t-1} as there is between the columns headed Y_t and X_t. Each column in the table is treated as though it consists of observations on quite distinct variables. The term 'lagged variables' is simply a convenient description for what are, in fact, slightly different sets of observations on the basic variables, Y and X. Having made this point, it is permissible to talk of a transformation which generates the lagged variables: obviously, this could be done by hand, but then both the original and lagged variable observations have to be supplied as input. It is simpler if there is a transformation which creates the lagged variables directly from the original observations. The final possibility is that *all* the necessary transformations of the variables are carried out by hand, in which case the transformed variables have to be supplied as input. This may be very tedious, but it is *possible* to obtain the GLS estimates, or the simplified estimates, by using a computer program which is designed for OLS regression and which has *no* additional transformation facilities.

The transformation method can obviously be used with a model containing several explanatory variables. All that we need to do is to apply the transformation to all the variables in the model. If there is an intercept in the original model, the transformation must also be applied to this term. So, for example

$$Y_t = \alpha + \beta X_t + u_t; t = 1, 2, \ldots, n$$

becomes

$$Y_t - \rho Y_{t-1} = \alpha(1 - \rho) + \beta(X_t - \rho X_{t-1}) + v_t; t = 2, 3, \ldots, n$$

with an additional observation

$$(\rho^* Y_1) = \alpha \rho^* + \beta(\rho^* X_1) + (\rho^* u_1)$$

in the full GLS method. Using the simplified version, it is possible to treat $\alpha(1 - \rho)$ as a single parameter attached to a 'variable' which is always equal to 1. One can then estimate $\alpha(1 - \rho)$ as a whole and, since the value of ρ is assumed to be known, it is possible to 'unscramble' an estimate of α, the intercept in the original model. In the full GLS method, α is attached to a quantity which differs between the first observation and all other observations and this has to be treated as a true variable, with observations

$$\sqrt{(1 - \rho^2)}, (1 - \rho), (1 - \rho), \ldots, (1 - \rho)$$

So, in general, the full GLS method involves a regression on k genuine variables, with no *additional* intercept term.

The most serious difficulty with the method that we have described is that it is necessary to know the value of ρ. This is a parameter of the disturbance process and disturbance parameters seldom have known values. We should therefore try to find an estimate of ρ and, given the form of the relationship

$$u_t = \rho u_{t-1} + v_t; t = 1, 2, \ldots, n \qquad (4.3.13)$$

one would naturally think in terms of an estimate obtained from a regression run on (4.3.13). Unfortunately, the relationship involves the unobservable disturbances u_t; $t = 0, 1, \ldots, n$ and all that we can do is to replace these disturbances by residuals. If the model used is

$$Y_t = \beta X_t + u_t; t = 1, 2, \ldots, n \qquad (4.3.14)$$

the residuals that we would want are

$$e_t = Y_t - \hat{\beta} X_t; t = 1, 2, \ldots, n \qquad (4.3.15)$$

where $\hat{\beta}$ is the OLS estimator for the parameter β. A moment's thought will show that these are the appropriate residuals. We require a set of values to replace the disturbances to the *original* model, (4.3.14), and so we should use residuals based on the original model. And we cannot even approximate a GLS estimate of β, since we do not yet have an estimate of ρ. So it is the OLS estimator that appears in (4.3.15).

Instead of a regression of u_t on u_{t-1}, we now consider a regression of e_t on e_{t-1}. We can only use observations for periods $t = 2$ to $t = n$, since we do not have a value for the residual that would be written as e_0. The estimator for ρ is therefore

$$\hat{\rho} = \sum_{t=2}^{t=n} e_t e_{t-1} \left/ \sum_{t=2}^{t=n} e_{t-1}^2 \right. \qquad (4.3.16)$$

At this stage, we shall not worry about the properties of the estimator shown in (4.3.16): there is an obvious complication caused by the use of residuals in place of the unobservable disturbances and there are other problems besides. What we do have is a regression on the residuals that will produce an estimate of ρ and, with this development, we can describe a complete procedure for the estimation of the parameter β in (4.3.14). The same method can be applied to a model containing several explanatory variables.

What we have is essentially a *two-step* procedure, the first step involving regressions based on to the original model and the second step involving the transformed model. The first step actually consists of two regressions, one to find an OLS estimate of β and the second, using the residuals, to obtain an estimate of ρ. The second step consists of a regression on the transformed model, to provide an approximation to the GLS estimate of β. It is an approximation, because the transformation uses an estimate of ρ rather than the true value: if the simplified transformation is used, a further approximation is involved.

This procedure is very similar to that described at the end of the previous section, in which an estimated disturbance variance is used in a transformation to correct for the heteroscedasticity induced by the addition of a stochastic constraint. So we can think in terms of a general class of two-step procedures. The first step consists of an OLS regression on the original model and the residuals from this are used to generate estimates of one or more disturbance parameters. The model is then transformed by making use of the estimated disturbance parameters and the second step consists of a regression run on the transformed model. It is this regression which provides the final estimates of the parameters of the deterministic part of the model. As we have said before, the use of estimated disturbance parameters does have implications for the properties of the final estimators obtained from the second stage. We consider this further in Section 4.5.

Before leaving this section, we should mention an alternative technique that is sometimes used in an attempt to correct for the effects of serial correlation. Suppose that, instead of trying to estimate the value of ρ, we proceed as though it were true that $\rho = 1$. This would suggest that the model

$$Y_t = \beta X_t + u_t; t = 1, 2, \ldots, n \tag{4.3.17}$$

should be transformed as

$$(Y_t - Y_{t-1}) = \beta(X_t - X_{t-1}) + (u_t - u_{t-1}); t = 2, 3, \ldots, n \tag{4.3.18}$$

The variables in (4.3.18) are *first differences* of the original variables and, if it were true that $\rho = 1$, the disturbances in the transformed model would be independent. But we have suggested that ρ should always be less than 1 and, usually, the correct value will be considerably less than 1. If so, the disturbances in (4.3.18) will follow a rather complicated pattern and they may actually be less 'well-behaved' than the disturbances to the original model.

We can get some idea of what may happen by considering a related problem. Suppose now that the disturbances in (4.3.17) are actually independent, but that the investigator believes that there is serial correlation and proceeds to transform the model accordingly. The correct value for the parameter ρ would be zero, but the investigator uses some non-zero value, say λ, and transforms as

$$(Y_t - \lambda Y_{t-1}) = \beta(X_t - \lambda X_{t-1}) + (u_t - \lambda u_{t-1}); t = 2, 3, \ldots, n$$
$$(4.3.19)$$

Far from improving the model, this would actually *induce* serial correlation, but it is interesting to note that the disturbances in (4.3.19) do *not* follow a first order autoregressive process. Instead, there is a *moving average* disturbance scheme in the transformed model. If we write

$$v_t = u_t - \lambda u_{t-1}; t = 2, 3, \ldots, n \qquad (4.3.20)$$

it is clear that v_t and v_{t-1} cannot be independent, since both involve the term u_{t-1}. If λ is positive, there will actually be a *negative* correlation between v_t and v_{t-1}. But v_t and v_{t-2} will be independent, so long as u_t; $t = 1, 2, \ldots, n$, are independent. This is not true of an autoregressive process.

We have established the fact that trying to correct for positive serial correlation, when the disturbances are actually independent, will induce *negative* serial correlation in the form of a moving average process. This suggests that one would get a somewhat similar effect from using the first difference transformation, when the disturbances in the original model follow an autoregressive scheme with a value of ρ which is considerably less than 1. The other point that emerges from the example above is that we have two possible types of representation for serial correlation of the disturbances. In the example, the moving average process arises as the result of a mistake in the specification, but this is not generally true and, in several different contexts, a moving average process would be a more appropriate representation than an autoregressive process. Unfortunately, the transformations required for GLS estimation are rather more complicated in the moving average case and, in practice, the autoregressive process is often used as an approximation, even when the disturbances are thought to follow a moving average scheme.

4.4 The Durbin-Watson Test

There are many stages in the construction of a model which involve choices between alternative courses of action and, for the deterministic part of the model, we have various test procedures that can be used. But the choice between OLS and GLS estimation depends on disturbance properties and this suggests that we should also have tests which can be applied to the disturbance specification. In principle, we could use such tests to choose between two alternative patterns of disturbance behaviour, both of which would imply GLS estimation, but the more fundamental problem is to test the assumptions which are critical to the choice between OLS and GLS. Ideally, the tests would be based on the disturbance values, but these cannot be observed and residuals must be used instead. So a typical procedure would be as follows. A preliminary regression on the model provides OLS estimates and residuals. The residuals are then used, in lieu of the unobservable disturbances, to test disturbance assumptions which, if true, would indicate the optimality of OLS. If any assumption is rejected, it is possible that an alternative method would produce better estimates of the parameters of the model.

One would certainly envisage using this type of test procedure if there was any reason to believe that a particular disturbance problem *might* occur. But if there are tests which are relatively simple, it might be sensible to apply the tests, as a matter of course, to the residuals from *any* OLS regression. We have identified heteroscedasticity and serial correlation as major disturbance problems and one would therefore expect tests of the constant variance and independence assumptions to be widely used in practice. In fact, this is not the case. There are tests designed to show the presence of heteroscedasticity, but there is no single test that is universally accepted as the obvious one to use and even when a test is chosen and the constant variance assumption is rejected, there is still the problem of choosing an alternative hypothesis on which to base GLS estimation. The examples of Section 4.2 illustrate the fact that there can be many different patterns of heteroscedasticity. In the case of the independence assumption, the situation is different. There is one test that has become widely accepted, to the extent that the value of the test statistic will often be provided as part of the output from *any* OLS regression calculation. And if the null hypothesis of independence is rejected, the first order autoregressive scheme, shown in (4.3.1), is an obvious alternative, which is widely used, at least as a first approximation.

If the alternative to independence *is* considered to be a first order autoregressive process, *both* possibilities are covered by the statement

$$u_t = \rho u_{t-1} + v_t; \; t = 1, 2, \ldots, n \qquad (4.4.1)$$

If $\rho = 0$, then

$$u_t = v_t; t = 1, 2, \ldots, n \qquad (4.4.2)$$

and the disturbances $u_t; t = 1, 2, \ldots, n$ *are* independent. Any other value of ρ means that the disturbances are serially correlated. A suitable test would therefore be concerned with the null hypothesis that $\rho = 0$. For this purpose, the analogy between (4.4.1) and earlier examples of regression models is not particularly useful. The disturbances $u_t; t = 1, 2, \ldots, n$, cannot be observed and, in any case, our existing theory for testing a hypothesis concerning a regression parameter would not be appropriate. The role of the explanatory variable is taken by u_{t-1}, which is obviously random and our test procedures have been derived on the assumption that explanatory variables can be considered to be non-random. So a rather different approach is used.

The *Durbin-Watson* test statistic, denoted as d, is given by

$$d = \sum_{t=2}^{t=n} (e_t - e_{t-1})^2 \Bigg/ \sum_{t=1}^{t=n} e_t^2 \qquad (4.4.3)$$

where $e_t; t = 1, 2, \ldots, n$ are the OLS residuals. Equation (4.4.3) shows that the value of d can be computed directly from a given set of residuals and, as we have said, many computer programs provide the value of d as a part of the output from any regression calculation. Obviously, the next step is to consider the information contained in a given value of d.

The first thing to notice is that d cannot be negative, since it is a ratio of sums of squares. Next, the value of d will tend to be small if successive residuals are close to one another. To the extent that the residuals represent the behaviour of the disturbances, this will happen when successive disturbances *are* largely determined by the preceding value, so long as ρ is *positive*. If ρ is *negative*, successive disturbances will tend to be of *different* signs. So d will tend to be relatively small if ρ is positive and relatively large if ρ is negative. But d is a random variable and any *single* value of ρ could give rise to many different values of d. What ρ determines is the *probability* of finding a value of d within any given range. If (4.4.3) is used to test the null hypothesis that $\rho = 0$, it is of particular interest to know the probabilities appropriate to this value of ρ.

In earlier examples of test procedures, we have found that the distribution of the test statistic can depend on the number of observations

(n) and the number of explanatory variables (k). When this happens, we have different critical values for different values of n and k. In the case of the Durbin-Watson test, the distribution also depends on something else. Suppose that we have a model

$$Y_t = \alpha + \beta X_t + u_t; t = 1, 2, \ldots, n \qquad (4.4.4)$$

where, as before, the values of the explanatory variable are considered to be non-random. The residuals would be

$$e_t = Y_t - \hat{\alpha} - \hat{\beta} X_t; t = 1, 2, \ldots, n \qquad (4.4.5)$$

where $\hat{\alpha}$ and $\hat{\beta}$ are OLS estimators. The Durbin-Watson statistic depends on the residuals, which in turn depend on the particular X values used in any given application. This, in itself, is not remarkable, but unfortunately there is no way of correcting d to make the distribution independent of the X values. This means that, in general, the critical values depend on the explanatory variable observations as well as on n and k. It is obviously impossible to tabulate critical values for all possible sets of explanatory variables and, if we wanted exact critical values, we would have to compute them for each separate regression that is run. This hardly qualifies as a simple and routine test procedure.

Fortunately, it is possible to put *bounds* on the critical values: this means that an exact critical value, for any given application, will fall between two extremes and these bounds have been tabulated, for given n and k and for various probabilities of type I error (rejecting the null hypothesis $\rho = 0$ when, in fact, this is true). The tables are used in the following way. First, a decision is made as to whether the alternative to $\rho = 0$ is a positive value of ρ or a negative value of ρ. In either case, there are *three* possible outcomes to the test. Suppose that the alternative is that ρ is positive. If the calculated value of d is less than the *lower* bound (usually denoted as d_L), the null hypothesis of independence is rejected in favour of the alternative of positive serial correlation. If d is greater than the *upper* bound (usually denoted as d_U), the null hypothesis is not rejected. If d falls *between* the bounds, we simply do not know the relationship between d and the *exact* critical value and the test is inconclusive. The tables do not give bounds for the case in which the alternative is that ρ is negative, but we can proceed as follows. If d is greater than $(4 - d_L)$, the null hypothesis of independence is rejected in favour of the alternative of negative serial correlation. If d is less than $(4 - d_U)$, the null hypothesis is not rejected and, if d falls between $(4 - d_U)$ and $(4 - d_L)$, the test is inconclusive. Notice that the test is used with one or other of the two possible alternatives and not with both together. We say that this is a *one-tailed* test.

This procedure may still seem to be rather complicated and, instead of providing complete tables for the test, we now suggest some simple rules of thumb. A value of d between 0 and 1 will generally indicate positive serial correlation and a value between 3 and 4 will indicate negative serial correlation. A value between 1 and 3 can, somewhat cautiously, be interpreted as being consistent with independence of the disturbances: the closer the value is to 2, the more confidence one would have in drawing this conclusion. It should be noted that our rule of thumb effectively takes both alternatives together and so the tables are not strictly appropriate to checking the accuracy of the rules: but the tables do suggest that we should pay some attention to the value of n, the number of observations. The rules given above are appropriate to a fairly small value, say $n = 20$. As n is increased, the bounds shown in the tables move in towards 2 and this suggests that for larger values of n, say $n = 50$, the range of values consistent with the null hypothesis should be more like $1·5-2·5$.

Before we leave the Durbin-Watson test, two limitations should be noted. The theoretical development does assume that the explanatory variables in the model can be considered to be non-random and, when this assumption breaks down, there can be definite distortions in the behaviour of the test statistic. We return to this in the next chapter. Rather less important, but still worthy of note, is an implicit assumption that the model contains an intercept: the tables are not appropriate to a model which does not contain an intercept term.

Considerable attention has been given to the Durbin-Watson test because it is a widely used procedure, designed to reveal an important disturbance problem. Many applications of econometric method do contain some reference to the test and, although we have suggested a rather crude interpretation of the test procedure, we have certainly said enough to enable the significance of such a reference to be understood. But, in concentrating on formal test procedures, one should not overlook an important source of information. A simple visual inspection of the residuals can often provide valuable evidence concerning the model specification. If the residuals show long runs of values with the same sign, then, to the extent that the residuals reproduce the behaviour of the disturbances, this might indicate positive serial correlation. If some subset of residuals seem to exhibit greater variation than the rest, this may indicate heteroscedasticity. And if the residuals seem to show some systematic behaviour that can be linked to a variable that has been excluded from the model, this would suggest a specification error that could be corrected by including that variable. In particular, the presence of one or two oddly behaved residuals may be sufficient to remind the investigator of some shock to the system that should be allowed for by using a dummy variable. These procedures are somewhat *ad hoc*, but the residuals can provide useful evidence and this source of information should not be ignored.

4.5 Two-Step and Iterative Methods

On introducing the GLS method, it was possible to obtain the properties of the estimators directly, by noting that GLS estimation applied to the original model is equivalent to OLS estimation applied to an appropriate transformed model. Indeed, this equivalence was actually used to *define* the GLS estimators. But, in some cases, it is not possible to obtain GLS estimates, because the transformation procedure involves an unknown disturbance parameter. One might then decide to use a two-step procedure, in which an *estimate* of the disturbance parameter is used to carry out the transformation. Such a procedure is an approximation to GLS, but the two-step estimators are not the same as the GLS estimators and we cannot assume that the estimator properties are exactly the same.

The crucial difference between a known disturbance parameter and an estimate is that a known parameter is non-random, whereas an estimate is a particular value taken by a random variable. Now suppose that we have an *original* model

$$Y_t = \beta X_t + u_t; t = 1, 2, \ldots, n \tag{4.5.1}$$

and a *transformed* model

$$Y_t^* = \beta X_t^* + u_t^*; t = 1, 2, \ldots, n \tag{4.5.2}$$

It may be perfectly reasonable to treat X_t; $t = 1, 2, \ldots, n$ as a set of non-random quantities, but if (4.5.2) is formed by a transformation which uses an estimate of a disturbance parameter, it is *not* true that X_t^*; $t = 1, 2, \ldots, n$, represents a set of non-random quantities. This obviously has implications for the properties of the two-step estimators.

If we had some general properties for OLS estimators obtained from models with random explanatory variables, we could still make use of the fact that the two-step procedure is equivalent to OLS applied to a transformed model. In fact, this approach is not particularly fruitful in terms of providing general results. When the appropriate disturbance parameters are known, we have essentially the *same* estimation problem, for each different type of disturbance specification, but when the disturbance parameters are unknown, there is an *additional* estimation problem, which varies somewhat from case to case. So there is a distinction between the estimation of a disturbance variance, required for the transformation appropriate to heteroscedasticity and the estimation of the parameter of an autoregressive process, required for the transformation appropriate to serial correlation. The essential difference is the *dynamic* nature of the serial correlation problem: it is generally true that the analysis of estimation problems based on dynamic models is more complicated than that for static models and the results obtained may well be weaker in the dynamic case.

The implication of all this is that the rules governing estimator choice are no longer clear-cut. So long as the explanatory variables in the *original* model can be considered to be non-random, it is usually possible to show that the two-step estimators have the asymptotic property of *consistency* (see Section 2.7). Results which hold for any number of observations, however small, are considerably more difficult to obtain. It should be remembered that the whole point of introducing GLS is to improve the *efficiency* of estimation, that is, to reduce the estimator variances. If we were simply concerned about unbiased estimation, we could have used OLS on the original model. To replace unbiased but inefficient estimators by two-step estimators, which are merely consistent, may seem to be a rather poor bargain, but there are several points to note. First, we have not said that the two-step estimators *are* biased. To answer this question, one has to distinguish between the different types of disturbance problem to a greater extent than has hitherto been necessary and the analysis does become more difficult. If there is a bias, it need not be large and it may be outweighed by a gain in efficiency from using the two-step procedure. It seems likely that the two-step procedure *would* produce a gain in efficiency, since it is an approximation to GLS, but again, we do not know that this is so, without conducting a detailed analysis of some specific type of model. In any case, we have not said that consistency is the only property of the two-step estimators. What we did suggest is that consistency is one of the few properties that is relatively easy to establish. Finally, there are many cases in which the OLS alternative does *not* give unbiased estimators. As assumptions are relaxed, to allow for more realistic types of model, questions of estimator choice are, more often than not, resolved in terms of asymptotic properties.

If there is some uncertainty as to whether a suggested method of estimation is a sensible choice, one should obviously be prepared to consider a wider class of alternatives. One possibility is a natural extension of the two-step method. Suppose that we have the model

$$Y_t = \beta X_t + u_t; t = 1, 2, \ldots, n \tag{4.5.3}$$

$$u_t = \rho u_{t-1} + v_t; t = 1, 2, \ldots, n \tag{4.5.4}$$

where the disturbances $v_t; t = 1, 2, \ldots, n$, are 'well-behaved'. In the two-step method, we would first apply OLS to (4.5.3), to produce a preliminary estimate of β. We would then use the residuals to obtain an estimate of ρ and, using the estimate in place of the unknown true value, we would transform (4.5.3). Finally, by the application of OLS to the transformed model, we would produce a revised estimate of β, But the *complete* model involves at least *two* unknown parameters, β and ρ, and one might wish to improve the estimate of ρ, by using the revised estimate of β to generate a new set of residuals. This, in turn, would allow us to find a new estimate of β and so the process would continue. This describes an *iterative* method for the estimation of β and ρ and we can summarize the steps as follows. Let $\beta_{(i)}$ and $\rho_{(i)}$ be the estimates of β and ρ obtained during step i and let

$$e_{(i)t} = Y_t - \beta_{(i)}X_t; t = 1, 2, \ldots, n \tag{4.5.5}$$

be the residuals obtained by using the estimate $\beta_{(i)}$. Then, with $\rho_{(0)} = 0$ as the starting point, each step consists of

1. a transformation

$$(Y_t - \rho_{(i-1)}Y_{t-1}) = \beta(X_t - \rho_{(i-1)}X_{t-1}) + (u_t - \rho_{(i-1)}u_{t-1});$$
$$t = 2, 3, \ldots, n \tag{4.5.6}$$

or alternatively, a full transformation, to include the first observation.

2. A regression on the transformed model, to produce an estimate, $\beta_{(i)}$. This estimate is used in (4.5.5) to produce residuals $e_{(i)t}$; $t = 1, 2, \ldots, n$.

3. A regression of $e_{(i)t}$ on $e_{(i)t-1}$, to produce an estimate, $\rho_{(i)}$.

Since $\rho_{(0)} = 0$, the transformation has no effect during step 1 and the first observation can *always* be used. Notice also that the residuals are based on the *original* variables and that, at each step, the transformation starts again from the original variables.

At some point, we have to stop the iterations and, with any iterative process, we must consider whether the estimates will *converge*, so that there is no longer any appreciable difference between successive values. In this case, it can be shown that convergence should occur, but this is not true of iterative methods in general and, even when convergence can be guaranteed, the number of iterations required can be rather large. Although it would be possible to carry out this particular iterative procedure by repeated runs of an OLS regression program, it would clearly be very tedious to do so and, in general, special computer programs are needed for iterative calculations.

There is another way of looking at the method that we have described. Suppose that we consider the application of the least squares principle to the transformed model

$$(Y_t - \rho Y_{t-1}) = \beta(X_t - \rho X_{t-1}) + (u_t - \rho u_{t-1}); t = 2, 3, \ldots, n$$

$$(4.5.7)$$

where β and ρ are the unknown true values. The least square principle would suggest that we should choose that value for β that minimizes the sum of squares

$$\sum_{t=2}^{t=n} [(Y_t - \rho Y_{t-1}) - \beta(X_t - \rho X_{t-1})]^2 \qquad (4.5.8)$$

and that we should use the resulting value as an estimate of β. But ρ is also an unknown parameter and, instead of substituting a prior estimate of ρ, we could minimize (4.5.8) with respect to β *and* ρ. Both parameters would then be estimated together, using the least squares principle. Unfortunately, this is a *nonlinear* least squares problem and an iterative method has to be used to obtain the solution. The particular iterations described above represent one possible approach.

Finally, we should consider the possibility that the least squares criterion itself is no longer the best approach to estimation. The criterion was first suggested as an intuitively plausible method for fitting a line to a two-dimensional scatter of points and this was subsequently reinforced by the fact that the estimators have desirable properties under certain conditions. But, if these conditions no longer hold, the criterion itself is called into question. We mention this because there is an important group of alternative methods, based on the *maximum likelihood principle*.

The technical details of the maximum likelihood (ML) approach are beyond the scope of this book, but we can explain the principle by making use of a simple example. Suppose that we have the model

$$Y_t = \beta X_t + u_t; t = 1, 2, \ldots, n \tag{4.5.9}$$

where, for simplicity, the explanatory variable observations are taken to be non-random. According to the model, the dependent variable observations are particular values taken by a set of random variables. This follows from the direct linkage between the dependent variable observations and the random disturbances. If we assume some particular probability distribution for each disturbance, it is possible to derive the implied probability distribution for each dependent variable observation. These distributions will involve the unknown parameter β. Now our data consists of *one* set of observations on the dependent variable and, for any given value of β, there would be a certain probability of obtaining this set of observations. Strictly speaking, we should say that there would be a certain probability of obtaining values in a small range around those which are observed, since the dependent variable observations are treated as continuous random variables, but this is a technicality. The maximum likelihood principle suggests that we should choose that value of β that gives the maximum probability of observing what we have actually observed and this value of β is used as the ML estimate.

It should be noted that we do have to assume a specific form of distribution for each disturbance and, not surprisingly, the normal distribution is almost invariably the form that is chosen. If this is the case and (4.5.9) has 'well-behaved' disturbances, the ML estimator for β is identical to the OLS estimator. In more complicated forms of model, this is not always the case. If, for example, we have a first-order autoregressive scheme for the disturbances, with an unknown value for ρ, the ML principle can be used to obtain estimates of β *and* ρ and the ML estimators are *not* the same as the least squares estimators defined by the minimization of (4.5.8), although the asymptotic properties of the estimators *are* the same. The usual reason given for using the maximum likelihood method is in fact concerned with asymptotic properties. For a wide variety of models, the ML estimators can be shown to be consistent, asymptotically efficient and to have asymptotic normal distributions. Roughly speaking, this means that, with a large number of observations, the estimators are not subject to systematic distortions, they do have minimum variance and they are approximately normally distributed. But asymptotic distribution theory is an extremely difficult subject and statements concerning ML estimation are sometimes based on the folklore of econometrics, rather than on careful analysis.

4.6 Some Further Disturbance Problems

In Section 3.10, we introduced the idea of a model in which a given form of relationship may have different parameter values in different regions. Despite the basic similarity of the individual relationships, this was actually our first example of a *multiple equation* model, a model which involves several different underlying equations. If the parameters are *all* different, it is possible to treat each equation in isolation and to run a separate regression on the data for each region. If, on the other hand, some parameters take the same value in different regions, there are restrictions which apply *between* equations and, in order to impose these restrictions, it is necessary to find a way of combining all the individual equations into a single relationship. We showed how this can be done by making use of dummy variables and, for the purpose of estimation, we can treat a model with several equations as though it were a model with just one equation, applied to the data from all regions.

As soon as we take the step of combining the equations, we introduce the possibility of heteroscedasticity. It may well be that, *within* each region, we have a constant disturbance variance, but there may be a different constant variance appropriate to each region. If this is so, combining the equations to give a single relationship will introduce heteroscedasticity. The reason for combining equations is to enable cross-equation restrictions to be imposed and so what we have is a problem of restricted estimation with heteroscedastic disturbances. We can handle this by treating each component problem in turn. Suppose that there are two regions, with disturbance variances given by

$$\text{var}(u_t) = \sigma^2 \lambda_1^2 \text{ ; in region 1} \tag{4.6.1}$$
$$= \sigma^2 \lambda_2^2 \text{ ; in region 2}$$

The first step would be to create the dummy variables. In theory, one would introduce a full set of dummies and then the restrictions would be imposed by making the appropriate deletions. In practice, one would simply fail to insert those dummies which are not needed under the restrictions. Then, if λ_1 and λ_2 are known, all observations relating to region 1 would be divided by λ_1, including observations on the dummy variables and, where appropriate, those on the artificial variable which allows for an intercept term. All observations relating to region 2 would be divided by λ_2. After all these preliminary transformations, the application of OLS to the transformed model would produce restricted GLS estimates. Notice that we do not need to know the value of σ^2, the common scale factor in (4.6.1).

It should be remembered that the purpose of using any available restrictions is to improve the efficiency of estimation, that is, to reduce the variance of the estimators. But combining the equations introduces heteroscedasticity and, if heteroscedasticity is present, GLS estimation is more efficient than OLS estimation. So we have the result that the restricted GLS estimators are generally more efficient than the restricted OLS estimators which, in turn, are more efficient than the unrestricted OLS estimators. In this example, two separate problems are dealt with by a combination of the methods appropriate to the individual problems.

If λ_1 and λ_2 are not known, a two-step procedure could be used. There would no longer be any point in writing the disturbance variances in terms of two components, since both σ^2 and the λ values are unknown. So (4.6.1) is now written as

$$\text{var}\,(u_t) = \sigma_1^2\,;\ \text{in region 1} \qquad\qquad (4.6.2)$$
$$\phantom{\text{var}\,(u_t)} = \sigma_2^2\,;\ \text{in region 2}$$

and the GLS procedure that we are trying to approximate would involve division by σ_1 and σ_2 respectively, rather than λ_1 and λ_2. The two-step procedure would be as follows. Fitting separate unrestricted regressions to each region would produce a set of residuals for each region and the disturbance variances could then be estimated in the usual way. These estimates are denoted as $\hat\sigma_1^2$ and $\hat\sigma_2^2$. The equations for the two regions would then be combined, as before, and the appropriate restrictions imposed, but the transformation for heteroscedasticity would involve division by $\hat\sigma_1$ and $\hat\sigma_2$, instead of the unknown values σ_1 and σ_2. The final estimates of the parameters of the deterministic part of the model would then be *approximations* to the restricted GLS estimates.

The argument above illustrates an important point. One can have an absolutely standard disturbance specification for the individual equations in a model, but the very fact that there is more than one equation means that there are additional possibilities to consider. So, within each equation, there may be a constant disturbance variance, but this does not necessarily mean that the disturbance variance is the same for each equation. Similarly, one may rule out the possibility of serial correlation within the individual equations, but there can be various patterns of correlation between disturbances taken from *different* equations.

To illustrate this point, suppose that time series data are available, at the regional level, on aggregate consumers' expenditure (C) and

158 *Understanding Econometrics*

aggregate disposable income (D). Suppose also that there are two regions, with m observations for each region, and that the model is

$$C_t = \alpha_1 + \beta_1 D_t + u_t; \text{ in region 1} \qquad (4.6.3)$$

$$C_t = \alpha_2 + \beta_2 D_t + v_t; \text{ in region 2}$$

where v_t; $t = 1, 2, \ldots, m$ is now used to represent the disturbances for region 2, as distinct from u_t; $t = 1, 2, \ldots, m$, the disturbances for region 1. Now consider a particular disturbance term, say u_1. It may be that u_1 is independent of $u_2, u_3, \ldots, u_m$ and of $v_2, v_3, \ldots, v_m$. Similarly, u_2 may be independent of $u_1, u_3, \ldots, u_m$ and of $v_1, v_3, \ldots, v_m$. If this pattern is repeated, there is no *serial* correlation in the model, but there can still be *contemporaneous* correlation, between disturbances to *different* equations, during the *same* period of time. This would mean that u_1 is correlated with v_1, u_2 with v_2, and so on. The distinction between serial correlation and contemporaneous correlation is illustrated in Fig. 4.1: in each case, there are arrows linking certain disturbances and, where linkages exist, it is impossible to assume independence between those particular disturbance terms.

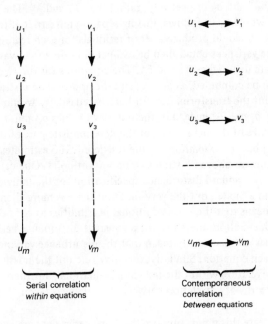

Serial correlation
within equations

Contemporaneous correlation
between equations

Figure 4.1

If there is contemporaneous correlation in the model, it would generally be assumed that the same *pattern* of correlation holds between each pair of disturbances and this assumption would usually be expressed in terms of the *covariance* between each pair. The covariance between two random variables is a measure of the extent to which the variables 'move together' and it is a property of two random variables, just as the variance is a property of a single random variable. Using the concept of covariance and the notation $\text{cov}(u_t, v_t)$, the assumption of a constant pattern of contemporaneous correlation can be expressed as

$$\text{cov}(u_t, v_t) = \sigma_{uv}; t = 1, 2, \ldots, m \tag{4.6.4}$$

This says that there is a constant covariance for all values of t, the constant value being written as σ_{uv}. If this constant is not equal to zero, there *is* contemporaneous correlation in the model. Notice the analogy between (4.6.4) and the assumption of constant variance within each equation. In both cases it is assumed that there are disturbance parameters which do not change through time.

Now consider a possible reason for contemporaneous correlation of the disturbances in (4.6.3). The disturbances represent all influences on consumption, except for disposable income and, in any given time period, it is quite possible that disturbances in the two regions have at least some components in common. This could be the case if the disturbances include factors which represent national rather than regional characteristics. Such factors would tend to affect consumption in both regions in the same way and this would perhaps suggest a positive correlation between the disturbances. But our example is purely illustrative: in other, more complex models, there can be a very definite reason for contemporaneous correlation of the disturbances. The important point is that, in considering a multiple equation model, one must make *some* assumption concerning the relationship between the disturbances to the different equations. If the assumption of independence is acceptable, well and good. But if the theory underlying the model suggests contemporaneous correlation or if there is no clear indication one way or another, the existence of a possible disturbance problem must be recognized.

If the two equations in (4.6.3) were combined, the complete set of disturbances could not be considered to be independent and this suggests that one should use some form of GLS to ensure efficiency. But this leaves unanswered the question as to whether it is actually necessary to combine the individual equations. In the previous example, the equations were combined in order that cross-equation restrictions could be imposed. It was the existence of the restrictions that established a connection between the equations. The fact that the disturbance variance differed between equations did not, of itself, establish any connection. In (4.6.3), it is implicit that the parameters are different as between regions 1 and 2 and there are no cross-equation restrictions. But, if there is contemporaneous correlation, there is a connection, albeit a subtle one, between the two equations. A model of this kind is actually said to consist of *seemingly unrelated regressions*: there does not *seem* to be any connection between the equations, but closer inspection of the disturbance specification shows that there is a connection. The correct estimation procedure would be to combine the equations, using the dummy variable technique to allow the parameters to vary between regions and then to apply GLS to the resulting single relationship. The transformations appropriate to this particular disturbance problem are complicated and we shall not give details, but the principles which lie behind the choice of GLS can be understood. The contemporaneous correlation establishes a connection between the equations and one should then consider the model as a whole. But if the equations are combined, it is obvious that the disturbances are not mutually independent and some form of GLS estimation has then to be applied to the combined equation. In principle, this should improve the efficiency of estimation *vis-à-vis* OLS.

The model shown in (4.6.3) is a perfectly valid example of a multiple equation model, but it is not entirely typical. Both equations have consumption as the dependent variable and income as the explanatory variable. One can therefore interpret the consumption observations in the two regions as being different sets of observations on the *same* economic variable and similarly for income. This makes it easy to combine the equations, without necessarily imposing equality of the parameters, by making use of dummy variables. Even if one chose to regard consumption in region 1 as a *different* variable from consumption in region 2, it would make no difference to the method of estimation. One could still combine the equations in exactly the same way. This leads us to an interesting possibility. If one can combine equations involving similar, but conceptually distinct variables, it must also be possible to combine equations involving completely different variables. This idea is very useful when we consider the estimation of complete models in a more general context and we shall explain the methodology in more detail in Section 6.5. For the moment, we shall merely note that one can combine equations for the purposes of estimation. One possible reason for doing this is to impose cross-equation restrictions, but another, more subtle reason is that, in a multiple equation model, there can be correlation of the disturbances *between* the individual equations.

Exercises (Solutions on page 235)

4.1 Can one impose the stochastic constraint

$$0 \cdot 5 = \beta + v; \operatorname{var}(v) = 0 \cdot 1$$

on the model

$$Y_t = \alpha + \beta X_t + u_t; t = 1, 2, \ldots, n$$

using only a standard least squares program?

4.2 The model

$$Y = \alpha + \beta X_t + u_t; t = 1, 2, \ldots, n$$

is applied to quarterly data and it is thought that disturbances in the same quarters of successive years are serially correlated

$$u_t = \rho u_{t-4} + v_t; t = 1, 2, \ldots, n$$

If the value of ρ were known, how could one transform the model so as to remove the serial correlation? Would OLS applied to the transformed model produce GLS estimates?

5 Distributed Lags and Dynamic Economic Models

5.1 Introduction

The next step in moving towards more realistic forms of economic model is to allow for lags in the relationships between economic variables. We have already considered the use of lags in the disturbance specification: we now consider the implications of including lags in the deterministic part of the model.

The simplest case is that in which Y and X represent two economic variables, connected by a relationship which shows that the current value of Y is linked to a past value of X. A specific example is

$$Y_t = \beta X_{t-1} + u_t; t = 1, 2, \ldots, n \tag{5.1.1}$$

There is no *particular* reason why this model should not satisfy the full list of assumptions under which the OLS estimator would be best linear unbiased. Indeed, the only difference between (5.1.1) and

$$Y_t = \beta X_t + u_t; t = 1, 2, \ldots, n \tag{5.1.2}$$

lies in the data requirement: the observations $X_{t-1}; t = 1, 2, \ldots, n$ are equivalent to the observations $X_t; t = 0, 1, \ldots, n - 1$. But it is possible to extend (5.1.1), in such a way that the dependent variable reacts to *several* past values of the explanatory variable and, although this does not necessarily lead to the violation of assumptions, there are some practical problems of estimation, which are discussed in Section 5.2, under the heading of *distributed lags*.

With the introduction of lags there is another possibility. The current value of the dependent variable may be determined in part by its *own* past values. We shall give reasons for such a hypothesis in due course. The immediate objective is to identify the characteristics of this new type of model. The simplest formal example is that in which we use a first order autoregressive process, applied now to the dependent variable observations

$$Y_t = \beta Y_{t-1} + u_t; t = 1, 2, \ldots, n \tag{5.1.3}$$

The only explanatory variable in (5.1.3) is the lagged dependent variable and, apart from the random disturbance terms, the current values of the dependent variable are determined entirely by past values. More generally, there would be some other explanatory variables, but (5.1.3) does serve to illustrate the characteristics which make this type of model different from those considered earlier.

The first point to note is that we have a problem of terminology. In (5.1.3), there is only one economic variable, which is both 'dependent' and 'explanatory'. As variables in a standard form of statistical model, the current and lagged versions of Y are distinct: but both represent the same economic variable and, if the model is designed to explain the behaviour of this variable, it is inevitable that the behaviour of the 'explanatory' variable is also explained.

Now consider the model shown in (5.1.1). In this case, there are two quite distinct economic variables and, whilst the model attempts to explain the behaviour of Y, there is no attempt to explain the behaviour of X. In terms of the underlying economic model, Y would be described as an *endogenous* variable and X as an *exogenous* variable. We have not needed to make use of these terms before: the dependent variable is, by definition, endogenous and it has hitherto been assumed that, in formulating the model, all explanatory variables can be treated as exogenous. The characteristics which were assumed to hold for explanatory variables are those which, in a more general context, one would assume for exogenous variables. It is still convenient to use 'dependent' and 'explanatory' to refer to 'left hand side' and 'right hand side' variables respectively: but now explanatory variables can be either exogenous or lagged endogenous variables.

The use of a lagged endogenous variable does lead to problems of estimation. In a model which contains random disturbances, each *dependent* variable observation must be treated as a particular value taken by a random variable. But, if $Y_t; t = 1, 2, \ldots, n$ represents a set of random quantities, so does $Y_{t-1}; t = 2, 3, \ldots, n$. Note that the starting value, Y_0, is not determined within the model and this could be considered to be non-random. The implication is that we have a model in which all but one of the *explanatory* variable observations must also be particular values taken by a set of random variables. We have already come across this problem in the context of a *transformed* model, when the transformation involves an estimated disturbance parameter. In the lagged endogenous variable case, the randomness of the explanatory variable observations is an inherent property of the model. But we do have specific information as to the nature of the random variation and this can be used in looking at the estimator properties. These properties are discussed in Section 5.3.

The other novel feature of (5.1.3) is that it is a simple example of a *dynamic* model. Ignoring the random disturbances, we can say that a dynamic model is one which is designed to show how an endogenous variable can change through time, even though any exogenous variables that are present may not change at all. In (5.1.3), there are no exogenous variables, but each successive value of the endogenous variable is determined by the previous value and, in this way, the model does generate a complete time path for the endogenous variable. The decision as to whether (5.1.1) is also a dynamic model is less straightforward. The concept of time is certainly used in specifying the relationship between Y and X, but, apart from the effect of the random disturbances, Y can only change in response to a past change in the value of X. It is convenient, for our purposes, to say that a dynamic model should contain at least one lagged endogenous variable. This is slightly restrictive, but it does serve to identify a class of models associated with a specific type of estimation problem and our definition does correspond to what is *usually* meant by a dynamic model.

There is one further complication. If the *disturbances* follow an autoregressive process, a dynamic element is added to what may otherwise be an essentially static *economic* model. We shall not pursue this point, but if the parameter of the autoregressive disturbance scheme is unknown, the resulting problems of estimation are very similar to those that arise from a dynamic economic model. Before we consider these problems, we return to the case in which the model involves only lagged *exogenous* variables.

5.2 Distributed Lags

In the model shown in (5.1.1), the explicit assumption that Y_t is related to X_t is replaced by the equally explicit assumption that Y_t is related to X_{t-1}. There are, of course, many other possibilities. The one period lag could be replaced by a lag of two or more periods. Alternatively, we may have a *distributed lag*, in which the current value of Y is related to *several* past values of X. A typical example for this type of model is that of investment in plant and machinery, where the flows of investment expenditure during any given period result from the investment decisions of earlier periods. The explanatory variables will primarily be those which affect the investment decisions, but there can be many types of lag in the translation of decisions into actual flows of investment expenditure. We shall assume that our example relates to aggregate investment in the national economy and, given that this aggregate is taken over many firms, each of which may, in any period, have several projects at different stages of completion, it is not difficult to see why a distributed lag formulation is appropriate.

If we knew exactly which past values of X were relevant in determining the behaviour of Y, it would be possible to specify the lag model precisely. But, typically, there is some uncertainty as to which lagged values of X should be included and the model is then specified by choosing a maximum lag and a minimum lag and including all lagged values of X between these extremes. To simplify, we shall assume that the minimum lag is 0 and we shall represent the maximum lag as s. This would give a model in the form

$$Y_t = \beta_0 X_t + \beta_1 X_{t-1} + \ldots + \beta_s X_{t-s} + u_t; t = 1, 2, \ldots, n \qquad (5.2.1)$$

More generally there would be other explanatory variables and an intercept term, but our concern here is with the estimation of the parameters of the distributed lag relationship and, for this purpose, (5.2.1) is an adequate representation.

The first point to note is that (5.2.1) is in the form of a k variable model, with $k = s + 1$. The explanatory variables are actually current and lagged versions of the *same* economic variable, but the parameters can be estimated by treating each version of X as a distinct variable in a multiple regression calculation. The data for the regression would consist of observations

$$Y_t; t = 1, 2, \ldots, n, \ X_t; t = 1, 2, \ldots, n,$$
$$X_{t-1}; t = 1, 2, \ldots, n, \text{etc.}$$

If the computer program allows for a lag transformation, it would obviously be convenient to generate the lagged variable observations directly from a *single* set of observations on the variable X. The complete input data would then consist of n observations on Y and X, together with some additional observations on the values of X for the s periods immediately prior to $t = 1$. If X is taken to be exogenous and the disturbances are well behaved, the OLS estimators would be best linear unbiased. Of course, if there is a particular disturbance problem, the appropriate GLS estimators would be used instead, but there is no *inherent* property of the model that suggests a violation of assumptions.

Although OLS can be applied to (5.2.1), the practical difficulty that we referred to earlier is that there will inevitably be some degree of intercorrelation between the current and lagged versions of X. Since X is treated as exogenous, the explicit representation of any association between successive values of X is not within the scope of the present model but, invariably, some measured correlation would be found and if there is any regularity in the behaviour of X over time, the degree of intercorrelation between the explanatory variables in (5.2.1) can be very high. So we would, in general, have a problem of severe multicollinearity and this means that we would tend to get rather imprecise estimates of the individual parameters. Specifically, the estimators would tend to have relatively high variances.

We know, from the discussion in Section 3.9, that the estimator variances can be reduced by imposing restrictions on the model. If (5.2.1) is specified in an attempt to cover all possible lags, there may well be scope for deleting some of the lagged variables and this amounts to imposing exclusion restrictions. Unfortunately, under conditions of severe multicollinearity, the t test applied to individual coefficients does not give a very reliable method for choosing the variables to be deleted and, in the context of a distributed lag model, there are other forms of restriction that can be used.

Equation (5.2.1) shows how the current value of Y reacts to several past values of X, but the model also shows how Y would adjust, over time, to a given change in X. Ignoring the effect of the random disturbances, consider an extremely simple example

$$Y_t = \beta_0 X_t + \beta_1 X_{t-1} ; t = 1, 2, \ldots, n \qquad (5.2.2)$$

and suppose that

$$X_t = 0; \text{ for all values prior to } t = 1$$

and

$$X_t = X_c; t = 1, 2, \ldots, n$$

where X_c is a *single* fixed value of X. So X does not change after the value X_c is established in period $t = 1$. The behaviour of Y is then given by

$$Y_1 = \beta_0 X_c + \beta_1 \cdot 0 = \beta_0 X_c$$
$$Y_2 = \beta_0 X_c + \beta_1 X_c = (\beta_0 + \beta_1) X_c$$
$$Y_3 = (\beta_0 + \beta_1) X_c, \text{ etc.}$$

After an initial period of adjustment, there is no further change in the value of Y and we can write

$$Y_t = Y_c = (\beta_0 + \beta_1)X_c; t = 2, 3, \ldots, n$$

If X_c is set to 1, it becomes obvious that the parameter β_0 measures the immediate response of Y to a unit change in X and that the parameter β_1 measures the additional response after a lag of one period. The sum, $\beta_0 + \beta_1$, measures the *total* or long-run response

More generally, we have a set of *response coefficients*, β_i; $i = 0, 1, \ldots, s$ and the long-run response is measured by

$$\beta = \beta_0 + \beta_1 + \ldots + \beta_s \tag{5.2.3}$$

We can then express the individual coefficients as

$$\beta_i = \beta w_i; \, i = 0, 1, \ldots, s \tag{5.2.4}$$

where

$$w_i = (\beta_i/\beta); i = 0, 1, \ldots, s \tag{5.2.5}$$

The weights defined in (5.2.5) show how the total response is distributed through time. It is usually the case that all the response coefficients have the same sign. If they are positive, β is positive. If they are negative, β is negative. In either case, the *weights* are non-negative. There can be exceptions to this rule, but this is relatively unimportant. As we shall shortly discover, it is very convenient to be able to express the response pattern in a way which is independent of the sign of the long-run coefficient, β, and we could still do this if one or two of the individual coefficients were of a different sign to the rest. The majority of weights would still be non-negative.

Suppose now that we were to draw a graph, showing how the *weights* change with the value of the *lag length, i*. Fig. 5.1 shows an example in which the largest weight corresponds to a lag of 2 periods, with smaller weights on lags of 0, 1, 3 and 4 periods. This indicates that the peak response of Y to X occurs with a lag of 2 periods, with smaller responses for other lag lengths up to a maximum lag of 4 periods. We could represent this pattern by means of a graph of β_i against i, but if the long run coefficient, β, is negative, the pattern shown would be the inverse of that on the graph of weights. It seems more satisfactory to represent the peak response as the highest point on a graph, irrespective of the sign of the overall effect and this is the advantage of using the weights rather than the original response coefficients.

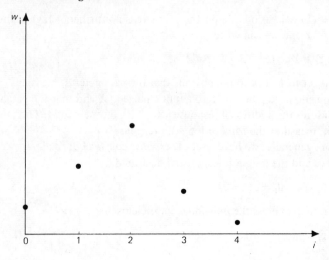

Figure 5.1

The information shown on the graph of weights is described as the *lag distribution*. The graph actually consists of a set of points, but the points do trace out a shape and, whilst it is unrealistic to suppose that the values of the weights would be known exactly, one may have some rough idea of the shape appropriate to a particular case. In the distribution shown in Fig. 5.1, the weights rise and then fall as the lag length is increased. If we knew this, without knowing the exact pattern, we could choose the weights accordingly. For example, we could set

$$w_0 = 1/9, w_1 = 2/9, w_2 = 3/9, w_3 = 2/9, w_4 = 1/9 \qquad (5.2.6)$$

where the scale is chosen to ensure that the weights add to one. These weights trace out an 'inverted V' shape and, if this is thought to be appropriate, the model (5.2.1) could be written as

$$Y_t = \beta[(1/9)X_t + (2/9)X_{t-1} + (3/9)X_{t-2} + (2/9)X_{t-3}$$
$$+ (1/9)X_{t-4}] + u_t; t = 1, 2, \ldots, n \qquad (5.2.7)$$

or as

$$Y_t = \beta X_t^* + u_t; t = 1, 2, \ldots, n \qquad (5.2.8)$$

where X_t^* represents the term in the square brackets on the right of (5.2.7). The observations on X^* can be formed from the observations on the original lagged variables and the regression of Y on X^* would produce an estimate of β, which is now the only unknown parameter.

The imposition of a certain shape on the lag distribution amounts
to the use of a set of restrictions on the parameters of the original
model and, by using these restrictions, we have apparently overcome
the effects of multicollinearity. But the chosen weights are unlikely
to correspond exactly to the 'true' values and, as a result, the implicit
estimators

$$\hat{\beta}_0 = (1/9)\hat{\beta}; \ \hat{\beta}_1 = (2/9)\hat{\beta}; \ \ldots, \hat{\beta}_4 = (1/9)\hat{\beta}$$

will be subject to a certain amount of bias. This price would be
acceptable if the inverted V shape is a reasonably good approximation,
for then the bias would tend to be small. Otherwise, the bias may be
very serious and, in the absence of any firm information as to the shape
of the lag distribution, we have to find yet another way of choosing the
restrictions to be imposed. The discussion which follows is based on a
simplified version of a method proposed by Shirley Almon, known
generally as the *Almon* method.

In Fig. 5.1, the lag distribution is represented by a set of points
and, as we have said, a similar representation could be used for the
original response coefficients. If we consider this latter case, an
alternative way of expressing the linkage between the response
coefficients and the lag length would be to find the equation of a
curve passing through all the points. There is, however, a difficulty.
The coefficients, β_i, are only defined for the lag lengths $i = 0, 1, \ldots, 4$
or, more generally, for $i = 0, 1, \ldots, s$, but the equation of a curve
must involve *continuous* variables. To get round the problem, we
treat i as a continuous variable and we define a second continuous
variable, b, the value of which is determined by the value of i. If an
equation linking b to i is to pass through all the points on a graph of
β_i against i, the value of b at any of the lag lengths $i = 0, 1, \ldots, s$,
must be equal to the corresponding coefficient, β_i. So, as part of the
definition of b, we have

$$b = \beta_i; i = 0, 1, \ldots, s \qquad (5.2.9)$$

If there were just two response coefficients, there would only be
two points on a graph of β_i against i and a straight line would be a
suitable form for an equation passing through the points. But three
or more points would be unlikely to lie exactly along a single straight
line and the equation of a curve would have to be used instead. There
is actually a general rule concerning a type of equation that can be
guaranteed to fit exactly to a given number of points. For just two

points, a straight line

$$b = a_0 + a_1 i \qquad (5.2.10)$$

would be sufficient but, for three points, we would need

$$b = a_0 + a_1 i + a_2 i^2 \qquad (5.2.11)$$

and, for $(s + 1)$ points, we would need

$$b = a_0 + a_1 i + \ldots + a_s i^s \qquad (5.2.12)$$

In each case, a_0, a_1, etc, are parameters of the equation form and these would take particular values for particular examples of lag distributions. Equations (5.2.10), (5.2.11) and (5.2.12) are *polynomials* of degree 1, 2 and s respectively. When the maximum lag length is s, equation (5.2.12) is a general form for the equation of a curve passing through all the points on a graph of β_i against i. But, having defined b in order to write down the equation, our interest centres on the particular values of b which correspond to $\beta_i; i = 0, 1, \ldots, s$, and, for these values, we can write

$$\beta_i = a_0 + a_1 i + \ldots + a_s i^s \qquad (5.2.13)$$

If the $(s + 1)$ values $a_0, a_1, \ldots, a_s$ were known, we could derive the value of β_i appropriate to any of the lag lengths $i = 0, 1, \ldots, s$. Thus, we would have

$$i = 0: \beta_0 = a_0 + a_1(0) + \ldots + a_s(0)^s = a_0$$

$$i = 1: \beta_1 = a_0 + a_1(1) + \ldots + a_s(1)^s = a_0 + a_1 + \ldots + a_s$$

$$i = 2: \beta_2 = a_0 + a_1(2) + \ldots + a_s(2)^s, \text{ etc.} \qquad (5.2.14)$$

But we are trying to establish a technique that can be used when nothing is known about the lag distribution, except for the value of the maximum lag length, s, and so $a_0, a_1, \ldots, a_s$ represent a set of *unknown* parameters. In fact we have expressed the unknown values $\beta_i; i = 0, 1, \ldots, s$, in terms of an *equal* number of unknown values $a_i; i = 0, 1, \ldots, s$. The substitution does, however, have an advantage, which can best be understood by means of a particular example.

Suppose that we have the model

$$Y_t = \beta_0 X_t + \beta_1 X_{t-1} + \beta_2 X_{t-2} + \beta_3 X_{t-3} + u_t; t = 1, 2, \ldots, n \qquad (5.2.15)$$

In this case $s = 3$ and we would need a third degree polynomial

$$b = a_0 + a_1 i + a_2 i^2 + a_3 i^3 \qquad (5.2.16)$$

to give an exact fit through the *four* points corresponding to the values $\beta_i; i = 0, 1, 2, 3$. In this case, the equations in (5.2.14) would give

$$\beta_0 = a_0$$

$$\beta_1 = a_0 + a_1 + a_2 + a_3$$

$$\beta_2 = a_0 + 2a_1 + 4a_2 + 8a_3$$

$$\beta_3 = a_0 + 3a_1 + 9a_2 + 27a_3 \qquad (5.2.17)$$

and so (5.2.15) becomes

$$Y_t = a_0 X_t + (a_0 + a_1 + a_2 + a_3)X_{t-1} + (a_0 + 2a_1 + 4a_2 + 8a_3)X_{t-2}$$
$$+ (a_0 + 3a_1 + 9a_2 + 27a_3)X_{t-3} + u_t; t = 1, 2, \ldots, n$$

Rearranging this equation, we obtain

$$Y_t = a_0(X_t + X_{t-1} + X_{t-2} + X_{t-3})$$
$$+ a_1(X_{t-1} + 2X_{t-2} + 3X_{t-3})$$
$$+ a_2(X_{t-1} + 4X_{t-2} + 9X_{t-3})$$
$$+ a_3(X_{t-1} + 8X_{t-2} + 27X_{t-3}) + u_t; t = 1, 2, \ldots, n \qquad (5.2.18)$$

or

$$Y_t = a_0 X_{0t}^* + a_1 X_{1t}^* + a_2 X_{2t}^* + a_3 X_{3t}^* + u_t; t = 1, 2, \ldots, n$$
$$(5.2.19)$$

where $X_{it}^*; i = 0, 1, 2, 3$, represent the bracketed terms in (5.2.18). What we have done is to define a new set of explanatory variables, which are actually linear combinations of the original lagged variables. The parameters attached to these new variables are a_0, a_1, a_2, a_3. The advantage of having carried out the rearrangement is that there is now a restriction which may be appropriate. A third degree polynomial is needed to guarantee an *exact* fit to the points on the graph of β_i against i, but a second degree polynomial may be a sufficiently good approximation. Equation (5.2.16) can be converted into a second degree polynomial by deleting the last term, that is, by setting $a_3 = 0$. The values a_0, a_1 and a_2 would no longer be unique, because there are many different second degree polynomials that could be used to provide an approximation, but we shall see that this does not matter. If a_3 is set to zero then, following through to (5.2.19), we see that one of the new explanatory variables is completely removed. There would then only be *three* unknown parameters, and a regression of Y on

X_0^*, X_1^* and X_2^* would provide estimates of a_0, a_1 and a_2. If these estimates are used in (5.2.17), together with $a_3 = 0$, it is possible to obtain estimates of the *four* parameters β_0, β_1, β_2 and β_3. The deletion of X_3^* implies a restriction on (5.2.19) and, indirectly, a restriction on the *original* response coefficients. The estimators obtained in this way are thus restricted estimators, which will generally have lower variances than the corresponding unrestricted estimators. Instead of the complete deletion of one of the lagged variables, this method involves the deletion of a small part of the information contained in all the lagged variable observations. This may remind the reader of the use of *principal components*, discussed in Section 3.9 and, indeed, there are similarities. But the rationale for the restriction is different in the Almon method: the fundamental idea is that a polynomial of relatively high degree can be successfully approximated by a polynomial of a lower degree. To the extent that this can be done, the implied restriction on the response coefficients will be almost 'true', the bias introduced will be relatively small and the reduction in variance should more than compensate for the bias.

Our example was chosen for relative simplicity and two comments are in order. We have described a single version of the Almon method and there are variations. But we have said enough to enable the reader to understand the basic principles and to appreciate the significance of any reference to the method which may be found in the literature. Indeed, one could carry out the calculation of the coefficients by using a standard regression program, preferably one with transformation facilities. This would be used to run the regression on (5.2.19), with X_3^* deleted. From the estimates of a_0, a_1 and a_2 and the restriction $a_3 = 0$, one could use (5.2.17) to calculate estimates of β_0, β_1, β_2 and β_3. But it is more difficult to work back to the variances of the original coefficients and, in this respect, our description is incomplete.

The other point concerns the lag length in our example. A second degree polynomial may be too restrictive for general use, but a third degree polynomial will often be a good approximation for polynomials of higher degree. In principle, one could test the approximation by conducting *t* tests on the coefficients of the transformed relationship corresponding to (5.2.19). But the results do have to be treated with caution, because the transformed model will still be subject to multicollinearity. The advantage of the Almon method is that it suggests restrictions that can be justified on *a priori* grounds and, in practice, a third degree polynomial will often be adequate.

As a final example of the methods used to estimate the parameters

of a distributed lag model, we consider the case in which an *infinite*
lag distribution is used. Instead of assuming that there is a maximum
lag length, s, we impose a pattern under which the weights in the lag
distribution decline as the lag length is increased but, except in one
special case, the weights never become exactly zero. To achieve this,
the weights are expressed as

$$w_0 = (1 - \lambda); w_1 = (1 - \lambda)\lambda; w_2 = (1 - \lambda)\lambda^2 ; \text{ etc.} \qquad (5.2.20)$$

where λ is a single unknown parameter. We shall exclude the
special case in which $\lambda = 0$, for then $w_0 = 1$, all other weights are zero
and, effectively, there is no lag distribution. For any other value of λ,
the sequence of weights is assumed to continue indefinitely and, to
ensure that the weights are positive and steadily declining, λ must be
positive and less than 1. Under these conditions, the *infinite series*

$$1 + \lambda + \lambda^2 + \ldots$$

converges to the value $1/(1 - \lambda)$. By including the term $(1 - \lambda)$ in
each of the weights, we define a set of weights which do add to 1.

The implication of the lag distribution shown in (5.2.20) is that the
current value of Y is determined by *all* past values of X, going back
indefinitely. As an original hypothesis, this seems to be rather bizarre
and a better approach might be to argue that (5.2.20) is an approximation to a finite lag distribution. As such, it could obviously be
useful, because the unknown weights are expressed in terms of a *single*
unknown parameter and, given that λ is less than 1, the weights do
become *close* to zero as the lag length is increased. If the response
coefficients are constrained to follow the infinite lag distribution, we
would have

$$\beta_0 = \beta(1 - \lambda); \beta_1 = \beta(1 - \lambda)\lambda; \beta_2 = \beta(1 - \lambda)\lambda^2 ; \text{ etc.}$$

As before, β is a single parameter measuring the total or long-run
response. The distributed lag model could then be written as

$$Y_t = \beta(1 - \lambda)[X_t + \lambda X_{t-1} + \lambda^2 X_{t-2} + \ldots] + u_t; t = 1, 2, \ldots, n$$
$$\qquad (5.2.21)$$

The deterministic part of (5.2.21) involves just two parameters
but, given that λ is unknown, (5.2.21) is certainly not in the standard
form for a linear model. The parameter λ actually enters the model
in a highly nonlinear fashion. Moreover, a strict interpretation of the
infinite lag distribution means that the data requirement would be an
infinitely long run of past values of X. As a matter of fact, neither of

these problems is insurmountable. One can treat the values of X for which no observations are available as a type of nuisance effect, for which an allowance can be made: and it is possible to solve nonlinear problems by iterative methods. But the approach that has been most widely used in practice is based on a transformation of (5.2.21).

The transformation is actually that which is used in the case of an autoregressive disturbance scheme: its use in the present context was pioneered by L. M. Koyck and it is often described as the *Koyck* transformation. Equation (5.2.21) implies that we can write

$$Y_{t-1} = \beta(1 - \lambda)[X_{t-1} + \lambda X_{t-2} + \dots] + u_{t-1}; t = 2, 3, \dots, n$$
(5.2.22)

and

$$\lambda Y_{t-1} = \beta(1 - \lambda)[\lambda X_{t-1} + \lambda^2 X_{t-2} + \dots] + \lambda u_{t-1}; t = 2, 3, \dots, n$$
(5.2.23)

The subtraction of (5.2.23) from (5.2.21) gives

$$(Y_t - \lambda Y_{t-1}) = \beta(1 - \lambda)X_t + (u_t - \lambda u_{t-1}); t = 2, 3, \dots, n \quad (5.2.24)$$

All other terms cancel out and a final rearrangement gives

$$Y_t = \lambda Y_{t-1} + \beta(1 - \lambda)X_t + (u_t - \lambda u_{t-1}); t = 2, 3, \dots, n \quad (5.2.25)$$

In principle, we could treat Y_{t-1} and $X_t; t = 2, 3, \dots, n$, as explanatory variable observations, associated with parameters

$$\beta_1^* = \lambda; \beta_2^* = \beta(1 - \lambda)$$

A regression run on (5.2.25) would then provide estimates of β_1^* and β_2^*, from which estimates of λ and β could be obtained. But one of the explanatory variables is actually a lagged endogenous variable and the disturbances in the transformed model follow a moving average scheme. As we shall see in the next section, the use of OLS under these conditions leads to estimators which can be seriously biased. We could, of course, take steps to correct for the moving average disturbances: but to do this, we would actually have to transform *back* to (5.2.21). The one advantage of the Koyck transformation, followed by OLS estimation applied to the transformed model, is the relative simplicity of the calculation and this is the historical reason for the widespread use of the method. But the apparent simplicity does have a cost. Apart from anything else, the shape of the lag distribution is severely constrained and, whilst it is possible to use alternative forms of infinite lag, the application of a Koyck type transformation will still produce a combination of lagged endogenous variables and moving average disturbances.

5.3 Dynamic Economic Models: Estimation

The first order autoregressive process

$$Y_t = \beta Y_{t-1} + u_t; t = 1, 2, \ldots, n \qquad (5.3.1)$$

is a special case, but it does serve to illustrate the nature of the estimation problem in a dynamic model. Initially, it is assumed that the disturbances $u_t; t = 1, 2, \ldots, n$ are *serially independent*, with zero means and constant variance. Since the model explicitly involves the observations $Y_t; t = 1, 2, \ldots, n$ *and* the starting value Y_0, it is assumed that all $(n + 1)$ observations on Y are available. If this is the case then, given that there is no intercept in (5.3.1), the OLS estimator for β would be

$$\hat{\beta} = \sum_{t=1}^{t=n} Y_{t-1} Y_t \bigg/ \sum_{t=1}^{t=n} Y_{t-1}^2 \qquad (5.3.2)$$

Having established the range of summation in (5.3.2), the range is excluded from subsequent statements.

To investigate the properties of the estimator, it is necessary to consider the nature of the random variation in $\hat{\beta}$. If equation (5.2.1) is used to substitute for Y_t, (5.3.2) can be written as

$$\hat{\beta} = \frac{\Sigma Y_{t-1}(\beta Y_{t-1} + u_t)}{\Sigma Y_{t-1}^2} = \frac{\beta \Sigma Y_{t-1}^2}{\Sigma Y_{t-1}^2} + \frac{\Sigma Y_{t-1} u_t}{\Sigma Y_{t-1}^2}$$

or

$$\hat{\beta} = \beta + \Sigma Y_{t-1} u_t / \Sigma Y_{t-1}^2 \qquad (5.3.3)$$

The corresponding equation for the model

$$Y_t = \beta X_t + u_t \qquad (5.3.4)$$

is

$$\hat{\beta} = \beta + \Sigma X_t u_t / \Sigma X_t^2 \qquad (5.3.5)$$

Notice that (5.3.5) is slightly different from the expression used in Section 2.3. In that case, the algebra is complicated by the presence of an intercept term, the effect of which is that the observations on X appear in *deviation* form. Although the models used in practice do generally contain an intercept, it is possible to explain the essential point of our argument by comparing equations (5.3.3) and (5.3.5).

At this stage, it is necessary to recall the arguments used in Section 2.3. If the explanatory variable observations in (5.3.4) are considered to be non-random, the assumption of zero expectation for the disturbance distributions leads directly to the result that the random term

$$\Sigma X_t u_t / \Sigma X_t^2 \qquad (5.3.6)$$

has an expectation equal to zero. Then, in Section 2.7, it was suggested that one could obtain the same result if the explanatory variable observations are considered to be random, so long as each $X_t; t = 1, 2, \ldots, n$ is distributed independently of *all* disturbances $u_t; t = 1, 2, \ldots, n$. In either case, the implication is that the OLS estimator is unbiased.

Now consider the autoregressive model. The explanatory variable observations are $Y_{t-1}; t = 1, 2, \ldots, n$ and, with the possible exception of Y_0, these are random variables which are *not* completely independent of the disturbances. This follows directly from (5.3.1) but, to avoid any confusion with the time subscripts, we take $t = 3$ as an example of one particular time period. According to (5.3.1)

$$Y_3 = \beta Y_2 + u_3$$

but

$$Y_2 = \beta Y_1 + u_2$$

and

$$Y_1 = \beta Y_0 + u_1$$

Combining these equations, we have

$$Y_3 = \beta(\beta Y_1 + u_2) + u_3$$
$$= \beta[\beta(\beta Y_0 + u_1) + u_2] + u_3$$

or

$$Y_3 = \beta^3 Y_0 + \beta^2 u_1 + \beta u_2 + u_3 \qquad (5.3.7)$$

This shows that Y_3 depends on u_3 and on all earlier disturbances. If β lies between -1 and $+1$, without reaching either extreme value, the contribution of earlier disturbances diminishes as the time lag is increased, but it cannot be assumed that Y_3 is independent of *any* of the disturbances on the right of (5.3.7). On the other hand, it *would* be possible to assume that Y_3 is independent of all *future* disturbances, *so long as the disturbances are serially independent.* Under this last condition, we can say that, in general, Y_t is independent of u_{t+1}, $u_{t+2}, \ldots$, or that Y_{t-1} is independent of $u_t, u_{t+1}, \ldots$. The importance of the independence assumption, in considering the product of two random variables, is that, given independence, the expectation of the product is the product of the expectations. Again, this was explained in Section 2.7. If Y_{t-1} is independent of u_t, the expectation of the term $(Y_{t-1}u_t)$ would also be zero and, if the independence condition holds for *all* pairs, Y_{t-1}, u_t; $t = 1, 2, \ldots, n$, the expectation of the sum, $\Sigma Y_{t-1}u_t$, would be zero. This is an important result, but it does not imply that the expectation of

$$\Sigma Y_{t-1} u_t / \Sigma Y_{t-1}^2 \qquad (5.3.8)$$

is zero. If we rearrange slightly, (5.3.8) can be written as

$$\Sigma (Y_{t-1}/\Sigma Y_{t-1}^2) u_t$$

or

$$\Sigma w_t u_t \qquad (5.3.9)$$

where

$$w_t = Y_{t-1}/\Sigma Y_{t-1}^2 ; t = 1, 2, \ldots, n$$

Each term in (5.3.9) is the product of a disturbance u_t and a weight, w_t. But it is *not* true that w_t is independent of u_t, because the weight involves ΣY_{t-1}^2, which includes *all* observations on Y (except for Y_n). The result is that (5.3.8) does *not* generally have an expectation equal to zero and, in the autoregressive model, the estimator $\hat{\beta}$ *is* generally biased.

Given that the origin of the bias lies in the connection between each disturbance, u_t, and some of the terms in ΣY_{t-1}^2, we now consider what would happen if the number of observations, n, is large. Again, it is convenient to look at a particular disturbance term. A given disturbance, say u_3, would influence Y_3 and, indirectly, $Y_4, Y_5, \ldots$, but, so long as β lies between -1 and $+1$, without reaching either extreme value, the influence of u_3 would diminish over time. If n is very large, those values of Y which are strongly influenced by u_3 make a relatively unimportant contribution to the sum ΣY_{t-1}^2 and hence, to the weight w_3. In the limit, the contribution is negligible. This argument is merely indicative, but it does suggest the asymptotic property of *consistency*. So long as the dynamic model satisfies *stability* conditions, represented here by the restriction on the value of β, it *is* possible to prove consistency. But the argument does depend on the assumption that the disturbances are serially independent.

There is in fact no practical method of estimation which gives unbiased estimators of the parameters of a model containing one or more lagged endogenous variables. In this situation, the question of estimator choice is often resolved by looking at asymptotic properties. Consistency is one such property and, as a rough approximation, we can take this to suggest that, when the number of observations is large, the bias inherent in the OLS estimator is small. The other property which is relevant to estimator choice is the asymptotic variance: again, this does have a precise technical definition, but the asymptotic variance can be taken to be indicative of the true variance of the estimator, so long as the number of observations is relatively large. In choosing between two consistent estimators, one would tend to use the one with the smallest asymptotic variance. On this basis, OLS is an acceptable method of estimation for the parameters of a model involving a lagged endogenous variable and serially independent disturbances.

If OLS is used then, *in terms of the actual calculation performed*, there is no difference between a model involving a lagged endogenous variable and one that does not. In the particular case of the simple autoregressive model, shown in (5.3.1), the estimator for $\hat{\beta}$ would be that shown in (5.3.2) and the assumed form for the variance would be

$$\text{var}(\hat{\beta}) = \sigma^2 / \Sigma Y_{t-1}^2 \qquad (5.3.10)$$

Equation (5.3.10) follows from treating the lagged endogenous variable exactly like any other single explanatory variable in an OLS regression calculation, but it also happens to be exactly the form suggested by the *asymptotic* variance. Moreover, it can be shown that the distribution of $\hat{\beta}$ is approximately normal, for large values of n. In short, we can say that our usual procedures do represent a valid approximation, so long as the number of observations is large. But it is also of interest to know what would happen when n is small. A limited number of analytic results are available and these suggest that, if β is positive, the OLS estimator tends to systematically *underestimate* the true value. Beyond this, the analysis does become difficult and an alternative source of information is that taken from *simulation* experiments.

In Chapter 2, the nature of an estimator was explained by considering what would happen if the estimation could be repeated for different sets of disturbance values. Using a computer, it is actually possible to generate a number of different sets of artificial disturbances, in such a way that the values look as though they *could* have been generated from independent normal distributions, with zero means and constant variance. Alternatively, some other pattern of disturbance behaviour could be imposed.

Suppose now that we wished to investigate the properties of the OLS estimator, under the conditions of the simple auto-regressive model (5.3.1). For given values of Y_0 and β, a single set of disturbances can be used to produce an artificial set of observations $Y_t; t = 1, 2, \ldots, n$. The procedure would be to use Y_0 and u_1 to generate Y_1, Y_1 and u_2 to generate Y_2, and so on

$$Y_1 = \beta Y_0 + u_1, \ Y_2 = \beta Y_1 + u_2, \ldots, \ Y_n = \beta Y_{n-1} + u_n$$

Then a regression of Y_t on Y_{t-1} would produce a single estimate of β, that is, a single value for $\hat{\beta}$. The process of using one set of artificial disturbances, to generate one set of observations and a single value for $\hat{\beta}$, is described as one *trial*. If the process is repeated for each different set of disturbance values, the result would be a whole set of different values for the estimator $\hat{\beta}$. This would constitute a single *experiment*, involving a certain number of trials. But the true value, β, is chosen by the investigator and so it is possible to look at the way in which the estimates are spread around the true value. For a reasonably large number of trials, say 50 or more, the shape of the experimental spread of $\hat{\beta}$ values should be a reasonably good approximation to the shape of the probability distribution of $\hat{\beta}$. This distribution corresponds to a single *true* value of β and so the entire experiment would now be repeated for different values of β. In the case of the simple auto-regressive model, one might use the sequence of values: -0.8, -0.6, -0.4, -0.2, 0, 0.2, 0.4, 0.6, 0.8. Having tried all these experiments, one would have a reasonably good indication of the behaviour of $\hat{\beta}$ under the specified disturbance conditions. Notice that one might also wish to vary the number of observations, n, and this would require further sets of experiments.

Simulation is expensive in terms of computer time but, if the analysis of estimator properties is difficult, simulation does at least give some indication as to how an estimator would behave under certain specified conditions. The use of simulation is not limited to cases in which the number of observations is small: it can also provide a check on whether the asymptotic properties give a reliable indication of estimator behaviour when the number of observations is large. Experiments which have been carried out on the autoregressive model do tend to confirm the analytic results. If the disturbances are serially independent, there is a bias for small values of n, but the bias tends to disappear as the value of n is increased.

The assumption of serial independence is clearly important to the arguments laid out above and we now consider the case in which the disturbances are serially correlated. Again, we shall use the simple autoregressive model for the behaviour of the endogenous variable, but it is now convenient to use $v_t; t = 1, 2, \ldots, n$ to represent the disturbances. This provides a distinction between

$$Y_t = \beta Y_{t-1} + v_t; t = 1, 2, \ldots, n \tag{5.3.11}$$

in which it is assumed that the disturbances are serially correlated and the model shown in (5.3.1), in which it is assumed that the disturbances are serially independent. If we continue to use $u_t; t = 1, 2, \ldots, n$ to represent a set of *independent* random variables, a first order autoregressive process for the disturbances to (5.3.11) can be written as

$$v_t = \rho v_{t-1} + u_t; t = 1, 2, \ldots, n \tag{5.3.12}$$

If this scheme is used, the model consists of *two* autoregressive processes, one for the endogenous variable and one for the disturbances. The other prototype form for serial correlation is the moving-average scheme

$$v_t = u_t - \lambda u_{t-1}; t = 1, 2, \ldots, n \tag{5.3.13}$$

Now consider the properties of the OLS estimator for β, in the presence of either of these forms of serial correlation of the disturbances. Equation (5.3.3) must be modified to allow for the use of $v_t; t = 1, 2, \ldots, n$ in place of $u_t; t = 1, 2, \ldots, n$ and this gives

$$\hat{\beta} = \beta + \Sigma Y_{t-1} v_t / \Sigma Y_{t-1}^2 \tag{5.3.14}$$

If it were true that v_t and Y_{t-1} were independent, for all values of t, our earlier arguments would suggest the consistency of $\hat{\beta}$. Indeed, it is possible to relax the independence assumption, without *necessarily* destroying the consistency property. But in this case, there is a definite linkage between the behaviour of v_t and Y_{t-1} and, with either pattern of serial correlation, it can be shown that $\hat{\beta}$ is *inconsistent*. We shall sketch out the linkage between v_t and Y_{t-1}, using one particular time period to provide an example.

If the disturbances follow the autoregressive form (5.3.12), with a positive value of ρ, a positive value of the disturbance v_2 would *tend* to lead to a positive value of v_3. Furthermore, it can be seen from (5.3.11) that a positive value of v_2, would *tend* to produce a positive value for Y_2, or at least a value that is 'less negative' than it would otherwise have been. This indicates that there is a *tendency* for positive values of Y_2 to occur with positive values of v_3. Had we started from a negative value of v_2, the result would have been a *negative* value for v_3. The argument is decidedly crude, but, it does suggest a *tendency* for the pairs $Y_{t-1}, v_t; t = 1, 2, \ldots, n$, to have the same sign: so the terms in $\Sigma Y_{t-1} v_t$ would tend to be positive, giving a positive value for the sum. The sum of squares, ΣY_{t-1}^2, is also positive, and so the tendency is for the entire random term

$$\Sigma Y_{t-1} v_t / \Sigma Y_{t-1}^2 \qquad (5.3.15)$$

to take a positive value.

If this argument is to be used to determine the probable sign of (5.3.15), it is important that the influence of individual terms in *both* autoregressive processes should diminish over time and there is an implicit assumption that both β and ρ lie between -1 and $+1$, without reaching either extreme value. Given this condition, it can indeed be shown that the inconsistency of $\hat{\beta}$ follows the pattern suggested by our argument. If ρ is positive, the *probability limit* of (5.3.15) is positive and the probability limit of $\hat{\beta}$ is *greater* than the true value. If ρ is negative, the probability limit of $\hat{\beta}$ is *less* than the true value. The extent of the inconsistency depends on the true values of β and ρ but, under the conditions stated above, the *sign* of the inconsistency depends only on the *sign* of ρ.

The inconsistency of $\hat{\beta}$ suggests that there is a bias in the OLS estimation of β and that this bias does *not* disappear as the number of observations is increased. Both the asymptotic theory and the results of simulation experiments lead to the conclusion that this bias can be relatively serious. The direction of the inconsistency also suggests that the direction of the bias depends on the sign of ρ, so that if ρ is positive, the bias is positive and $\hat{\beta}$ tends to *overestimate* the true value, β. This is reversed if ρ is negative. The inconsistency of $\hat{\beta}$ is a significant theoretical disadvantage of the OLS estimator, but the important practical implication is that, for any number of observations, there is likely to be a bias which can be relatively large.

If the serial correlation of disturbances follows the moving average scheme shown in (5.3.13), one can use a similar argument to suggest that $\hat{\beta}$ will again be inconsistent. A positive value for λ suggests a *negative* inconsistency, that is, the probability limit of $\hat{\beta}$ will be *less* than the true value. This is not surprising, since a positive value of λ implies *negative* serial correlation between successive pairs of disturbances, $v_t, v_{t-1}; t = 2, 3, \ldots, n$.

Given the inconsistency of the OLS estimator, there is now an incentive to look for alternative methods of estimation. The methods proposed divide roughly into two groups and those in the first group are based on the use of *instrumental variables*. Consider an estimator denoted as $\hat{\beta}_I$ and defined by:

$$\hat{\beta}_I = \Sigma Z_t Y_t / \Sigma Z_t Y_{t-1} \tag{5.3.16}$$

where Z_t; $t = 1, 2, \ldots, n$ represents a set of observations on a new variable, Z. As yet, no justification is offered for the introduction of Z: we simply want to consider the implications of using an estimator in the form of (5.3.16). This is an instrumental variable (IV) estimator and Z represents an instrumental variable.

By analogy with our earlier examples, we can use (5.3.11) to substitute for Y_t and (5.3.16) becomes

$$\hat{\beta}_I = \frac{\Sigma Z_t (\beta Y_{t-1} + v_t)}{\Sigma Z_t Y_{t-1}} = \frac{\beta \Sigma Z_t Y_{t-1}}{\Sigma Z_t Y_{t-1}} + \frac{\Sigma Z_t v_t}{\Sigma Z_t Y_{t-1}}$$

or

$$\hat{\beta}_I = \beta + \Sigma Z_t v_t / \Sigma Z_t Y_{t-1} \tag{5.3.17}$$

The inconsistency of the OLS estimator stems from the fact that there is a linkage between the values taken by Y_{t-1} and those taken by v_t, for any value of t. In the case of the IV estimator, the relevant question is whether Z_t and v_t are linked in a similar fashion. The answer is that Z would be chosen so as to *avoid* the problems inherent in OLS estimation: but we cannot actually justify the use of Z in the context of the simple autoregressive model. Having used (5.3.16) to show the *form* of the IV estimator, without the complication of further explanatory variables, we now move on to consider how one might use the IV method in practice. To do this, it is necessary to introduce a more realistic example.

Consider the model

$$Y_t = \beta_1 Y_{t-1} + \beta_2 X_t + v_t; t = 1, 2, \ldots, n \tag{5.3.18}$$

where X is an exogenous variable. This is the simplest form that is likely to be used as the basis for an economic model: in the previous example, nothing was said about the linkage between different *economic* variables. Given that there are now *two* explanatory variables, the expressions for both the OLS and IV estimators would change, but the essential characteristics are those revealed by the earlier example. Equation (5.3.16) does show that the IV method involves the partial replacement of the observations Y_{t-1}; $t = 1, 2, \ldots, n$ by the observations Z_t; $t = 1, 2, \ldots, n$. It is a partial replacement in the sense that Y_{t-1} still appears in the formula for the IV estimator. To the extent that Z is to serve as a proxy for the lagged endogenous variable, it is important to find instrumental variable observations that do move fairly closely in step with those on the lagged endogenous variable. But equally, it is important that Z should be chosen to ensure the consistency of the IV estimators and this requires that Z_t should be independent of v_t, or should at least satisfy some weaker criterion that will lead to consistency. One possibility is to make use of an *exogenous* variable, for then the observations on Z can be considered to be non-random. Because the lagged endogenous variable still appears in the random term of an expression like (5.3.17), the IV method does not lead to unbiased estimation, but the use of an exogenous variable will generally ensure consistency. So what we need is an exogenous variable, which does, as far as possible, replicate the behaviour of the lagged endogenous variable.

In (5.3.18), X is the only exogenous variable and the behaviour of Y depends, in part, on the behaviour of X. In particular, the values taken by Y_{t-1}; $t = 2, 3, \ldots, n$, are partially determined by the values X_{t-1}; $t = 2, 3, \ldots, n$. So we might use the lagged *exogenous* variable as an instrument for the lagged *endogenous* variable which means that

$$Z_t = X_{t-1}; t = 1, 2, \ldots, n \qquad (5.3.19)$$

To make use of the full number of observations covered by the model, we do need one extra observation on X, namely X_0.

Although the IV method gives consistent estimators, other properties depend on how closely the behaviour of the endogenous variable follows that of the exogenous variable. There are several clues which suggest that the variance of the IV estimators might be relatively high and the results of simulation experiments tend to confirm this. But the only analytic result that can be established under fairly general conditions is that the asymptotic variances are higher than those obtained by an alternative method which we shall shortly consider. This is not surprising, since the IV procedure does not involve any attempt to correct for the disturbance problem, in the sense of transforming the model to obtain well-behaved disturbances. The sole motivation for using the IV approach is to obtain consistency: but, by analogy with the use of GLS for pure serial correlation, there ought to be a possible gain of efficiency from using a transformation to produce serially independent disturbances. This leads us to the second group of estimation methods.

If the necessary disturbance parameters were known, it *would* be possible to transform the model, so as to remove the disturbance problem. The use of OLS on the transformed model would then be equivalent to the use of GLS on the original model. Even though the transformed model may still contain lagged endogenous variables, there would no longer be serial correlation of the disturbances and, in principle, this approach should give consistent estimators. The difficulty that arises in practice is that the disturbance parameters are not known.

One might then think in terms of using a two-step procedure of the kind described in the previous chapter. Consider the model shown in (5.3.18) and suppose that the disturbances follow the autoregressive scheme in (5.3.12). In principle, one could estimate ρ from the residuals to an OLS regression run on (5.3.18) and this estimate could be used to transform the model. But given the problems inherent in the OLS estimation of β_1 and β_2, it is unlikely that the estimate of ρ would be satisfactory. If a two-step procedure is used, the first step should consist of IV estimation of β_1 and β_2: the IV estimates would be used to compute the residuals and the procedure could then continue as before. The purpose of the second step would be to try to increase the efficiency of estimation, that is, to reduce the estimator variances.

As a final possibility, we consider a nonlinear method which is analogous to the procedures described at the end of Section 4.5. Instead of trying to carry out the transformation with a preliminary estimate of ρ, the problem can be specified in such a way that β_1, β_2 and ρ are to be estimated simultaneously. The usual framework for this approach is that of maximum likelihood estimation and, under certain conditions, the ML estimators are consistent and asymptotically efficient, that is, the asymptotic variances are as small as possible. A similar approach can be used when the disturbances follow a moving average process. The technical details of these methods are beyond the scope of this book, but the *principle* of transforming the model to remove the disturbance problem can be understood. The reader should at least appreciate the significance of any reference to ML methods in the context of a model involving a lagged endogenous variable and serially correlated disturbances.

We have not given sufficient detail for either the IV method or the ML method to be used and, in any case, both methods do generally require the use of additional computer programs. Because of this, one might decide to use OLS estimation, despite the known disadvantages of doing so. In this situation, one must at least appreciate that the estimators are likely to be biased and that the bias can be serious. The

one encouraging result to emerge from simulation experiments is that
the presence of additional exogenous variables does tend to reduce the
bias. This may offer some small consolation if OLS has to be used.

One final problem is that the investigator may not be aware of
the presence of serial correlation. In principle, one could employ the
Durbin-Watson test but, unfortunately, the assumptions underlying the
test procedure are no longer valid and the value of the test statistic is
not a reliable indicator of the disturbance behaviour. Specifically, one
cannot assume that a value in the region around 2 indicates independence
of the disturbances, as is the case in the absence of a lagged endogenous
variable. There is actually an alternative test, proposed by James Durbin,
which is based once more on asymptotic theory: we simply state the
procedure for this test, without offering a justification. The test statistic
can be computed as

$$h = (1 - 0.5d) \sqrt{\frac{n}{(1 - n\mathrm{var}(\hat{\beta}_1))}} \qquad (5.3.20)$$

where d is the Durbin-Watson statistic, n is the number of observations
and $\mathrm{var}(\hat{\beta}_1)$ is the estimate of the variance of coefficient of Y_{t-1},
obtained from a *standard OLS calculation*, applied to the original model.
Under the null hypothesis of serial independence of the disturbances,
the statistic, h, has an *asymptotic* normal distribution and, following the
principle of the original Durbin-Watson test, a *one-tailed* procedure is
used. For a 0·05 probability of type I error and for the alternative of
positive serial correlation, the critical value would be 1·64 (in place of
1·96, the value appropriate to a *two-tailed* test). If h is greater than
1·64, the null hypothesis of serial independence is rejected in favour of
the alternative of positive serial correlation. If the alternative is
negative serial correlation, a value *less* than −1·64 would lead to
rejection of the null hypothesis. Since the test is based on the asymptotic distribution of (5.3.20), the assumed probabilities of error are
purely nominal and, for a relatively small number of observations, the
behaviour of the test statistic is uncertain. So, in the presence of a
lagged endogenous variable, it may be very difficult to establish
whether there is also the additional problem of serial correlation of
the disturbances. In general, it is likely that these problems do tend
to go together and, given the difficulties associated with the test of
serial independence, it is often safer to assume that the disturbances
are serially correlated.

5.4 Alternative Dynamic Hypotheses

In the previous sections of this chapter, we have seen two ways in which one can arrive at a specification involving a lagged endogenous variable. One might choose such a hypothesis directly: alternatively, it could arise as a result of the Koyck transformation applied to a model with an infinite distributed lag. The lag model is

$$Y_t = \beta(1-\lambda)[X_t + \lambda X_{t-1} + \lambda^2 X_{t-2} + \dots] + u_t; t = 1, 2, \dots, n$$

$$(5.4.1)$$

and, after transformation, we obtain

$$Y_t = \lambda Y_{t-1} + \beta(1-\lambda)X_t + (u_t - \lambda u_{t-1}); t = 2, 3, \dots, n \qquad (5.4.2)$$

The equivalence between these forms is instructive. It is not immediately obvious that a model with an *infinite* distributed lag is, within our definition, a dynamic model. But it is certainly possible to transform so as to obtain an equation involving a lagged endogenous variable and, ignoring the random disturbances, (5.4.1) *could* generate a time path in which each value Y_t; $t = 1, 2, \dots, n$ is different, without there being any change in the values of X between periods $t = 1$ and $t = n$. This happens because Y reacts to *all* past values of X and any changes in X *prior* to period $t = 1$ would have some effect, however small, on the values Y_t; $t = 1, 2, \dots, n$. So the hypothesis of an infinite distributed lag is at least equivalent to a dynamic model and (5.4.1) does imply that the current behaviour of the endogenous variable is linked to the immediate past value of that variable. Equally, the direct specification implies that the current value of the endogenous variable is determined by past values of any *exogenous* variables that are present. If the model is

$$Y_t = \beta_1 Y_{t-1} + \beta_2 X_t + v_t; t = 1, 2, \dots, n \qquad (5.4.3)$$

then, starting at period $t = 1$, we have

$$Y_1 = \beta_1 Y_0 + \beta_2 X_1 + v_1$$

$$Y_2 = \beta_1 Y_1 + \beta_2 X_2 + v_2$$

$$= \beta_1(\beta_1 Y_0 + \beta_2 X_1 + v_1) + \beta_2 X_2 + v_2$$

$$= \beta_2(X_2 + \beta_1 X_1) + \beta_1^2 Y_0 + (v_2 + \beta_1 v_1)$$

The general form for this expression would be

$$Y_t = \beta_2[X_t + \beta_1 X_{t-1} + \dots + \beta_1^{t-1} X_1] + \beta_1^t Y_0 + \text{disturbance terms}$$

$$(5.4.4)$$

Given that the parameters are *unknown*, the only formal difference
between this and (5.4.1) lies in the treatment of the observations
immediately prior to $t = 1$ and, possibly, in the behaviour of the
disturbance terms. The infinite lag model would relate Y_t to *all* past
values of X: in (5.4.4) we have a term in the starting value, Y_0, and the
model does not state explicitly that Y_0 could be replaced by an
expression involving values of X prior to period $t = 1$. But, just as
(5.4.1) can generate a model which is *similar* to (5.4.3), so (5.4.3) can
generate a model which is similar to (5.4.1). Indeed, we can strengthen
this conclusion to say that, under certain conditions, the two forms of
model may be *observationally equivalent*. To see what this means,
consider a specific example.

Suppose that two investigators decide to examine the behaviour of
consumers' expenditure (C) and that the first postulates an infinite lag
reaction to present and past values of disposable income (D), whilst the
other specifies a model in which consumers' expenditure is linked to
the present value of disposable income and to the immediate past value
of consumers' expenditure. Then suppose that the first investigator
transforms his model, to give a specification equivalent to (5.4.2)

$$C_t = \lambda C_{t-1} + \beta(1 - \lambda)D_t + (u_t - \lambda u_{t-1}); t = 1, 2, \dots, n \qquad (5.4.5)$$

The second investigator would write directly

$$C_t = \beta_1 C_{t-1} + \beta_2 D_t + v_t; t = 1, 2, \dots, n \qquad (5.4.6)$$

For convenience, we have assumed that both investigators have the
same set of observations, including C_0. Finally suppose that both
proceed to estimate their respective models and, finding a reasonably
good fit, both claim to have an acceptable theory of consumers'
behaviour, during the period of time to which the models refer. Let
us examine this proposition.

First note that no amount of econometric analysis can *prove*
the validity of a given theory. The best that one can do is to find that
the observed behaviour in the real system does correspond to the
predictions of the theory. Similarly, when faced with the choice
between alternative theories, there is no way of *proving* that one
theory is correct. Each theory gives rise to a formal specification and
it is the formal specifications that are tested. If the specifications are
distinct, one may be able to accumulate evidence in favour of one
theory as opposed to the other. There is no question of proof and the
quality of the discrimination depends on the extent of the difference
between the alternatives and on the statistical properties of the

methods used. The other possibility is that the specifications are formally equivalent, in which case there is no question of discriminating between alternatives, despite the fact that the investigators may have different beliefs as to the economic behaviour underlying the formal specification. Ideally, these beliefs should be made explicit and should be part of the model that is tested but, as we shall see, this is not always possible.

In our example, the two models can only be distinguished if there is *known* to be some formal difference between them. If the theory giving rise to (5.4.6) requires that the disturbances $v_t; t = 1, 2, \ldots, n$ should be serially independent then, given that the disturbances to (5.4.5) follow a moving average scheme, a formal distinction would exist. There is then the separate question of whether a test procedure, based on a given set of data, can offer satisfactory discrimination in practice. In our example this is unlikely, given the problems of testing for serial correlation in the presence of a lagged endogenous variable. So, if the investigators do have different ideas as to the underlying economic behaviour, there is little chance of being able to make a choice between the two possibilities, either because the formal models are *exactly* equivalent or, alternatively, because it is difficult to choose between similar but formally distinct models on the basis of the given data. To complete the discussion, we look at some possible forms for the underlying economic behaviour.

The first example is the *partial adjustment* hypothesis. In the context of the consumption–income relationship, the argument would be that there exists some *desired* level of consumption, which is determined by the current value of disposable income. For a variety of reasons, it may be impossible to adjust the actual value of C to the desired value, within a single time period. It is then necessary to add a second hypothesis about the way in which the actual value *is* adjusted. For example, one might assume that the desired value, C^*, is determined as

$$C_t^* = \beta D_t; t = 1, 2, \ldots, n \tag{5.4.7}$$

and that the actual adjustment between periods is some proportion of the desired adjustment

$$(C_t - C_{t-1}) = \delta(C_t^* - C_{t-1}); t = 1, 2, \ldots, n \tag{5.4.8}$$

It is difficult to see how one could possibly expect to observe the behaviour of the variable C^* and so neither of these hypotheses could be tested directly. But (5.4.8) implies that

$$C_t = (1 - \delta)C_{t-1} + \delta C_t^*; t = 1, 2, \ldots, n \tag{5.4.9}$$

and, using (5.4.7) to substitute for C_t^*, this becomes

$$C_t = (1 - \delta)C_{t-1} + \delta\beta D_t; t = 1, 2, \ldots, n \qquad (5.4.10)$$

Equation (5.4.10) involves the same explanatory variables as both (5.4.5) and (5.4.6). As yet there are no disturbances in (5.4.10) but, if disturbance terms were added to either (5.4.7) or (5.4.8) or, for that matter, to both, this would imply a set of disturbances to (5.4.10). Note that there is no particular reason to assume that these would follow a moving average scheme.

A second example is one in which the basic hypothesis involves an explanatory variable that is unobservable. Suppose that the behaviour of consumption is believed to be determined by *permanent* income, excluding any transitory or 'windfall' components. The model for this process might be

$$C_t = \beta D_t^* + u_t; t = 1, 2, \ldots, n \qquad (5.4.11)$$

where D^* represents permanent income. Once again, we have a hypothesis which cannot be tested directly and we need a second hypothesis about the way in which permanent income is derived from measured income. One possibility is to specify that D_t^* is a weighted average of current and past values of D and, in particular, we might have

$$D_t^* = (1 - \lambda) [D_t + \lambda D_{t-1} + \lambda^2 D_{t-2} + \ldots]; t = 1, 2, \ldots, n \qquad (5.4.12)$$

where λ is positive and less than 1. We already know that the weights $(1 - \lambda), (1 - \lambda)\lambda, (1 - \lambda)\lambda^2, \ldots$, do add to 1 and so this *is* a weighted average, including *all* past values, with steadily declining weights. This is, of course, a single possibility, but it does show another way in which one might arrive at our basic dynamic model. If (5.4.12) is used to eliminate D_t^* from (5.4.11), we would obtain the infinite lag model and, indirectly, a model in the form of (5.4.5). In this case the disturbances to the dynamic model would probably follow a moving average process.

A very similar example arises when the behaviour of the dependent variable is determined by the *anticipated* value of one or more explanatory variables. Although one could envisage situations in which consumption is determined by anticipated income, the example is not entirely satisfactory and we revert to a general description in terms of variables Y and X. The model might then be

$$Y_t = \beta X_{t+1}^* + u_t; t = 1, 2, \ldots, n \qquad (5.4.13)$$

where the current value of Y is determined by a prediction of the value that X will take in the following period. Yet again, we have an unobservable variable which has to be eliminated and again, it could be argued that the predictions are formed as a weighted average of known values of X

$$X_{t+1}^* = (1 - \lambda)[X_t + \lambda X_{t-1} + \lambda^2 X_{t-2} + \dots]; t = 1, 2, \dots, n$$
(5.4.14)

With this secondary hypothesis, we obtain a model which, in terms of observable variables, is again equivalent to an infinite lag model and thus, indirectly, to our basic dynamic model. The hypothesis shown in (5.4.14) is sometimes written as

$$(X_{t+1}^* - X_t^*) = (1 - \lambda)(X_t - X_t^*); t = 1, 2, \dots, n$$
(5.4.15)

and the process is described as an *adaptive expectations* hypothesis. We can interpret (5.4.15) as saying that the prediction of the behaviour of X is revised by taking the change in the prediction as some proportion, $(1 - \lambda)$, of the extent to which anticipations are not realized in the current period. Repeated substitution for X_t^*, X_{t-1}^*, etc. will show that (5.4.14) and (5.4.15) are formally equivalent, except possibly for the treatment of the starting value X_1^*. An example of the application of this type of model would be to a hypothesis concerning the relationship between wage claims and *anticipated* changes in the price level. The model would be more elaborate, but the assumed process for the determination of anticipated price changes could well be similar to that used here.

In one sense, it is reassuring to find that there can be several different reasons for using a certain basic type of model, but all that this really does is to justify the time spent on considering problems of estimation that will arise quite frequently. On closer examination, it is disturbing to find that the same derived model can be consistent with several different types of underlying behaviour. Of course, the problem would not arise if we could observe desired, anticipated and permanent versions of the relevant variables: and it would not arise if the theory suggested restrictions which would make one derived model quite different from the rest. But the possibility that there may be alternative justifications for a single formal model must always be borne in mind.

Exercises (Solutions on page 235)

5.1 Derive equation (5.4.14) from equation (5.4.15).

5.2 The partial adjustment and adaptive expectations hypotheses can be combined, as in the following simple model

$$Y_t^* = \beta X_{t+1}^*$$

$$Y_t - Y_{t-1} = \delta(Y_t^* - Y_{t-1}) + u_t$$

$$(X_{t+1}^* - X_t^*) = (1 - \lambda)(X_t - X_t^*); t = 1, 2, \ldots, n$$

where Y_t^* is a desired value and X_{t+1}^* is an anticipated value. Derive an equation which contains only observable variables and point to any problems of estimation associated with this equation.

6 Simultaneous Equation Models

6.1 Introduction

Despite all the modifications discussed in previous chapters, there is still a divergence between the type of statistical model that has been described and the way in which one typically envisages the working of an economic system. In particular, we have been concerned almost exclusively with models suitable for partial analysis, designed to explain the behaviour of a single endogenous variable. In those cases in which we have considered a multiple equation model, all dependent (left hand side) variables have been endogenous and all explanatory (right hand side) variables have been exogenous. But typically, the representation of a complete economic system would involve several equations and the dependent variable in one equation might well appear as an explanatory variable elsewhere. If all dependent variables are taken to be endogenous, we may have an equation with one endogenous variable on the left and other *current* endogenous variables on the right. There are two types of analysis in which this can occur. Obviously, it can happen when the intention is to build a model for the complete system. But it is also relevant to the analysis of a single equation, when it is explicitly recognized that this is taken from a larger model.

As usual, it is possible to explain the essential points of the argument by using an extremely simple example. Consider a representation of the circular flow of income, in which income is allocated between consumption and non-consumption expenditure and in which total income is equal to total expenditure. Let C be consumers' expenditure, Z be non-consumption expenditure and D be total income. The model might then be

$$C_t = \alpha + \beta D_t + u_t; t = 1, 2, \ldots, n \tag{6.1.1}$$

$$D_t = C_t + Z_t; t = 1, 2, \ldots, n \tag{6.1.2}$$

The second equation in this model is somewhat atypical, for it is an *exact* relationship, representing the equality between income and expenditure. This is essentially a convention of accounting at the level of the macro-economy. A relationship of this kind is called an *identity*, to distinguish from a *behavioural relationship*, such as the consumption function.

It is readily apparent that this is a case in which the dependent variable in one equation is an explanatory variable elsewhere in the model. It also seems reasonable to assume that C and D are both endogenous variables: the way in which we have written the equations certainly suggests that the values of C_t and D_t are determined by the operation of the model. But although it may be natural to think of the consumption function as determining consumption and of the identity as determining income, a strict interpretation of the mathematical formulation does not lead to this conclusion. It *is* our intention that C and D should be endogenous variables, but what the model actually says is that *both* equations *together* determine the values of consumption and income. In fact the model consists of a pair of *simultaneous equations* in C_t and D_t.

In any given time period and for any particular values of α and β, Z_t and u_t, there are two linear equations in two unknowns and, since we can safely rule out those cases in which there is no unique solution, the model can be assumed to determine unique values for C_t and D_t. In practice, α, β and u_t would be unknown, but what the model suggests is that the economic system behaves *as though* it were a set of simultaneous equations, which together determine the values of the endogenous variables in each time period. The model used here is not likely to be a sufficiently informative representation for the macro-economy, but the same logic would apply in a more realistic case.

Several questions remain to be answered. Given that the model is supposed to generate values of the endogenous variables by the solution of linear equations, there must be as many equations as there are endogenous variables. This rule determines the *number* of endogenous variables for any given set of equations, but the decision as to *which* variables are to be endogenous is based on economic analysis and not on the mathematics of the model. In modelling a system, the ideal situation is one in which the only variables that are *exogenous* are those that can really be thought of as imposed from outside the system. In the context of the national economy, one might think of variables for which values are determined by policy decision or for which values are 'imported' from abroad. But, given the degree of inter-dependence in both the national and international economic systems, very few variables are truly exogenous and, in practical model-building, some compromise must be reached.

In our example, there are three economic variables, one of which must be treated as exogenous and we have assumed that non-consumption expenditure (Z) would be that variable. Ideally we should like to explain the behaviour of some of the components of non-consumption expenditure but, given the present structure of the model, the most natural choice is to designate Z as exogenous. Actually, this puts the question the wrong way round. We have written down two equations which are intended as a 'theory' of the determination of consumption and income. As a mathematical proposition, there is no reason why one should not argue that the equations determine C_t and Z_t for given values of D_t. But, unless this makes sense in terms of the underlying economics, one would not admit this possibility in interpreting the model. Since Z includes components which would be difficult to explain in terms of other economic variables, notably government expenditure, it is unlikely that we would accept this interpretation. Once again, we have a distinction between the mathematical properties of the model and the assumed behaviour that lies behind the formal specification. Indeed we must make precisely this distinction in considering what a simultaneous model actually represents.

To an observer, taking measurements relating to a certain time period, consumption and income may appear to be determined simultaneously. The underlying process could be envisaged as a continuous loop, in which changes in income lead to changes in consumption, possibly with some delay, and in which changes in consumption generate changes in income by a process that we have subsumed in the accounting identity. If the lags in the process are shorter than the frequency of observation of the data, we have a situation in which consumption and income *do* appear to be determined simultaneously. Although there are implicit directions of causality, these are not made explicit in the formal model.

When a decision has been taken, as to which variables are endogenous, we can adopt the convention of writing an endogenous variable on the left hand side of each equation. It can also be assumed that all exogenous variable observations can be treated as non-random quantities. Having added this assumption, one could still rearrange the equation to write an exogenous variable on the left, but it would be somewhat misleading to do so, for it would violate the convention for understanding what the equation means. But if there are two or more *endogenous* variables in a single equation, there *is* an element of choice as to which variable to write on the left hand side. To see exactly what is meant by this, start with the consumption function as written and follow through the algebraic manipulation necessary to write D on the left of the equation

$$C_t = \alpha + \beta D_t + u_t; t = 1, 2, \ldots, n$$

or

$$-\beta D_t = \alpha - C_t + u_t; t = 1, 2, \ldots, n$$

so that

$$D_t = (-\alpha/\beta) + (1/\beta)C_t + (-u_t/\beta); t = 1, 2, \ldots, n \qquad (6.1.3)$$

This is still a linear equation subject to disturbance, for $(-\alpha/\beta)$ and $(1/\beta)$ represent unknown parameters and $(-u_t/\beta)$ is a random disturbance term. And there is still an endogenous variable on the left. Equation (6.1.3) is written in a particular way because we started from a conventional specification of the consumption function. This does not alter the fact that the equation is

$$D_t = \text{intercept} + (\text{slope} \times C_t) + \text{disturbance} \qquad (6.1.4)$$

which is a perfectly valid formal statement of the hypothesis that C and D are connected by an inexact linear relationship, in a situation in which C and D are both endogeous variables in a simultaneous model.

It is clear from this argument that the decision to write C on the left of the consumption function is, in a formal sense, arbitrary. This does not imply that it is undesirable to write C on the left hand side: on the contrary, since it is natural for an economist to write the consumption function in this way and, since there is freedom of choice, the original formulation is sensible. The point is just that a choice must be made. In each equation of a simultaneous model, one endogenous variable is written on the left. This is known as the *normalization* of the equation.

The reader may, at this stage, have anticipated the problems of estimation in a simultaneous model, given that each equation can contain current values of endogenous variables on the right hand side. We shall consider estimation in Sections 6.4 to 6.6 but, first, there is another aspect of using a simultaneous model, the question of *identification*, to which we now turn.

6.2 Identification

To illustrate the concept of identification we use a simple model of a single market. Let Q^D be quantity demanded, Q^S be quantity supplied and P be price. The model may then be written as

$$Q_t^D = \alpha + \beta P_t + u_t; t = 1, 2, \ldots, n \tag{6.2.1}$$

$$Q_t^S = \gamma + \delta P_t + v_t; t = 1, 2, \ldots, n \tag{6.2.2}$$

where u_t and v_t are both random disturbances. As it stands, this multiple equation model is not simultaneous, because quantity demanded and quantity supplied are quite distinct concepts, represented by two different variables. It is quite possible to think of price as determining each variable separately. It is, however, very unusual to be able to find a way to *observe* quantities demanded and supplied, and what is usually observed is the result of the operation of the market. The simplest assumption is that the market is cleared by the equalization of supply and demand and, in this case, there is a third equation in the model, to represent the identity between Q^S and Q^D. But if the model is to be written using only observable variables, Q^S and Q^D must be eliminated: let Q represent the market clearing quantity and, with the identity implicit, we have

$$Q_t = \alpha + \beta P_t + u_t; t = 1, 2, \ldots, n \tag{6.2.3}$$

$$Q_t = \gamma + \delta P_t + v_t; t = 1, 2, \ldots, n \tag{6.2.4}$$

The model now consists of two relationships between the same two variables, it is clearly simultaneous and it happens to have been normalized by using the same variable on the left of each equation. There are no exogenous variables.

As it stands, the model consists of two observationally equivalent equations. To the investigator, who does not know the true parameter values, the demand and supply relationships have exactly the same form

$$Q_t = \text{intercept} + (\text{slope} \times P_t) + \text{disturbance} \tag{6.2.5}$$

Any attempt to estimate a relationship between quantity and price is utterly futile, because there would be no way of knowing to which set of parameters the estimates refer. There is simply not enough information to *identify* the equation that is estimated. Hence the name given to this phenomenon, the problem of *identification*.

There is one piece of information that has not yet been used. It might be said that if the estimated equation slopes downwards, it is a demand equation and conversely, if it slopes upwards, it is a supply equation. Unfortunately, there are more than two possible lines having the same form as the demand and supply equations. If it is true that

$$Q_t = \alpha + \beta P_t + u_t; t = 1, 2, \ldots, n$$

$$Q_t = \gamma + \delta P_t + v_t; t = 1, 2, \ldots, n$$

then, for any constant value, represented as λ, it must also be true that

$$\lambda Q_t = \lambda\alpha + \lambda\beta P_t + \lambda u_t; t = 1, 2, \ldots, n \qquad (6.2.6)$$

and, for any constant value, represented as μ, that

$$\mu Q_t = \mu\gamma + \mu\delta P_t + \mu v_t; t = 1, 2, \ldots, n \qquad (6.2.7)$$

Again, it must also be true that the sum of (6.2.6) and (6.2.7) represents a valid equation, so that

$$(\lambda + \mu)Q_t = (\lambda\alpha + \mu\gamma) + (\lambda\beta + \mu\delta)P_t + (\lambda u_t + \mu v_t); t = 1, 2, \ldots, n \qquad (6.2.8)$$

or

$$Q_t = \frac{(\lambda\alpha + \mu\gamma)}{(\lambda + \mu)} + \frac{(\lambda\beta + \mu\delta)}{(\lambda + \mu)} P_t + \frac{(\lambda u_t + \mu v_t)}{(\lambda + \mu)}; t = 1, 2, \ldots, n \qquad (6.2.9)$$

This looks complicated but, for *any* particular values of λ and μ, the first term on the right of (6.2.9) would represent an (unknown) intercept, the term attached to P_t would represent an (unknown) slope and the final term would represent a random disturbance. In other words, (6.2.9) is again of the form

$$Q_t = \text{intercept} + (\text{slope} \times P_t) + \text{disturbance} \qquad (6.2.10)$$

If $\lambda = 1$ and $\mu = 0$, (6.2.9) would be the demand equation. If $\lambda = 0$ and $\mu = 1$, it would represent the supply equation. For non-zero values of *both* λ and μ, (6.2.8) would be a *linear combination* of the two equations, with *weights* λ and μ and (6.2.9) would represent the same equation normalized on Q. Depending on the values of λ and μ, equation (6.2.9) might slope up or down. Either way, it is indistinguishable, to the observer, from one or other of the original 'true' relationships. So information on the direction of slope is not sufficient to identify the original equations and, since λ and μ can take any values, the demand and supply equations imply an infinite number of combinations, all indistinguishable, one from another and from the original equations, as far as the observer is concerned.

The model shown in (6.2.3) and (6.2.4) would only be used if the investigator considered it to be appropriate. The extra information about the sign of the slopes is a part of the hypothesis and should be written down with the equations of the model, but once the model is fully defined, it must not be changed simply because the equations cannot be identified. Indeed, the model may still be appropriate, but the lack of identification means that the investigator can neither estimate the parameters nor test to see whether this is the case.

To see that identification depends upon the amount of information available, consider a different example, a model that might be appropriate to the market for a farm product. Suppose that supply depends not only upon price but on an exogenous variable, say rainfall (R). The new model is

$$Q_t^D = \alpha + \beta P_t + u_t; t = 1, 2, \ldots, n \tag{6.2.11}$$

$$Q_t^S = \gamma + \delta P_t + \epsilon R_t + v_t; t = 1, 2, \ldots, n \tag{6.2.12}$$

$$Q_t^S = Q_t^D; t = 1, 2, \ldots, n \tag{6.2.13}$$

Any weighted combination of the supply and demand equations now contains rainfall as a variable, except in the case where the wieght on supply is zero. But this is trivial: it simply gives the demand equation and it is already known that the demand equation does *not* include rainfall. So the demand equation is distinct from supply and all (non-trivial) combinations and is therefore identified, but the supply equation is indistinguishable from the combinations, and is *not* identified. This example shows that one can consider the identification of individual equations, that the presence of exogenous variables in the model aids identification and that it is the information that rainfall does *not* enter the demand equation which leads to identification in that equation.

The formal analysis of identification is rather complex, but it is possible to summarize by saying that, in order to identify a particular equation, it must be possible to show that there is no combination of equations in the model that appears, to the observer, to be indistinguishable from the particular equation in question. It is the *restrictions* on particular equations that provide the information necessary to make the distinction between an equation and possible combinations. There are various types of restriction that may be used. One example is the exclusion of variables from individual equations, the formal restrictions being zero parameter values for those variables in that equation. This form of restriction is used in the example above. Again, the fact that an identity does not have a disturbance and that it has *known* parameters, serves to distinguish an identity from possible combinations. Identities, not surprisingly, are always identified.

As a final example, consider the consumption–income relationship used in the first section of this chapter. It might aid the reader if the equations are written

$$C_t = \alpha + \beta D_t + u_t; t = 1, 2, \ldots, n \qquad (6.2.14)$$

$$C_t = D_t - Z_t; t = 1, 2, \ldots, n \qquad (6.2.15)$$

Any linear combination of the two equations will contain an intercept, a term in Z_t and a disturbance and the combinations are therefore distinct from both the consumption function and the identity. The key fact in distinguishing between the consumption function and combinations is that the consumption function does not contain Z_t. Because of this, there is just enough information to identify the consumption function. The identity can be distinguished either by the known parameter on D_t (the parameter value is 1), the known parameter on Z_t (a value of -1) or the absence of a disturbance. Combinations have none of these characteristics. Formally, the consumption function is said to be *exactly identified*, whereas the identity is *over-identified*, because there is more than enough information available to distinguish it from combinations.

In building a macro-economic model, one is not usually faced with the problem of equations that are not identified. On the contrary, the equations are often over-identified. When a problem of under-identification does arise, it is often because the initial specification of the model involves unobservable variables. The simple example of a single market illustrates this perfectly: if quantity demanded and quantity supplied could be observed directly, there would *not* be an identification problem. But, given that the unobservable variables must be eliminated, we have a model *in observables*, in which neither equation is identified. We have come across a similar problem before, in the context of the single equation dynamic model. This may be derived from a *two* equations in unobservables such as desired or anticipated values and, because the values of these variables cannot be observed, the model has to be reduced to a single equation. Since the derived model *does* only have a single equation, there is no identification problem of the kind described in this section. In the context of a simultaneous equation model, the question is whether each equation in the *observable* version of the model can be identified. But, at another level, there is the very similar question of whether an underlying hypothesis can be uniquely identified and this may be a much more difficult question to answer.

6.3 The Reduced Form

A simultaneous equation model is supposed to operate by the solution of equations in the endogenous variables, for given values of the exogenous variables. It is instructive to carry through this solution process algebraically, using the consumption–income model as an example. The model states that

$$C_t = \alpha + \beta D_t + u_t; t = 1, 2, \ldots, n \qquad (6.3.1)$$

$$D_t = C_t + Z_t; t = 1, 2, \ldots, n \qquad (6.3.2)$$

and, if (6.3.2) is used to substitute for D_t in (6.3.1), we obtain

$$C_t = \alpha + \beta(C_t + Z_t) + u_t$$

or

$$(1 - \beta)C_t = \alpha + \beta Z_t + u_t$$

or

$$C_t = \frac{\alpha}{(1 - \beta)} + \frac{\beta}{(1 - \beta)} Z_t + \frac{u_t}{(1 - \beta)} ; t = 1, 2, \ldots, n \qquad (6.3.3)$$

A similar process gives an equation for D_t. Using (6.3.1) to substitute for C_t in (6.3.2)

$$D_t = (\alpha + \beta D_t + u_t) + Z_t$$

or

$$D_t = \frac{\alpha}{(1 - \beta)} + \frac{1}{(1 - \beta)} Z_t + \frac{u_t}{(1 - \beta)}; t = 1, 2, \ldots, n \qquad (6.3.4)$$

By this stage, the reader should be familiar with the idea that terms like $\alpha/(1 - \beta)$, $\beta/(1 - \beta)$ and $1/(1 - \beta)$ merely represent different unknown parameters and that $u_t/(1 - \beta)$ is a random disturbance term. Equation (6.3.3) is therefore a linear relationship, subject to disturbances, between C and Z. Equation (6.3.4) gives a similar relationship for D and Z. What we have done is to express each *endogenous* variable in terms of the *exogenous* variables in the model. In this example, there is only one exogenous variable (apart from the artificial variable that allows for an intercept) but, more generally, any *linear* simultaneous model can be expressed in a similar fashion, to give what is known as the *reduced form*. In this context the requirement is for linearity in the endogenous variables, because it is a set of equations in the endogenous variables that we wish to solve. Nonlinear models do have reduced forms, but it can be difficult to solve the equations explicitly. We shall return to this point later in the discussion.

If the model can be expressed in terms of reduced form equations, it may be thought that the original specification is redundant, but this is not so. When the model is written down in terms of a consumption function, it is presumably because that is the relationship of interest and because it is the parameters of that relationship that we wish to know. It is certainly true that, having written down the original specification, which is called the *structural form*, one can then derive the reduced form as a mathematical construction. Indeed, the reduced form parameters do have a useful interpretation. But the model is a formal representation for linkages which we believe to exist in the real system and we have an interest in isolating the parameters of the relationship which is intended to show how changes in income lead to changes in consumption. It is also interesting to see that the model implies that changes in non-consumption expenditure would lead to changes in consumption, as shown by the reduced form, but our primary purpose is to estimate the parameters of structural form. Incidentally, the exogenous component of expenditure is often described as *autonomous* expenditure: in our model, autonomous expenditure includes all non-consumption expenditure.

The reduced form parameters can be interpreted in the following way. If we take equation (6.3.4) and ignore the random disturbance term, the parameter attached to Z_t measures the effect on income of a unit change in autonomous expenditure. This parameter is $1/(1 - \beta)$, where β is the marginal propensity to consume and, in the terminology of economics, this is a *multiplier*. To be more specific it is the autonomous expenditure multiplier, since it shows the effect on income of a change in autonomous expenditure. In fact we can define a multiplier showing the effect on *any* endogenous variable of a unit change in *any* exogenous variable and the 'true' values of these multipliers are the parameters of the reduced form equations.

So far, it has not been explicitly stated that the *endogenous* variable observations would have to be treated as random variables, although the reader may well have assumed this to be the case. The reduced form equations show that this assumption is correct. If the *exogenous* variable observations are taken to be non-random then, using (6.3.3) as an example, it may be seen that C_t does depend on a random disturbance and, since no other term on the right of (6.3.3) could take up the random variation, it does follow that C_t has a random component. Exactly the same argument applies to D_t. In this particular case, D_t is subject to the *same* random disturbances as C_t. More generally, for any value of t, *each* reduced form disturbance involves *all* the structural form disturbances, but the way in which these are combined differs between the various equations in the reduced form.

We shall refer back to the reduced form at various stages in the discussion which follows, but now, we move on to consider the problems of estimation in a simultaneous model. Before we start, it is worth restating the fact that our concern is with the estimation of the parameters of the *structural* form.

6.4 Estimation: A Single Equation from a Simultaneous Model

The preceding sections of this chapter contain a liberal scattering of clues to the effect that there are some problems of estimation which are due entirely to the use of a simultaneous model. To see exactly what these problems are, we shall start by considering the application of OLS to a single equation which is taken from a simultaneous model and, once again, we can use the consumption–income example to illustrate the argument.

Suppose that we were to apply OLS directly to the consumption function

$$C_t = \alpha + \beta D_t + u_t; t = 1, 2, \ldots, n \qquad (6.4.1)$$

If the observations D_t; $t = 1, 2, \ldots, n$ could be considered to be non-random and if the disturbances were well-behaved, the OLS estimators for α and β would be unbiased. For the moment, we shall assume that the disturbances *are* well-behaved, but the reduced form equations show that the observations on income must be treated as values taken by a set of random variables and, what is more, there exists a direct connection between each observation D_t and the corresponding disturbance u_t. It is possible to analyse the effect on the OLS estimators by using a form of argument that has been employed several times in earlier discussions. Given that there is an intercept in (6.4.1), the OLS estimator for β would be

$$\hat{\beta} = \Sigma d_t c_t / \Sigma d_t^2 \qquad (6.4.2)$$

where c_t, d_t; $t = 1, 2, \ldots, n$ represent observations expressed as deviations from the respective means. The appropriate expression in terms of the random disturbances would be

$$\hat{\beta} = \beta + \Sigma d_t u_t / \Sigma d_t^2 \qquad (6.4.3)$$

In earlier chapters, we have used an expression like (6.4.3) to suggest that a given estimator is unbiased or, failing this, to argue that an estimator might be consistent. But, in one case, that of a single equation dynamic model with serially correlated disturbances, it was possible to construct an argument suggesting that the estimator would *not* be consistent. The essential ingredient of such an argument is the existence

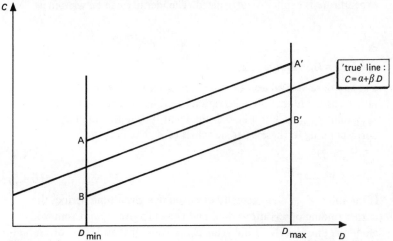

Figure 6.1

of a connection between each observation on one of the 'explanatory' variables and the *corresponding* disturbance term. This is precisely what we have in (6.4.1). So, by analogy, we might reach the tentative conclusion that $\hat{\beta}$ is *not* consistent, given that (6.4.1) is taken from a simultaneous model. Alternatively, we could follow through the type of analysis used in Section 5.3, to make sure that the analogy is appropriate. Our tentative conclusion turns out to be entirely correct. The OLS estimator is not consistent but, in this case, we shall present the argument in a slightly different way.

In a partial analysis, in which it is *not* recognized that the consumption function is taken from a larger model, one could construct a diagram such as that shown in Fig. 6.1. The observations on D *could* be taken to be non-random and one could assume that D can only take values between D_{min} and D_{max}. The lines AA' and BB' are intended to show that, without any connection between the values of D_t and u_t, observed points *must* lie between the lines drawn above D_{min} and D_{max} and are *likely* to lie between the lines AA′ and BB′. So we would have a scatter of points which would tend to fall in the area AA′B′B and, for a relatively large number of observations, the pattern of observed points in the area would tend to approximate to that suggested by the disturbance distributions. The minimization of squared residuals would then give a line which, with high probability, would be close to the true line.

Now consider the case in which the identity between income and expenditure is explicitly recognized. The identity can be written as

$$D_t = C_t + Z_t; t = 1, 2, \ldots, n$$

or as

$$C_t = D_t - Z_t; t = 1, 2, \ldots, n$$

and any observed values of C and D *must* satisfy this equation. It can now be assumed that all observations on Z lie between two points, Z_{min} and Z_{max} and, in Fig. 6.2, the identity is represented by lines corresponding to these extreme values of Z. The lines are

$$C = D - Z_{min} \tag{6.4.4}$$

$$C = D - Z_{max} \tag{6.4.5}$$

If the value Z_{min} were actually observed in a given time period, the corresponding observations on C and D would give a point somewhere along the line (6.4.4). If the value Z_{max} were observed, the corresponding observations on C and D would give a point somewhere along the line (6.4.5). Note that both (6.4.4) and (6.4.5) are 45° lines. All other observed values of C and D must correspond to a point in the area between these two 45° lines.

With the addition of the identity, it is impossible to argue that the area AA′B′B represents the likely scatter of observed points. There is no longer an absolute minimum income value, D_{min}, nor is there an absolute maximum value, D_{max}. All that we can do is to find two points, $D_{(1)}$ and $D_{(2)}$, which represent the income values that would be generated from the reduced form, by Z_{min} and Z_{max} respectively, for a *zero* value of the random disturbance

$$D_{(1)} = \frac{\alpha}{(1 - \beta)} + \frac{1}{(1 - \beta)} Z_{min} + 0$$

$$D_{(2)} = \frac{\alpha}{(1 - \beta)} + \frac{1}{(1 - \beta)} Z_{max} + 0$$

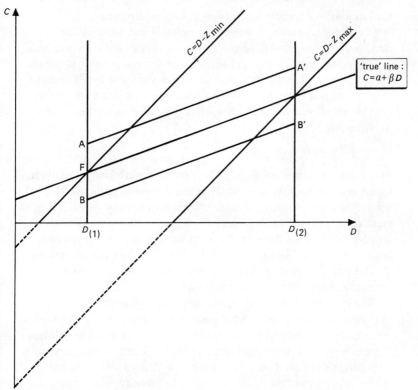

Figure 6.2

But a negative disturbance could give a value of D to the left of the point $D_{(1)}$ and a positive disturbance could give a value of D to the right of the point $D_{(2)}$. One could therefore have an observed consumption–income point lying *outside* the lines drawn above $D_{(1)}$ and $D_{(2)}$. The observed points must, however, lie between the two extreme 45° lines. So the scatter of points represented by the area AA′B′B has now been replaced by a scatter lying between the two 45° lines and this would tend to pull the slope of estimated line up towards that of the 45° lines. This is very similar to the example that was mentioned in Section 2.7, where we used a diagrammatic approach to show why the OLS estimator might sometimes be inconsistent. No matter how many observations there are, it is impossible to generate a 'proper' scatter of points around the true line. In this case, the slope of the consumption function is systematically overestimated. This corresponds to a positive inconsistency, but the direction of the inconsistency is specific to the chosen example and, in other cases, simultaneity might lead to negative inconsistency of the OLS estimator.

It is shown quite clearly, in Fig. 6.2, that it is not possible to obtain a pair of observations on consumption and income that would lead to an observed point directly above the point F, but, if one were to start with income $D_{(1)}$ and a positive value of the disturbance, then surely the equation

$$C_t = \alpha + \beta D_t + u_t$$

would suggest an upward shift in the observed point? The question can be answered by looking again at the reduced form equation for D. The whole point of our argument is that D_t depends directly on u_t. It is not possible to argue in terms of fixing D_t at $D_{(1)}$ and *then* choosing a positive value for u_t, since a positive disturbance means that *income cannot be at* $D_{(1)}$. The point $D_{(1)}$ corresponds to the minimum value of Z and a *zero disturbance*. A *positive* disturbance shifts income to the right as well as shifting consumption upwards.

This argument shows why OLS is deficient, at least in terms of lack of consistency, and it does give some clue as to what may be done to correct the deficiency. If the observations on income could be adjusted in some way, so as to prevent the movement of income values along the horizontal axis, then it would be possible to observe points outside the boundaries imposed by the identity. The identity refers to *actual* values of income, not to values that are adjusted in some way. The nature of the adjustment required is also indicated by the argument above. It is the fact that income is random that causes the difficulty. At this point, the reduced form equation for income again proves to be useful: equation (6.3.4) states that

$$D_t = \frac{\alpha}{(1-\beta)} + \frac{1}{(1-\beta)} Z_t + \frac{u_t}{(1-\beta)} \; ; t = 1, 2, \ldots, n \quad (6.4.6)$$

and shows that, if the term $u_t/(1-\beta)$ were subtracted from D_t, the result would be a variable that is not influenced by u_t at all. Unfortunately $u_t/(1-\beta)$ is not observable, so the suggested adjustment cannot be implemented directly. There is, however, a fairly simple approximation that can be used.

The reduced form equation can be written

$$D_t = \Pi_1 + \Pi_2 Z_t + v_t; t = 1, 2, \ldots, n \quad (6.4.7)$$

where Π_1, Π_2 represent an intercept and slope respectively and

v_t; $t = 1, 2, \ldots, n$ represent the reduced form disturbances. The disturbances cannot be observed, but the residuals from an *estimated* line could be obtained. What is more, the variable Z_t is exogenous and OLS *on this equation* is not subject to the difficulty of having an endogenous variable on the right hand side. If OLS is used to estimate Π_1 and Π_2, we would obtain a fitted line

$$\hat{D}_t = \hat{\Pi}_1 + \hat{\Pi}_2 Z_t; t = 1, 2, \ldots, n \qquad (6.4.8)$$

where the estimated or predicted values, $\hat{D}_t$; $t = 1, 2, \ldots, n$, differ from the true values, D_t; $t = 1, 2, \ldots, n$, by a set of residuals, which are written as $\hat{v}_t$; $t = 1, 2, \ldots, n$

$$D_t = \hat{D}_t + \hat{v}_t; t = 1, 2, \ldots, n \qquad (6.4.9)$$

The subtraction of the residual from a single observation, D_t, is thus equivalent to replacing that observation by the corresponding predicted value, determined by equation (6.4.8). This is only an approximation to the subtraction of the true disturbance, which would be the ideal adjustment to income.

The method outlined here is *two stage least squares* (2SLS). In the first stage, D_t is regressed on Z_t, to give predicted values, $\hat{D}_t$; $t = 1, 2, \ldots, n$. The second stage consists of a regression run on the consumption function, but the values D_t; $t = 1, 2, \ldots, n$ are replaced by $\hat{D}_t$; $t = 1, 2, \ldots, n$. In terms of Fig. 6.2, it can be argued that what we have done is to allow adjusted observations to fall outside the bounds imposed by the identity. For a given value of Z, say $Z_{\min}$, a positive disturbance would move the value of consumption upwards and the value of income to the right. But if income is corrected for the effect of the disturbance, albeit approximately, one could have a case in which consumption is moved upwards, but the *corrected* income value is *not* moved to the right. This would give a point $(C_t, \hat{D}_t)$ which lies *above* the line $C = D - Z_{\min}$. To the extent that one can now have a 'proper' scatter of points, this argument suggests that 2SLS *does* give consistent estimators. We shall shortly consider an algebraic argument, in an attempt to reinforce this conclusion, but first, consider a possible alternative to two stage least squares.

The first stage of 2SLS consists of an OLS regression run on one of the reduced form equations and, since the explanatory variables in the reduced form are assumed to be exogenous, the OLS estimators *of the reduced form parameters* would be consistent *and* unbiased. Equations (6.3.3) and (6.3.4) show that the reduced form parameters are related to the parameters of the structural form and so it might be possible to work back to estimates of the structural parameters from estimates obtained from the reduced form regressions. This is a recognized method of estimation, known as *indirect least squares* (ILS), but it does not turn out to be particularly useful. It is only possible to work back to unique estimates of structural form parameters when the equation in question is exactly identified and, when this condition is satisfied, the estimates obtained are identical to those given by 2SLS. This does not mean that the 2SLS estimators are unbiased in the exactly identified case, because the unbiasedness property of the reduced form estimators does not survive the transformation back to the structural form. There is in fact no generally applicable method of obtaining unbiased estimators of the structural parameters of a simultaneous model and questions of estimator choice are usually resolved by considering asymptotic properties.

Although the idea of working back from reduced form estimates has not produced a generally applicable alternative to 2SLS, we can make use of the fact that the reduced form estimators are consistent in considering an alternative argument for the consistency of 2SLS. In our example, the 2SLS estimators are obtained from an OLS regression of C on $\hat{D}$ and, given that there is an intercept in the consumption function, we can write the 2SLS slope estimator as

$$\hat{\beta}_{(2SLS)} = \Sigma \hat{d}_t c_t / \Sigma \hat{d}_t^2 \qquad (6.4.10)$$

where $c_t, \hat{d}_t; t = 1, 2, \ldots, n$ represent the observations $C_t, \hat{D}_t; t = 1, 2, \ldots, n$, expressed as deviations from the means. The corresponding expression in terms of the structural form disturbances is

$$\hat{\beta}_{(2SLS)} = \beta + \Sigma \hat{d}_t u_t / \Sigma \hat{d}_t^2 \qquad (6.4.11)$$

This expression is correct but, again, we omit the algebraic detail and concentrate on the interpretation of the expression. The deviations, $\hat{d}_t; t = 1, 2, \ldots, n$ are random variables, because they are derived from the predictions of the first stage regressions. And the deviations are not independent of $u_t; t = 1, 2, \ldots, n$, because they are indirectly related to the reduced form disturbances which, in turn, depend on the structural form disturbances. But it *is* possible to argue that the probability limit of the random term in (6.4.11) *is* zero, for the following reason. If the observations $D_t; t = 1, 2, \ldots, n$ could be adjusted for the *true* reduced form disturbances, the adjusted values would no longer depend on $u_t; t = 1, 2, \ldots, n$. As it is, we can only adjust the income values by using residuals, taken from a first stage (reduced form) regression. But the OLS estimators of the reduced form parameters *are* consistent, which suggests that as the number of observations is increased, the reduced form estimates do tend to get closer to the true values. In a limiting sense, the income observations *are* correctly adjusted, to remove the effect of the random disturbances and, in this same sense, there is no longer a connection between the adjusted income values and the random disturbances. This does lead to the conclusion that, in (6.4.11), the probability limit of the random term is zero. Hence, the two-stage least squares estimator is consistent.

Neither of the arguments that we have used is, in any sense, a formal proof of the consistency of the 2SLS estimators, but the reader may find one or other of the arguments to be helpful in understanding what the use of 2SLS achieves.

Before moving on, we restate the 2SLS method in a more general form. A single structural equation in a simultaneous model may have more than one *endogenous* variable on the right hand side. Each of these right hand side endogenous variables has to be replaced by a corresponding variable, the values of which are the predictions from the relevant reduced form regression. In the general case, each reduced form equation will express a single endogenous variable in terms of *all the exogenous variables in the model*. So the first stage consists of as many regressions as there are right hand side endogenous variables. Each of these regressions has a different dependent variable (one of the endogenous variables on the right of the *structural* equation), but the explanatory variables are the same in each case (all exogenous variables in the model). The second stage consists of a single regression, on the structural equation, in which the right hand side endogenous variable observations are replaced by the predicted values generated in the first stage.

There are other methods of estimation which can be applied to a single equation taken from a simultaneous model and which, like 2SLS, give rise to consistent estimators. But 2SLS is the most widely used of the possible methods and, as there is no unambiguous ranking that would lead to the choice of a 'better' procedure, the question of alternatives is not pursued here. The comparison between OLS and 2SLS shows that the latter gives consistent estimators whilst the former does not. It is very difficult to analyse the behaviour of the estimators for a relatively small number of observations, but there is some evidence from simulation experiments which suggests that there *is* less systematic distortion inherent in using 2SLS. On the other hand the estimator variances appear to increase *vis-à-vis* OLS. This is not surprising: by using estimated values for right hand side endogenous variables, we are using only those parts of the variation that can be explained in terms of exogenous variables in the model. Thus, for each right hand endogenous variable, we are discarding some of the observed variation and our earlier discussions would suggest that this would tend to *increase* the corresponding estimator variances. This conclusion is highly tentative, but it is important to realize that there may be a cost in achieving consistency of estimation. One further point that is worth noting is that 2SLS can be interpreted as an instrumental variable method. Equation (6.4.10) does not suggest this directly, but it can be shown that

$$\Sigma \hat{d}_t^2 = \Sigma \hat{d}_t d_t \qquad (6.4.12)$$

in which case

$$\hat{\beta}_{(2SLS)} = \Sigma \hat{d}_t c_t / \Sigma \hat{d}_t d_t \qquad (6.4.13)$$

A comparison with equation (5.3.16) will show that (6.4.13) is in the *form* of an IV estimator, the difference here being that it is possible to express the observations as deviations from the means, given that there is an intercept in the consumption function. The instrumental variable is $\hat{D}$, which is used as a proxy for D and this is a case in which it is possible to find a reasonable proxy, whilst at the same time satisfying the requirement that the IV estimator should be consistent. It is also interesting to note that, in Section 5.3, it was suggested that the IV method may involve an increase in variance as compared with OLS and this does correspond to our suggestion concerning 2SLS.

Given that 2SLS is the most widely used method of obtaining consistent estimates of structural parameters, it is important to consider some practical details. Ideally, one should use a computer program designed for 2SLS: such a program would presumably generate the parameter estimates and other information, such as standard errors and measures of goodness of fit. Since the only generally applicable statistical properties are these derived as *asymptotic* results, the standard errors would be based on the formulae for the asymptotic variances of the estimators. If a specially designed program is available, it is not necessary to know how the standard errors are computed but, in interpreting the results, it must be remembered that asymptotic approximations are being used. If a specially designed program is not available, it is still possible to carry out the computations, using an OLS program, but some care is needed.

In the first stage of the calculation, the OLS program would be used to generate predicted values for all endogenous variables which appear on the right hand side of the structural equation. This would be done by running a set of reduced form regressions, from which the predicted values are obtained. The predicted values would then be used as input to the second stage regression on the structural equation. One can certainly get the parameter estimates in this way, but there is a problem which centres around the computation of the residuals from the 2SLS estimation of the structural equation. The residuals should be obtained by substituting the 2SLS estimates into the original equation. So, in the consumption function example, the residuals are given by

$$\hat{u}_t = C_t - \hat{\alpha}_{(2SLS)} - \hat{\beta}_{(2SLS)}D_t; t = 1, 2, \ldots, n \qquad (6.4.14)$$

But when an OLS program is used for the second stage regression, it will automatically generate residuals from the given data and so the computed residuals would be

$$\hat{\hat{u}}_t = C_t - \hat{\alpha}_{(2SLS)} - \hat{\beta}_{(2SLS)}\hat{D}_t; t = 1, 2, \ldots, n \qquad (6.4.15)$$

The difference between (6.4.14) and (6.4.15) is that the latter has *predicted* income values on the right hand side, because predicted values are supplied as input to the second stage regression. The residuals shown in (6.4.15) are *not* the correct residuals to the original structural equation. As we shall see, this has implications for the standard errors and measures of fit computed by using an OLS program for the second stage regression.

In general, the estimate of the asymptotic standard error of a 2SLS estimator can be written as

$$se(\hat{\beta}_{j\,(2SLS)}) = \hat{\sigma}\sqrt{a_j} \qquad (6.4.16)$$

where β_j is a typical parameter, a_j is a quantity that *would* be correctly computed by using an OLS program for the second stage regression and $\hat{\sigma}$ is the square root of a consistent estimator for the disturbance variance of the structural equation. In the consumption function example, the second stage regression is a standard two variable case and the OLS calculation would determine a_j as

$$a_j = 1/\Sigma\hat{d}_t^2$$

In general, the expression is more complicated, but it would still be correctly computed by treating the second stage regression as a standard OLS calculation. But if an OLS program is used, the estimate of the disturbance variance would be computed as

$$\hat{\sigma}^2 = \Sigma\hat{\hat{u}}_t^2/(n - k) \qquad (6.4.17)$$

where $\hat{u}_t$; $t = 1, 2, \ldots, n$ represents a set of residuals computed with *predicted* values for the right hand side endogenous variables and k is the total number of variables (including any artificial variable) on the right of the structural equation. This is actually a consistent estimator, but in a specially written 2SLS program, $\hat{\sigma}^2$ would be computed either as

$$\hat{\sigma}^2 = \Sigma \hat{u}_t^2 / (n - k) \tag{6.4.18}$$

where $\hat{u}_t$; $t = 1, 2, \ldots, n$ represent the correct residuals, or as

$$\hat{\sigma}^2 = \Sigma \hat{u}_t^2 / n \tag{6.4.19}$$

This last version may be used because there is no longer any *theoretical* justification for dividing by $(n - k)$. Equation (6.4.18) does not define an unbiased estimator and the difference between n and $(n - k)$ is irrelevant in considering the consistency property.

We can now see that the essential problem in using an OLS program is that it produces estimates of the standard errors which are *different* to those obtained from a 2SLS program. Although there is no definite theoretical result which suggests using one method rather than the other, it does seem sensible to make use of the correct residuals. In fact the sum of squares calculated from $\hat{u}_t$; $t = 1, 2, \ldots, n$ is always *less* than that calculated from $\hat{u}_t$; $t = 1, 2, \ldots, n$, so the use of an OLS program will always produce *lower* standard errors than those obtained from a 2SLS program. This does seem rather undesirable: since the standard errors are based on asymptotic results, one should perhaps be conservative in interpreting the estimates, allowing for the possibility that the true standard errors are rather larger than those suggested by our formulae. The use of the correct residuals is therefore a move in the right direction. Incidentally, this also suggests that, for a relatively small number of observations, it might be a good idea to divide by $(n - k)$ rather than by n, even though there is no *theoretical* reason for doing so.

A similar problem arises in computing a measure of goodness of fit. Following the discussion in Section 3.3, we could compute a measure for the consumption function as

$$R^2 = 1 - \Sigma \hat{u}_t^2 / \Sigma c_t^2 \tag{6.4.20}$$

where the fact that the observations on consumption are in deviation form indicates that the measure does not give credit for the explanation achieved by the intercept. But if an OLS program is used for the second stage regression, the measure would automatically be computed

as
$$R^2 = 1 - \Sigma \hat{u}_t^2 / \Sigma c_t^2 \tag{6.4.21}$$
which would give a *higher* value to R^2. In this case we can argue that
the measure (6.4.21) is definitely misleading, as it overstates the degree
to which the behaviour of consumption is explained by the *original*
observations on income.

6.5 Estimation: Complete System Methods

In the consumption–income example, there is only one behavioural
equation and the estimation of this equation corresponds to the
estimation of all the structural parameters in the model. More generally,
in constructing a model of the complete economy, there would be
several behavioural equations. At the most highly aggregate level, the
endogenous variables might include components of expenditure such as
consumption and investment; components of income, such as wage
payments and profits; employment and output; and prices, including
wage rates and interest rates. There might be variables relating to
foreign trade. And there might be additional monetary and fiscal
variables. In putting the model together, there must be an equation, or
set of equations, representing a theory of the determination of each
endogenous variable: and there must be as many equations as there
are endogenous variables. When one starts to disaggregate, the number
of equations can become very large indeed and there are constructed
econometric models involving hundreds of equations. Very large
models do lead to particular problems of estimation, but we shall
not pursue this point. We shall take as typical the small to medium
sized model, in which the list of endogenous variables would include
at least some of those mentioned above.

To illustrate the discussion which follows, a new example is
introduced. Again, it must be emphasized that this is not intended to
be 'realistic'. In modelling a given system, a great deal of effort is
needed to achieve an appropriate specification and one cannot expect a
textbook example to be directly applicable. But our examples do
illustrate the methods used in a serious attempt at model construction.

With this in mind, consider the following equations

$$
\begin{aligned}
C_t &= \alpha + \beta D_t + u_t \\
I_t &= \gamma + \delta R_t + v_t \\
R_t &= \epsilon D_t + \theta M_t + w_t \\
D_t &= C_t + I_t + Z_t; \ t = 1, 2, \ldots, n
\end{aligned}
\tag{6.5.1}
$$

The new variables are I, investment; R, the interest rate; and M, the money stock. The disturbances are u_t, v_t and w_t; $t = 1, 2, \ldots, n$. Note that v_t is now a structural form disturbance whereas, previously, the same representation was used for a reduced form disturbance. This will not lead to any confusion, as we do not need to refer to reduced form disturbances again. As written, the model suggests that the endogenous variables are C, I, R and D, with M and Z exogenous. The third equation looks a little curious, but (6.5.1) is based on a simplified Keynesian model and the example *is* often used (without the disturbances) to show how C, I, R and D could be determined from given values of M and Z. If there were no disturbances, the third equation could be written as

$$M_t = \lambda D_t + \mu R_t \qquad (6.5.2)$$

where

$$\lambda = -\epsilon/\theta \text{ and } \mu = 1/\theta$$

In this form, the equation is more easily recognized as a linearized version of the liquidity preference function. But if M is to be exogenous in an 'econometric' formulation, it would violate our usual convention to write M on the left hand side. Any difficulties of interpretation stem largely from the fact that the model has been limited in size to three behavioural equations. We shall simply assume that ϵ and θ do represent parameters of interest and we shall proceed accordingly.

One could estimate the parameters of (6.5.1) by applying 2SLS to each behavioural equation in turn. But there is an alternative, which is to apply a *complete system* method, in which all the parameters of a model are estimated in one operation. In Section 4.6, this possibility was discussed in the context of a multiple equation model in which no equation had an endogenous variable on the right hand side. The reasons for considering the complete system approach were, firstly, that there might be cross-equation restrictions and, secondly, that there might be contemporaneous correlation of the disturbances to the individual equations. In (6.5.1), there are no cross-equation restrictions, but it is usually accepted that there can be contemporaneous correlation of the disturbances to a simultaneous model. If the analogy with our earlier argument is valid and if contemporaneous correlation does occur, one would expect a possible gain in efficiency from using a suitable complete system method.

It is worth restating briefly what is meant by contemporaneous correlation. In each time period, the value of the disturbance to each equation can be thought of as being generated according to the rules of a probability distribution. In a simultaneous model, there are several distributions for a single time period, corresponding to the several different disturbance terms on the individual structural equations. The existence of contemporaneous correlation means that these distributions are not independent and, roughly, we can say that there is some connection between the values taken by the different disturbance terms. To accept this as a general characteristic of simultaneous models may seem to be a violation of the principle of simplicity first. But, given that a simultaneous model is a representation for a highly interdependent system and that the disturbances are a summary representation for all the factors that are not explicitly included in the model, it is perhaps sensible to allow for the fact that there may be connections between the disturbances to the individual equations.

It is possible to construct a complete system method by putting together various ideas taken from earlier discussions. The method that we shall describe is *three stage least squares* (3SLS). In taking all the equations together, there is still the problem of having endogenous variables on the right hand side and, to overcome this, we use the same technique as in 2SLS. Each set of right hand side endogenous variable observations is replaced by the set of values predicted from the reduced form regressions. This represents the first stage of the process and we see that, in the first stage, the equations are still considered to be separate. Having taken this first step, let us consider how the equations could be combined.

The method is very similar to that described in the context of a non-simultaneous multiple equation model. To create a single set of 'dependent' variable observations, each left hand side endogenous variable is taken in turn and the observations are 'stacked' to give a single sequence of values. In our example, with R taken to be endogenous, this would give observations C_t; $t = 1, 2, \ldots, n$, followed by I_t; $t = 1, 2, \ldots, n$, followed by R_t; $t = 1, 2, \ldots, n$. Notice that D_t; $t = 1, 2, \ldots, n$ does *not* appear in this sequence, because we do not have to estimate the parameters of the identity. In fact all identities are removed before the equations are combined. The 'explanatory' variable observations are entered in a different way. Given that income appears in the first equation, with parameter β, and that income does *not* appear elsewhere *with this parameter*, we need a constructed set of observations $\hat{D}_t$; $t = 1, 2, \ldots, n$, followed by two sequences, each consisting of n

zeros. Notice that, since income is used here a *right hand side* endogenous variable, the predicted values are used in place of the original observations. So the complete set of observations on the constructed variable can be written as $\hat{D}_t$; $t = 1, 2, \ldots, n$, followed by 0; $t = 1$, $2, \ldots, n$; followed by 0; $t = 1, 2, \ldots, n$, where 0; $t = 1, 2, \ldots, n$ represents a sequence of n zeros. Income appears again in the third equation, but with a *different* parameter (ϵ). So another of the constructed 'explanatory' variables would have observations 0; $t = 1$, $2, \ldots, n$, followed by 0; $t = 1, 2, \ldots, n$, followed by $\hat{D}_t$; $t = 1, 2, \ldots, n$. We can summarize this description by presenting the complete set of data for the combined equation in the following table

Left Hand Side	Right Hand Side					
C_1	1	$\hat{D}_1$	0	0	0	0
.	.	.	.	.	.	.
.	.	.	.	.	.	.
.	.	.	.	.	.	.
C_n	1	$\hat{D}_n$	0	0	0	0
I_1	0	0	1	$\hat{R}_1$	0	0
.	.	.	.	.	.	.
.	.	.	.	.	.	.
.	.	.	.	.	.	.
I_n	0	0	1	$\hat{R}_n$	0	0
R_1	0	0	0	0	$\hat{D}_1$	M_1
.	.	.	.	.	.	.
.	.	.	.	.	.	.
.	.	.	.	.	.	.
R_n	0	0	0	0	$\hat{D}_n$	M_n
Associated Parameter	α	β	γ	δ	ϵ	θ

Once the observations have been combined in this way, we effectively have a single equation in the variables defined by the 'stacking' process. A complete system method is then equivalent to a single equation approach applied to the *derived* equation. By using predicted values for right hand side endogenous variables, we have allowed for the simultaneity problem but, having stacked the equations, we have implicitly stacked the disturbances and, if there are contemporaneous correlations in the disturbances to the original structural equations, there will be correlations between the individual disturbances to the derived equation. Suppose, for example, that there is contemporaneous correlation between the disturbances to the consumption function and those to the investment function. There will then be correlation between u_1 and v_1, u_2 and v_2, and so on. But these disturbances now appear in the derived single equation: to be specific, u_1 appears in the first disturbance and v_1 in disturbance $n + 1$, u_2 in the second disturbance and v_2 in disturbance $n + 2$, and so on. Since we do *not* have independent disturbances in the derived equation, the estimation procedure should be chosen accordingly. Given that we have taken care of the simultaneity problem by using predicted values for right hand side endogenous variables, one might think in terms of using OLS, just as OLS is used in the second stage of 2SLS. But if the disturbances are not independent, the obvious strategy would be to apply GLS instead. As before, the use of GLS is equivalent to a further transformation of the equation, after which OLS *can* be applied. Unfortunately, it is not possible to describe this transformation in simple terms and, in fact, it would be difficult to carry out the calculation without a specially designed computer program. But the *principles* underlying the method do follow from our earlier discussions and it has been possible to explain the essential nature of the complete system approach.

There is still one remaining problem. In practice, it is not possible to use the correct GLS transformation, as this requires that certain disturbance parameters be known. As before, it is necessary to use estimates in place of the true values. The unknown parameters are the disturbance variances for each structural equation and also the *covariances*, which measure the extent to which there is contemporaneous correlation. We have already seen how the disturbance variance for a single structural equation can be estimated from 2SLS residuals. After 2SLS estimation of the parameters of the consumption function, the estimate of the disturbance variance can be obtained as

$$\hat{\sigma}_u^2 = \Sigma \hat{u}_t^2/n \ \text{ or } \ \Sigma \hat{u}_t^2/(n-2) \tag{6.5.3}$$

The subscript u has been added to signify that this estimate refers to the consumption function. In like fashion, for the investment function, we would have

$$\hat{\sigma}_v^2 = \Sigma \hat{v}_t^2/n \ \text{ or } \ \Sigma \hat{v}_t^2/(n-2) \tag{6.5.4}$$

and, for the *covariance* between the disturbances to the consumption function and the investment function

$$\hat{\sigma}_{uv} = \Sigma \hat{u}_t \hat{v}_t/n \ \text{ or } \ \Sigma \hat{u}_t \hat{v}_t/(n-2) \tag{6.5.5}$$

The usual approach here is to divide by n: this avoids any difficulty caused by the fact that two different equations may not have the same number of variables on the right hand side.

It is now possible to explain the three stages which go to make up 3SLS. The first stage consists of reduced form regressions, used to obtain predicted values for the right hand side endogenous variables. The second stage consists of 2SLS estimation applied to each behavioural equation: the residuals from this stage are used to generate estimates of the disturbance parameters. And the third stage is an approximation to GLS estimation of the derived single equation. If there is contemporaneous correlation of the disturbances, the 3SLS estimators are more efficient than the corresponding 2SLS estimators, in the sense that the *asymptotic* variances are generally lower in the 3SLS case.

Three stage least squares is not the only complete system method that is available. An alternative is to apply the maximum likelihood principle, which leads to *full-information maximum likelihood* (FIML) estimates of the model parameters. Whereas the 3SLS method uses preliminary estimates of the disturbance parameters, which are then used to generate estimates of the remaining parameters, the FIML method generates both sets of estimates simultaneously. Beyond this, there is little that we can say about FIML. The technical details are complicated and, as the equations defining the estimators are highly nonlinear, an iterative solution procedure has to be used. One cannot possibly attempt FIML estimation unless a suitable computer program is available.

Throughout our discussion of the use of a simultaneous model, we have ignored the possibility that there might be lags in the system. There are no specific problems caused by the presence of finite lags in *exogenous* variables and a lagged exogenous variable is treated in exactly the same way as a current exogenous variable. But if there are lagged *endogenous* variables, the estimator properties may be altered and the model becomes dynamic. This final extension to the analysis is considered briefly in the next section.

6.6 Simultaneous Dynamic Models

As in the single equation case, the essential nature of a dynamic model is that it can generate a time path for the endogenous variables. There are actually two possibilities that we should consider. The model

$$C_t = \alpha + \gamma D_{t-1} + u_t$$
$$D_t = C_t + Z_t; t = 1, 2, \ldots, n \qquad (6.6.1)$$

is certainly dynamic and it does involve more than one equation. From a starting value, D_0, the model would generate a sequence of values of C and D, for given values of Z and for specific values of the disturbances. The process is

$$C_1 = \alpha + \gamma D_0 + u_1$$

$$D_1 = C_1 + Z_1$$

$$C_2 = \alpha + \gamma D_1 + u_2$$

$$D_2 = C_2 + Z_2, \text{ and so on}$$

But this is not actually a simultaneous model. The determination of the endogenous variables follows a definite sequence

$$D_0 \rightarrow C_1 \rightarrow D_1 \rightarrow C_2 \rightarrow D_2 \rightarrow \ldots$$

A second example provides a contrast. If the consumption function also involves the *current* value of income, we would have

$$C_t = \alpha + \beta D_t + \gamma D_{t-1} + u_t$$

$$D_t = C_t + Z_t; t = 1, 2, \ldots, n \tag{6.6.2}$$

and this *is* a simultaneous model. The logic of (6.6.2) is that, in any time period, the values of C_t and D_t are determined by the solution of the equations, for given values of Z_t and D_{t-1}. The value of Z_t is given in the sense that it is determined outside the model and the value of D_{t-1} is given in the sense that it has already been determined by the operation of the model in the previous period. Exogenous variables and lagged endogenous variables are therefore described collectively as *predetermined* variables.

The solution for the values of the current endogenous variables is represented by the reduced form and, in a dynamic model, the reduced form will have both exogenous *and* lagged endogenous variables on the right hand side. To illustrate the point, consider the reduced form equation for consumption, derived from the model shown in (6.6.2). Using the second equation to eliminate D_t from the consumption function, we obtain

$$C_t = \frac{\alpha}{1-\beta} + \frac{\beta}{1-\beta} Z_t + \frac{\gamma}{1-\beta} D_{t-1} + \frac{u_t}{1-\beta} ; t = 1, 2, \ldots, n \tag{6.6.3}$$

The corresponding equation for income would be

$$D_t = \frac{\alpha}{1-\beta} + \frac{1}{1-\beta} Z_t + \frac{\gamma}{1-\beta} D_{t-1} + \frac{u_t}{1-\beta} \; ; t = 1, 2, \dots, n \tag{6.6.4}$$

Now consider the use of OLS in estimating the parameters of the reduced form equation for income. It is immediately apparent that this is similar to the estimation of the parameters of a single equation dynamic model. If the disturbances u_t; $t = 1, 2, \dots, n$ are serially independent, so too are the disturbances $u_t/(1-\beta)$; $t = 1, 2, \dots, n$ and the OLS estimators will not be unbiased, but they will be consistent. The same analysis would apply to the reduced form equation for consumption: in this case, the lagged endogenous variable is not the same economic variable as that on the left of the equation, but the nature of the estimation problem will be the same. The next step is to consider 2SLS estimation of the structural form. Our arguments for the consistency of 2SLS require that the reduced form estimators should be consistent: it is not necessary that they should be unbiased. So it is reasonable to suppose that the 2SLS estimators *will* be consistent. There are, however, certain conditions. One element in our argument for the consistency of OLS applied to a single equation dynamic model was that the model should satisfy stability conditions. There is a similar requirement for the consistency of 2SLS applied to a simultaneous dynamic model. The essential meaning of such conditions can be explained in the following way. If we ignore the effect of the random disturbances and consider the effect of an initial shock, in the form of a once and for all change in one exogenous variable, then, if the stability conditions are satisfied, the endogenous variables should eventually attain values which no longer exhibit any discernible change from one period to the next. These conditions must be satisfied if the 2SLS estimators are to be consistent and there is similar requirement for the consistency of 3SLS. The other essential condition is that there should be no serial correlation of the disturbances. If this condition is violated, it *is* necessary to alter the estimation procedures. As in the single equation case, there are two basic approaches to the problem. The first is to extend the use of instrumental variables to the *lagged* endogenous variables and the second is to use a maximum likelihood method.

This account of the use of a simultaneous dynamic model has been very brief, but it does cover the essential points to emerge from a *combination* of simultaneity and dynamic behaviour. In fact the vast majority of constructed econometric models do involve lagged endogenous variables and this type of model is the final stage in our development of a representation for the economic system.

6.7 Forecasting and Policy Simulation

The estimation phase of the model-building process may involve several stages of testing and revision, but the end product will be a set of equations in which the unknown parameter values are replaced by estimates. If the intention is simply to assign values to key economic parameters, the exercise is then complete. But the estimated version of the model can also be used to generate forecasts and to conduct various experiments which obviously cannot be performed on the real system.

Suppose first that we wished to generate forecasts from the simplest version of consumption–income model

$$C_t = \alpha + \beta D_t + u_t$$
$$D_t = C_t + Z_t; t = 1, 2, \ldots, n \qquad (6.7.1)$$

At the end of the estimation process, we would have

$$C_t = \hat{\alpha} + \hat{\beta} D_t + \hat{u}_t$$
$$D_t = C_t + Z_t; t = 1, 2, \ldots, n \qquad (6.7.2)$$

where $\hat{\alpha}$ and $\hat{\beta}$ are now taken to refer to *particular estimates*, obtained by *any* chosen method of estimation and where $\hat{u}_t; t = 1, 2, \ldots, n$ are the residuals corresponding to the particular estimates obtained. Now suppose that we require forecasts for period $n + 1$. If the model still holds in period $n + 1$, it would be true that

$$C_{n+1} = \alpha + \beta D_{n+1} + u_{n+1}$$
$$D_{n+1} = C_{n+1} + Z_{n+1} \qquad (6.7.3)$$

and, for given values of α and β, Z_{n+1} and u_{n+1}, these equations would produce values for C_{n+1} and D_{n+1}. We have estimates of α and β but, if the forecast is made at the end of period n, the value of Z_{n+1} would be unknown and the value of u_{n+1} can never be observed. So, before a forecast can be made, it is necessary to predict the value of Z_{n+1} and, in the absence of any information as to the probable behaviour of the disturbance in period $n + 1$, the prediction of u_{n+1} would have to be a zero value. This means that the disturbance is simply omitted in making the forecast. The predictions for C_{n+1} and D_{n+1} would then be given as the solution to the equations

$$\hat{C}_{n+1} = \hat{\alpha} + \hat{\beta}\hat{D}_{n+1}$$
$$\hat{D}_{n+1} = \hat{C}_{n+1} + Z_{n+1} \tag{6.7.4}$$

The solutions are

$$\hat{C}_{n+1} = \hat{\alpha}/(1 - \hat{\beta}) + \hat{\beta}/(1 - \hat{\beta})Z_{n+1}$$
$$\hat{D}_{n+1} = \hat{\alpha}/(1 - \hat{\beta}) + 1/(1 - \hat{\beta})Z_{n+1} \tag{6.7.5}$$

These are reduced form equations in which the disturbance term is set to zero and in which the reduced form parameters are replaced by estimates taken from the structural form. It can happen that the resulting estimates of the reduced form parameters are exactly the same as those obtained by *direct* estimation of the reduced form equations, but this is not *generally* true.

The forecasts that are generated in this way are, in formal terms, particular values taken by a set of random variables. The statistical properties of these random variables are not exactly the same as those described in Section 2.6, in the context of a single equation, because the properties of the estimators used in defining the prediction rule are now rather different. But the most important conclusion drawn from our earlier discussion is still relevant. Even when the model is 'true', one cannot expect to obtain perfectly accurate point predictions.

Before a forecast can be generated, it is necessary to supply values for *all* the predetermined variables. So, for the model

$$C_t = \alpha + \gamma D_{t-1} + u_t$$
$$D_t = C_t + Z_t; t = 1, 2, \ldots, n \tag{6.7.6}$$

the forecasts for period $n + 1$ would be determined as

$$\hat{C}_{n+1} = \hat{\alpha} + \hat{\gamma}D_n$$
$$\hat{D}_{n+1} = \hat{C}_{n+1} + Z_{n+1} \tag{6.7.7}$$

for *given* values of Z_{n+1} and D_n. In practice, there are lags in the production of data and in the construction of the model and, if $n + 1$ is taken to refer to the period immediately after the data period, a more realistic situation would be that in which the model construction is completed during some later period, say $n + 2$, and in which the model is to be used to generate forecasts for period $n + 3$. The input required would be the values for D_{n+2} and Z_{n+3}. But the actual value of D_{n+2}

would not be available until some time after the end of period $n + 2$ and Z_{n+3} relates to the forecast period. So one would have to make subsidiary forecasts for each of these values. In the case of the exogenous variable, the forecast value is generated outside the model but, given that the model is dynamic, it is possible to make forecasts for the endogenous variables over two or more periods. Assuming that D_{n+1} is actually available and that values can be assigned to Z_{n+2} and Z_{n+3}, the two period forecast would be generated as

$$\hat{C}_{n+2} = \hat{\alpha} + \hat{\gamma}D_{n+1}$$
$$\hat{D}_{n+2} = \hat{C}_{n+2} + Z_{n+2}$$
$$\hat{C}_{n+3} = \hat{\alpha} + \hat{\gamma}\hat{D}_{n+2}$$
$$\hat{D}_{n+3} = \hat{C}_{n+3} + Z_{n+3}$$

In this way the forecasts can be carried forward to periods $n + 4$, $n + 5$, and so on, but the values of the exogenous variable do have to be supplied at each stage.

As described here, the forecasting exercise is very mechanical, but if one is faced with the problem of having to make the best possible point forecast, the approach may be rather different. The formal model will usually play an important part, but the forecasts may be adjusted to take account of any new information that is available at the time at which the forecast is made. Suppose that one had reason to anticipate a change in government policy. This might simply imply a revision of the subsidiary forecast for one of the exogenous variables. But the expected policy change may indicate a changed environment, unlike that operating during the period covered by the data used for estimation. Under these circumstances, one may adjust the parameter estimates or one may forecast a non-zero value for the disturbance to a particular structural equation. The model might then be used to work the implications of any adjustment though to all the endogenous variables in the system. Whatever form these adjustments may take, it is clear that it is unrealistic to suppose that a model is used as a forecasting machine, producing numbers which are untouched by human hand.

If one is not confident of the accuracy of the subsidiary forecasts for the exogenous variables, a range of possible values may have to be used to generate *conditional* forecasts of the endogenous variables. Alternatively, one might use exogenous variable values that are not necessarily considered to be forecasts, to see what *would* happen under certain alternative sets of assumptions. This is essentially what happens when the model is used for *policy simulation*. The underlying idea is that there are certain exogenous variables to which values are assigned by policy decision. These are the *policy instruments*. The model can be used to show how a change in policy is transmitted to one or more of the endogenous variables, these being the policy *objectives*. If the model does not involve lags, a change in policy will have a once and for all effect on the endogenous variables. If there are finite lags in the exogenous variables, the full impact of the policy change may only be apparent after a certain delay. Finally, if the model is dynamic, a once and for all change in a single exogenous variable can generate a complete time path for the endogenous variables. This type of experimentation may be performed by using the estimated version of the model as a deterministic equation system, or, alternatively, one may generate artificial disturbances, to allow for the fact that the underlying model does not assume exact relation-ships between the variables.

In both forecasting and policy simulation, each set of values for the endogenous variables is obtained by solving the equations of the estimated version of the model. In the examples that we have used, it is very simple to do this, but our examples have special characteristics. The number of equations is small and the equations are linear in the endogenous variables. In practice, the equations used may be linear in the *parameters*, but there will often be nonlinearities in the endo-genous variables. To illustrate this point, consider an equation taken from the model shown in (6.5.1). The equation states that

$$R_t = \epsilon D_t + \theta M_t + w_t; t = 1, 2, \ldots, n \qquad (6.7.8)$$

and this was identified as a *linearized* version of the liquidity preference function. But the relationship between the money stock and the interest rate is *not* usually considered to be linear. Indeed, in Section 3.4, we used essentially the same variables in a relationship which was interpreted as a money demand function and, in that case, the variables were expressed in logarithmic form. If the variables appear *only* in logarithmic form, there is no problem: one can treat $\log(R)$ and $\log(M)$ in exactly the same way as any other variable in the model. But if we had used logs in the third equation of (6.5.1), the interest rate would have appeared as $\log(R)$ in this equation *and* as R in the investment function. It would then have been necessary to use a rather different estimation procedure but, in general, the presence of nonlinearities in the *variables* does not cause serious problems of estimation. The difficulty arises when the estimated version of the model is used for forecasting or for policy simulation, for then one has to solve equations which are nonlinear in the variables for which solutions are required. In this situation, one has to use an iterative procedure to generate the predictions for a *single* time period. There is thus a qualification to be added to the conclusions reached in Section 3.4. The presence of nonlinearities in the variables may have little effect on estimation procedures. But when the model is put to work, the methods used are *not* exactly the same as those for a model which is linear in the variables.

6.8 Finale

The final version of our representation for an economic system is a set of simultaneous dynamic equations with random disturbances: this provides an 'econometric' formulation corresponding to a wide class of economic models. It is obvious that there are difficulties in using this representation. It is easy to point to the statistical problems of estimation and to the possible deficiencies of the data. It is easy to find examples of constructed econometric models in which there are exogenous variables that ought not to be exogenous and policy instruments that are not really instruments. But if we are to criticize in this way, we should have a clear idea as to what it is that we are attacking. It is true that there are certain aspects of real systems that have never been successfully modelled. For example, it is extremely difficult to find a representation for the way in which government policy is formulated and yet it is equally clear that governments do react to signals produced within the economic system. But this does not mean that we shall not eventually learn how to model the more difficult linkages in the economic system and this is not a criticism of the *type* of representation that has been suggested. And the fact that there are statistical difficulties and deficiencies of the data means simply that there are *practical* problems in model construction. It does not necessarily mean that the representation is invalid. What one can say is that it may be necessary to abandon some of the restrictions that are still present in the simultaneous dynamic model. The quantities that we have taken as parameters might more adequately be represented as random variables. One might perhaps replace the disturbance distributions that we have used. Indeed, one might choose to use a different framework of statistical inference in representing the fact that relationships are not exact. As the representation is extended, so there are new problems of estimation to be solved, new requirements in terms of data and new requirements in terms of economic theory. It is certainly true that model-building is difficult. But the methods of econometrics do at least provide an approach to understanding the way in which real systems operate.

Exercises (Solutions on page 236)

6.1 Consider the model

$$C_t = \alpha + \beta D_t + u_t$$
$$I_t = \gamma + \delta D_{t-1} + v_t$$
$$D_t = C_t + I_t + Z_t; t = 1, 2, \ldots, n$$

where C is consumers' expenditure, D is income, I is investment and Z is autonomous expenditure. C, I and D are endogenous. Find the reduced form equation for consumers' expenditure. Do you think that the consumption function is identified?

6.2 Consider the model

$$Q_t^D = \alpha + \beta P_t + u_t$$
$$Q_t^S = \gamma + \delta R_t + v_t$$
$$Q_t^D = Q_t^S$$

where Q^D is the demand for wheat, Q^S is the supply of wheat, P is the price of wheat and R represents a climatic variable. Which variables would you consider to be endogenous? Do you notice any special feature of this model?

Suggestions for Further Reading

There are a number of excellent textbooks which offer a more formal approach to the topics described in this book

Christ, C. F. (1966), *Econometric Models and Methods*, Wiley
Johnston, J. (1972), *Econometric Methods*, 2nd edition, McGraw-Hill
Kmenta, J. (1971), *Elements of Econometrics*, Collier-Macmillan
Wonnacott, R. J. and Wonnacott, T. H. (1970), *Econometrics*, Wiley

For the statistical background to econometrics, see

Hey, J. D. (1974), *Statistics in Economics*, Martin Robertson
Wonnacott, R. J. and Wonnacott, T. H. (1969), *Introductory Statistics*, Wiley

A rather more gentle introduction to statistics is

Allen, R. G. D. (1966), *Statistics for Economists*, Hutchinson

A very comprehensive discussion of the mathematics needed for many branches of economics is given in

Chiang, A. C. (1967), *Fundamental Methods of Mathematical Economics*, McGraw-Hill

Solutions to Exercises

1.1 (a) Let Y be the random variable for the modified game and note that $Y = V + 6$, where V is the random variable for the original game. The probability for each value of Y is $1/6$ and so

$$E(Y) = 1/6(7) + 1/6(8) + 1/6(9) + 1/6(10) + 1/6(11) + 1/6(12)$$
$$= 9{\cdot}5$$

$$\text{var}(Y) = 1/6(7 - 9{\cdot}5)^2 + 1/6(8 - 9{\cdot}5)^2 + 1/6(9 - 9{\cdot}5)^2$$
$$+ 1/6(10 - 9{\cdot}5)^2 + 1/6(11 - 9{\cdot}5)^2 + 1/6(12 - 9{\cdot}5)^2$$
$$= 2{\cdot}917 \ (\text{or, to two decimal places, } 2{\cdot}92)$$

It should be obvious that this method of computing the variance is exactly equivalent to that shown in the text (why?). In comparison with the original game, the expectation has increased by 6, but the variance has not changed. The general rule for expectations in this case is that if

$Y = V + c$, where c is constant

then

$$E(Y) = E(V + c) = E(V) + c$$

(b) Again, let Y be the random variable for the modified game and note that now $Y = 2V$. The probability for each value of Y is again $1/6$ and so

$$E(Y) = 1/6(2) + 1/6(4) + 1/6(6) + 1/6(8) + 1/6(10) + 1/6(12)$$
$$= 7$$

$$\text{var}(Y) = 1/6(2 - 7)^2 + 1/6(4 - 7)^2 + 1/6(6 - 7)^2 + 1/6(8 - 7)^2$$
$$+ 1/6(10 - 7)^2 + 1/6(12 - 7)^2$$
$$= 11{\cdot}67$$

In comparison with the original game, the expectation has been multiplied by 2, but the variance is multiplied by 4. The general rule for expectations in this case is that if

$Y = cV$, where c is a constant

then

$E(Y) = E(cV) = cE(V)$

There are also rules for the variance in each case

$\text{var}(V + c) = \text{var}(V)$

$\text{var}(cV) = c^2\text{var}(V)$

1.2 The random variable $[V - E(V)]$ takes the values $-2 \cdot 5, -1 \cdot 5, -0 \cdot 5, 0 \cdot 5, 1 \cdot 5$ and $2 \cdot 5$, each with a probability of $1/6$.

So

$$E[V - E(V)] = 1/6(-2 \cdot 5) + 1/6(-1 \cdot 5) + 1/6(-0 \cdot 5)$$
$$+ 1/6(0 \cdot 5) + 1/6(1 \cdot 5) + 1/6(2 \cdot 5)$$
$$= 0$$

This result holds for any random variable, V. Since $E(V)$ is a constant, we can use one of the rules from the previous solution. If $c = -E(V)$, then

$E(V + c) = E(V) + c$

so

$E[V - E(V)] = E(V) - E(V) = 0$

1.3 (i) $\sum_{t=1}^{t=n} (10) = 10 + 10 + \ldots + 10 = n(10)$

(ii) $\Sigma(cX_t) = 10(1) + 10(2) + 10(3) = 10(1 + 2 + 3) = c\Sigma X_t$

(iii) $\Sigma(X_t + Y_t) = (1 + 2) + (2 + 4) + (3 + 6) = 18$
$$= (1 + 2 + 3) + (2 + 4 + 6) = \Sigma X_t + \Sigma Y_t$$

Note, however, that $\Sigma X_t Y_t$ is not the same as $(\Sigma X_t)(\Sigma Y_t)$

$\Sigma X_t Y_t = 1(2) + 2(4) + 3(6) = 28$

$(\Sigma X_t)(\Sigma Y_t) = (1 + 2 + 3)(2 + 4 + 6) = 72$

1.4 The formula for the sample mean of C is

$$\bar{C} = \Sigma C_t / n$$

By adding the values of C and dividing the result by 10, we obtain $\bar{C} = 22\,445 \cdot 3$. Then

t	$(C_t - \bar{C})$	$(C_t - \bar{C})^2$
1	$-2315 \cdot 3$	$5\,360\,614 \cdot 09$
2	$-1615 \cdot 3$	$2\,609\,194 \cdot 09$
3	$-1248 \cdot 3$	$1\,558\,252 \cdot 89$
4	$-817 \cdot 3$	$667\,979 \cdot 29$
5	$-327 \cdot 3$	$107\,125 \cdot 29$
6	$241 \cdot 7$	$58\,418 \cdot 89$
7	$354 \cdot 7$	$125\,812 \cdot 09$
8	$967 \cdot 7$	$936\,443 \cdot 29$
9	$1586 \cdot 7$	$2\,517\,616 \cdot 89$
10	$3172 \cdot 7$	$10\,066\,025 \cdot 89$
	$0000 \cdot 0$	$24\,007\,482 \cdot 10$

This calculation shows that $\Sigma(C_t - C)^2 = 24\,007\,482 \cdot 10$. So the sample variance is

$$s_C^2 = 24007\,482 \cdot 10/10 = 2400748 \cdot 21$$

and the sample standard deviation is the square root of this quantity

$$s_C = 1549 \cdot 43$$

In a similar fashion, it can be shown that

$$\bar{D} = 24491 \cdot 8$$

$$\Sigma(D_t - \bar{D})^2 = 32188511 \cdot 60$$

and

$$s_D = 1794 \cdot 12$$

2.1 The values of L are as follows

if $V_1 = 0$ *and* $V_2 = 0$, then $L = 0$

if $V_1 = 0$ *and* $V_2 = 1$, then $L = 0 \cdot 8$

if $V_1 = 1$ *and* $V_2 = 0$, then $L = 0 \cdot 2$

if $V_1 = 1$ *and* $V_2 = 1$, then $L = 1$

Since each value for L is associated with a probability of $1/4$, we have

$$E(L) = 1/4(0) + 1/4(0\cdot8) + 1/4(0\cdot2) + 1/4(1) = 0\cdot5$$

Now consider the random variable V_1. This has two outcomes, each with a probability of $1/2$. So

$$E(V_1) = 1/2(0) + 1/2(1) = 0\cdot5$$

and, similarly

$$E(V_2) = 0\cdot5$$

Then note that

$$0\cdot2E(V_1) + 0\cdot8E(V_2) = 0\cdot5$$

which is the value of $E(L)$. So

$$E(L) = 0\cdot2E(V_1) + 0\cdot8E(V_2)$$

The significance of this result is that L is a linear combination of V_1 and V_2 and it can be seen that the expectation of the linear combination is the linear combination of the expectations. An analogous result in the context of the two variable regression model is that

$$E(\Sigma w_t u_t) = \Sigma[w_t E(u_t)]$$

2.2 In this application of the two variable model, C is equivalent to Y and D is equivalent to X. So

$$\hat{\beta} = \Sigma x_t y_t / \Sigma x_t^2 = 27\,734\,597\cdot6 / 32\,188\,511\cdot6$$
$$= 0\cdot861630$$

and

$$\hat{\alpha} = \overline{Y} - \hat{\beta}\overline{X} = 22\,445\cdot3 - (0\cdot861630)\,24\,491\cdot8$$
$$= 1342\cdot423$$

The estimated line is therefore

$$\hat{C} = 1342 + 0\cdot86D$$

Solutions 2.3 to 2.5 make use of the rules of summation, given in Section 1.6. A line which uses these rules is signified by an asterisk[*].

2.3 $\qquad \Sigma e_t^2 = \Sigma(Y_t - \hat{\alpha} - \hat{\beta}X_t)^2$

$$\frac{\partial(\Sigma e_t^2)}{\partial\hat{\alpha}} = \Sigma[2(Y_t - \hat{\alpha} - \hat{\beta}X_t)(-1)]$$

$$= -2\Sigma(Y_t - \hat{\alpha} - \hat{\beta}X_t) \qquad *$$

$$= -2(\Sigma Y_t - n\hat{\alpha} - \hat{\beta}\Sigma X_t) \qquad *$$

$$\frac{\partial(\Sigma e_t^2)}{\partial\hat{\beta}} = \Sigma[2(Y_t - \hat{\alpha} - \hat{\beta}X_t)(-X_t)]$$

$$= -2\Sigma X_t(Y_t - \hat{\alpha} - \hat{\beta}X_t) \qquad *$$

$$= -2(\Sigma X_t Y_t - \hat{\alpha}\Sigma X_t - \hat{\beta}\Sigma X_t^2) \qquad *$$

For a turning point

$$\frac{\partial(\Sigma e_t^2)}{\partial\hat{\alpha}} = 0 \quad \text{and} \quad \frac{\partial(\Sigma e_t^2)}{\partial\hat{\beta}} = 0$$

So

$$-2(\Sigma Y_t - n\hat{\alpha} - \hat{\beta}\Sigma X_t) = 0$$

$$-2(\Sigma X_t Y_t - \hat{\alpha}\Sigma X_t - \hat{\beta}\Sigma X_t^2) = 0$$

or

$$\Sigma Y_t = n\hat{\alpha} + \hat{\beta}\Sigma X_t$$

$$\Sigma X_t Y_t = \hat{\alpha}\Sigma X_t + \hat{\beta}\Sigma X_t^2$$

The second order conditions do in fact show that the solution is a minimum of Σe_t^2.

2.4 $\qquad \Sigma x_t y_t = \Sigma(X_t - \overline{X})(Y_t - \overline{Y}) = \Sigma(X_t Y_t - X_t\overline{Y} - \overline{X}Y_t + \overline{X}\overline{Y})$

$$= \Sigma X_t Y_t - \overline{Y}\Sigma X_t - \overline{X}\Sigma Y_t + n\overline{X}\overline{Y} \qquad *$$

where $\overline{X}$ and $\overline{Y}$ do not vary with t and so are treated as constants in applying the rules of summation. Now

$$\overline{Y}\Sigma X_t = (\Sigma Y_t/n)\Sigma X_t = (\Sigma X_t/n)\Sigma Y_t$$

and

$$n\overline{X}\overline{Y} = n(\Sigma X_t/n)(\Sigma Y_t/n) = (\Sigma X_t/n)\Sigma Y_t$$

So

$$\Sigma x_t y_t = \Sigma X_t Y_t - (\Sigma X_t/n)\Sigma Y_t$$

Similarly it can be shown that

$$\Sigma x_t^2 = \Sigma X_t^2 - (\Sigma X_t/n)\Sigma X_t$$

and the required result then follows.

2.5 First note the following

(i) $\Sigma x_t = \Sigma(X_t - \overline{X}) = \Sigma X_t - n\overline{X} = \Sigma X_t - \Sigma X_t = 0$ *

(ii) $\Sigma x_t y_t = \Sigma x_t(Y_t - \overline{Y}) = \Sigma x_t Y_t - \overline{Y}\Sigma x_t$ *

      $= \Sigma x_t Y_t$, since $\Sigma x_t = 0$

(iii) $\Sigma x_t^2 = \Sigma x_t(X_t - \overline{X}) = \Sigma x_t X_t - \overline{X}\Sigma x_t$ *

      $= \Sigma x_t X_t$, since $\Sigma x_t = 0$

(iv) $Y_t = \alpha + \beta X_t + u_t$

Then

$$\hat{\beta} = \Sigma x_t y_t/\Sigma x_t^2$$

$$= \Sigma x_t Y_t/\Sigma x_t^2, \text{ using (ii)}$$

$$= \Sigma x_t(\alpha + \beta X_t + u_t)/\Sigma x_t^2, \text{ using (iv)}$$

$$= (\alpha\Sigma x_t + \beta\Sigma x_t X_t + \Sigma x_t u_t)/\Sigma x_t^2$$ *

$$= (\alpha\cdot 0 + \beta\Sigma x_t^2 + \Sigma x_t u_t)/\Sigma x_t^2, \text{ using (i) and (iii)}$$

$$= \beta + \Sigma x_t u_t/\Sigma x_t^2$$

2.6 $\Sigma e_t^2 = \Sigma(C_t - \overline{C})^2 - \hat{\beta}\Sigma(D_t - \overline{D})(C_t - \overline{C})$

           $= 24007\,482\cdot10 - (0\cdot861630)\,27734597\cdot60$

           $= 11052\cdot07$

   $\hat{\sigma}^2 = 11\,052\cdot07/8 = 13815\cdot10$

     $\text{se}(\hat{\beta}) = \hat{\sigma}/\sqrt{\Sigma(D_t - \overline{D})^2} = 117\cdot537/5673\cdot492$

         $= 0\cdot020716$

   $t = 0\cdot861630/0\cdot020716 = 41\cdot59$

Without consulting a t table, it is obvious that the null hypothesis is very strongly rejected.

3.1 The unrestricted residual sum of squares can be found by fitting separate regressions to each region and adding the individual residual sums of squares together

$$S = S_1 + S_2 + S_3$$

Under the null hypothesis, there are restrictions which can be imposed on the following relationship

$$Y_t = \alpha_1 + (\beta_1 - \alpha_1)D_{2t} + (\gamma_1 - \alpha_1)D_{3t}$$
$$+ \alpha_2 X_{2t} + (\beta_2 - \alpha_2)(D_2 X_2)_t + (\gamma_2 - \alpha_2)(D_3 X_2)_t$$
$$+ \alpha_3 + (\beta_3 - \alpha_3)(D_2 X_3)_t + (\gamma_3 - \alpha_3)(D_3 X_3)_t + u_t$$

where

$D_{2t} = 1$; in region 2

$\quad\ = 0$; elsewhere

$D_{3t} = 1$; in region 3

$\quad\ = 0$; elsewhere

The restrictions are $\beta_3 - \alpha_3 = 0$ and $\gamma_3 - \alpha_3 = 0$ and these can be imposed by deleting the variables $(D_2 X_3)$ and $(D_3 X_3)$. The resulting regression calculation will give the restricted residual sum of squares S_R. The test statistic is.

$$F = \frac{(S_R - S)g}{S/(n - k)}$$

where $g = 2$, $k = 9$ and n is the *total* number of observations from all regions. If the calculated value is greater than the critical value for 2 and $(n - 9)$ degrees of freedom, the null hypothesis is rejected.

The disturbances are assumed to have normal distributions, with zero mean and the same variance in all regions.

3.2 The estimator $\hat{\beta} = \Sigma X_t Y_t / \Sigma X_t^2$ would be biased.

$$\hat{\beta} = \Sigma X_t(\alpha + \beta X_t + u_t)/\Sigma X_t^2$$

$$= \frac{\alpha \Sigma X_t}{\Sigma X_t^2} + \frac{\beta \Sigma X_t^2}{\Sigma X_t^2} + \frac{\Sigma X_t u_t}{\Sigma X_t^2}$$

$$E(\hat{\beta}) = \frac{\alpha \Sigma X_t}{\Sigma X_t^2} + \beta + E\left(\frac{\Sigma X_t u_t}{\Sigma X_t^2}\right)$$

$$= \frac{\alpha \Sigma X_t}{\Sigma X_t^2} + \beta + 0$$

The bias, $E(\hat{\beta}) - \beta$, is $\alpha \Sigma X_t / \Sigma X_t^2$. Since α is not zero (by assumption), the bias can only be zero if $\Sigma X_t = 0$.

4.1 Write the contraint as

$$0 \cdot 5 = \alpha(0) + \beta(1) + v$$

This suggests adding $0 \cdot 5$ as an extra observation on the dependent variable and 1 as an extra observation on the explanatory variable. But note that the 'observation' attached to α is 0, not 1, so the artificial variable observations in the augmented model consist of n 1's and one 0. The variance of v is known to be $0 \cdot 1$ and this is unlikely to be the same as disturbance variance in the main part of the model. So one would have to perform a transformation to allow for heteroscedasticity. The transformation would be based on an estimate of the disturbance variance, obtained from a preliminary regression on the unrestricted model.

4.2 $Y_t - \rho Y_{t-4} = \alpha(1 - \rho) + \beta(X_t - \rho X_{t-4}) + u_t - \rho u_{t-4};$
$$t = 5, 6, \ldots, n$$

Note that the disturbances are now independent, but four observations are lost. OLS applied to this equation is not exactly the same as GLS, because of the lost observations.

5.1 $X_{t+1}^* - X_t^* = (1 - \lambda)(X_t - X_t^*)$

$$= \delta \beta X_{t+1}^* = (1 - \lambda)X_t + \lambda X_t^*$$

$$= (1 - \lambda)X_t + \lambda((1 - \lambda)X_{t-1} + \lambda X_{t-1}^*)$$

and so on

$$X_{t+1}^* = (1 - \lambda)[X_t + \lambda X_{t-1} + \lambda^2 X_{t-2} + \ldots]$$

5.2 $Y_t = \delta Y_t^* + (1 - \delta)Y_{t-1} + u_t$

$$= \delta \beta X_{t+1}^* + (1 - \delta)Y_{t-1} + u_t$$

and, from the previous example

$$X_{t+1}^* = (1 - \lambda)[X_t + \lambda X_{t-1} + \lambda^2 X_{t-2} + \ldots]$$

So

$$Y_t = \delta \beta(1 - \lambda)[X_t + \lambda X_{t-1} + \lambda^2 X_{t-2} + \ldots] + (1 - \delta)Y_{t-1} + u_t$$

$$\lambda Y_{t-1} = \delta \beta(1 - \lambda)[\lambda X_{t-1} + \lambda^2 X_{t-2} + \ldots]$$

$$+ \lambda(1 - \delta)Y_{t-2} + \lambda u_{t-1}$$

and by subtraction, writing $\lambda = (1 - (1 - \lambda))$ to show the form of the equation

$$Y_t = \delta\beta(1 - \lambda)X_t + [(1 - \delta) + (1 - (1 - \lambda))]\,Y_{t-1}$$
$$- (1 - \delta)(1 - (1 - \lambda))Y_{t-2} + u_t - \lambda u_{t-1}$$

Problems

(i) The parameters of interest are δ, β and $(1 - \lambda)$ and there are three composite parameters. But δ and $(1 - \lambda)$ enter the composite parameters in a symmetrical fashion and, from estimates of the composite parameters alone, it is impossible to assign unique estimates to δ and $(1 - \lambda)$.

(ii) OLS estimation would lead to inconsistent estimates, since there are lagged dependent variables on the right, together with a moving average error.

6.1 $\quad C_t = \alpha + \beta(C_t + I_t + Z_t) + u_t$

$$= \frac{\alpha}{(1 - \beta)} + \frac{\beta}{(1 - \beta)}\,(I_t + Z_t) + \frac{u_t}{(1 - \beta)}$$

$$= \frac{\alpha}{(1 - \beta)} + \frac{\beta}{1 - \beta}\,(\gamma + \delta D_{t-1} + v_t) + \frac{\beta}{1 - \beta}\,Z_t + \frac{u_t}{(1 - \beta)}$$

$$= \frac{\alpha + \beta\gamma}{(1 - \beta)} + \frac{\beta\delta}{(1 - \beta)}\,D_{t-1} + \frac{\beta}{(1 - \beta)}\,Z_t + \frac{(u_t + \beta v_t)}{(1 - \beta)}$$

A linear combination of equations involving the identity would contain Z_t. A linear combination involving the investment function would contain D_{t-1}. The consumption function is therefore identified: in fact it is over-identified.

6.2 Climate is clearly exogenous and this leaves Q^D, Q^S and P as endogenous variables. Eliminating Q^D and Q^S leaves

$$Q_t = \alpha + \beta P_t + u_t$$
$$Q_t = \gamma + \delta R_t + v_t$$

and the model is no longer simultaneous. In fact R determines Q and Q determines P, despite the way in which the first equation is written. This is a *recursive* model.

Index

Adaptive expectations model, 190
Algol, 61
Almon method, 169–72
Asymptotic properties of estimators, 50–5, 152, 155, 177–8, 179, 208, 210
Asymptotic standard error, 210–12
Asymptotic variance, 178, 183, 210, 218
Autocorrelation; *see* Serial correlation of disturbances
Autonomous expenditure, 201
Autoregressive process:
   disturbances, 138–46, 147, 155, 180–1, 184
   dynamic model, 162, 175–85

Behavioural relationship, 193
Bias:
   dynamic model, 174, 177–80, 181
   omitted variables, 98–100, 107–9, 118, 169, 172
   random explanatory variable, 54, 152
   simultaneity, 202–8

Chow test, 116
Cobb-Douglas production function, 92–3
Coefficient; *see* Regression coefficient, Response coefficient
Coefficient of determination; *see* R^2
Complete system, methods of estimation, 214–18

Computer:
   language, 61
   program, 61
   simulation experiments, 178–80
   use of, 60–2, 68–70, 109, 115, 122, 184, 217, 218
      accuracy, 105–6
      Almon method, 172
      heteroscedasticity, 128–32
      iterative calculation, 154
      serial correlation, 142–4
      transformations of the data, 80, 91, 129–32, 142–3, 165
      two stage least squares, 210–13
Confidence intervals, 37–42, 83–4
Consistency:
   defined, 51–4
   instrumental variable estimator, 182–3
   maximum likelihood estimator, 155
   OLS, simple dynamic model, 177–8
   two stage least squares, 206–9
   two-step estimator, 152, 184
Constraint; *see* Restriction
Consumption function:
   contemporaneous correlation in, 157–61
   defined, 4
   in a simultaneous model, 192–5, 199, 200–23
   nonlinear forms for, 75–7
   partial adjustment model,

237

242   *Index*